The Shape of Music — Warren Schwartz

The Shape of Music — Warren Schwartz

FOREWORD by Nicholas Urie
INTRODUCTION by Mark Volpe
AFTERWORD by Warren Schwartz
EDITED by Oscar Riera Ojeda

OSCAR RIERA OJEDA
PUBLISHERS

I'd like to dedicate
this book jointly to
Sheila Fiekowsky, my
partner in life, and
Robert Silver, my partner
in architecture — without
them, none of this would
have been possible.

W.S.

CONTENTS

FOREWORD

— by Nicholas Urie

Something from Nothing

The conventional romanticized idea of creativity holds that a muse bestows fully-formed works of art on some lucky humans. This narrative insists that inspiration is spontaneous, given to artists by an external supernatural force. It suggests that creativity and inspiration are wholly different from other human endeavors where hard work is the required path to success. But follow any artist for a day and you will find them toiling at their trade, engaging it over and over with curiosity and resilience. When asked about creative inspiration Picasso said, "Inspiration exists, but it has to find you working."

The principal creative hurdle I encounter as a composer is making something where nothing yet exists, giving body to an idea. The music that lives in my mind's ear is ephemeral and difficult to coax out of the shadows. Though it is ever-present otherwise, it is conspicuously absent when I go searching for it. Because of this paradox and because music is my life's work, it is essential that I employ a practice that allows me to access my internal musical world on demand. The rituals of my creative practice trigger a state of mind that is conducive to spontaneous creation.

While the details of my ritual have changed considerably over the years, sketching is consistently the central avenue of access to my mind's ear. It offers a hunter's blind as I try to listen without disturbing anything, a quiet way of inviting my imagination to stay and play instead of running away. I start by quickly jotting down small musical moments without subjecting them to the realities and restraints of time. Rhythms are approximate or absent, and bar lines are the enemy. I scrawl these skeletal gestures onto large sheets of blank manuscript paper, putting ideas down with space around them so I can add whenever and wherever needed, so I can move freely from one idea to the next, filling the page at random. I am not concerned with how this stream-of-consciousness will fit together. Rather than looking like music, my notation resembles medieval neumes or some other kind of ancient and cryptic glyph, in other words, sketches.

When I am sketching I attempt to work without observing myself. My imagination flees at the first hint of criticism so I try to allow these small germs to exist outside of judgment. I want the ideas to exist apart from me, to breathe and grow, to be the catalyst for more ideas. Utility is not the point of the practice; I don't expect any single idea to be useful to me. Sketching is play and play does not want to be managed or interrupted or even observed.

At some point, the sketches begin to distill themselves into groups of melodies and harmonies that somehow work together. This is not a conscious decision; it is my mind uncovering a musical space that it wants to explore, and when this happens I begin to evaluate the material critically for the first time. I discard most of what I've written. I arrange and rearrange what is left of the small, amorphous gestures roughly into a possible chronological order, considering how I might develop and expand the gestures to fill the form that I imagine for the piece.

And now a different kind of writing begins, one that is newly fed and enhanced by critical assessment. You would recognize the notation as music and you would probably call the work composing. As I start to subject the sketch ideas to the confines of time, assigning specific rhythms, bar lines, tempo, and groove, this developed material reveals an outline that the listener can follow: the form. This is also when my original plans for the form of the piece meet with the realities of the sketch material, but once I understand what the piece is, what these ideas can come together to be, I can expand it into its final full score configuration. The piece now welcomes editing, refining, ornamenting, developing a sound world. A critical eye and deft technique, so destructive during the sketching process, bring this music to life adding colors, textures, and shapes.

For me, composing is the process of turning sketches into music. It is the process of moving from playful possibilities to a thoughtful and cohesive structure. Chuck Close said "Inspiration is highly overrated. If you sit around and wait for the clouds to part, it's not liable to ever happen. More often than not, work is salvation." Sketching invites my muse to visit. It is the opening salvo of my process, a beacon that lets inspiration find me prepared to receive it. Sketching gives corporality to the incorporeal, bridging the space between nothing and something.

Dr. A. H. McCoy Federal
Building Entry, Jackson

STANDARD
LIFE
STANDARD
LIFE

INTRODUCTION

— by Mark Volpe

For years (actually decades), I have attended Boston Symphony Orchestra concerts in Symphony Hall and at Tanglewood in the Berkshire hills in western Massachusetts where I have witnessed Warren Schwartz, a curly haired architect, sketching in his program book. Occasionally, he would share with me his drawings after the concert backstage as he waited for his wife, Sheila Fiekowsky, a long-time member of the BSO violin section. Sometimes, when he was excited by a notion or concept, he would find me at intermission in the first balcony hallway, close to his seat and my office, to show me his idea. Of course, I was interested as many of his sketches were very much correlated to the music on the program. Whether conscious or not, Warren had converted what he had heard into shapes and geometry that would morph into buildings and other structures. And some of those sketches would eventually be the inspiration for buildings that Warren and his partners would later design. As a student of the creative process, mostly within the music discipline, it was a fascinating glimpse into how a work of art is created in the visual realm.

Of course, the connection between music and architecture is well documented. Frank Lloyd Wright famously noted that, "music and architecture blossom on the same stem – sublimated mathematics" (with a nod to Pythagoras). Furthermore, in my frequent conversations with musicians and occasional talks with architects, it is abundantly clear that they share a vocabulary. Musicians talk about color, harmony, structure, balances, textures, scale, dynamics, tempo, etc., as do architects. Frequently, conductors will analyze the architecture (structure) of a piece of music before focusing on its details. In other words, studying the piece as a "whole" before "breaking it down to its elements". However, as Charles Jencks, the distinguished landscape designer and American cultural theorist, has noted, "music is experienced over time, whereas architecture is grasped as a spatial whole." So, it was a fascinating process to watch Warren in real time capture and transform the music permeating the hall into drawings. I suspect that other architects listen to recordings when working, but that is very different from a live orchestra performing in a hall full of people. Performances on recordings never change, the tempo is always the same, the balances and orchestral colors likewise. Contrast this with a live performance in which human nature mandates that each performance will be different and that "what comes next" in respect to tempo, dynamics, articulation, etc., is not known to the audience (and sometimes the orchestra as well) until it happens. Also, being part of an audience is a very different experience than sitting at a workstation and this undoubtedly impacts the artistic process of creation.

As noted, music is an art that exists in time, one note or chord disappearing into the next. It is linear and is primarily experienced through sound waves entering our ears. Conversely, architecture is three dimensional and is mostly experienced through light waves entering our eyes. Despite these distinctions, the two art forms have undeniably influenced and impacted each other since the advent of civilization. In his drawings, Warren has captured the essence of the relationship between music and architecture in a unique way. For some of the sketches, he even identifies the specific musical attribute that inspired the representation. In others, it is more abstract. The sum of Warren Schwartz's sketches is a work of art that should inspire the reader to fully embrace the notion articulated by the German writer Johann Wolfgang von Goethe who stated, "Music is liquid architecture; Architecture is frozen music."

SKETCHES

National Music Museum - Concept

— February 13, 2016

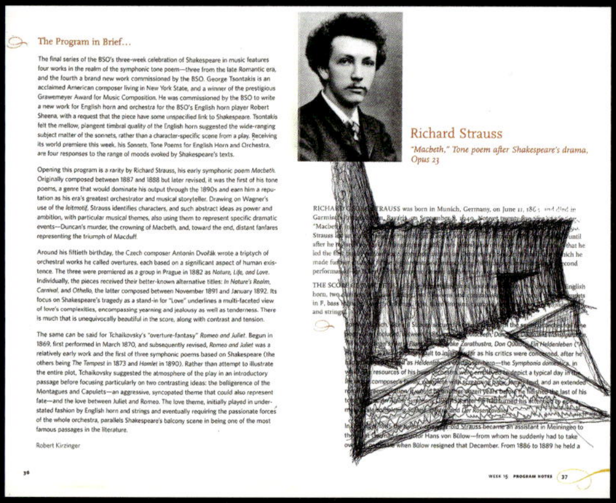

Vermillion, SD. Concept sketch.

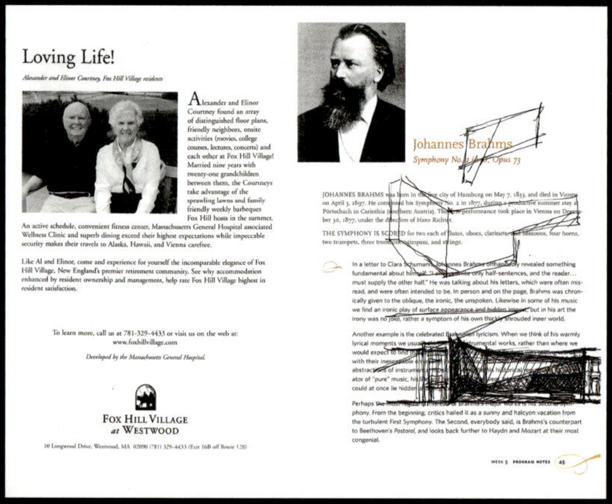

Concept - Music Museum

Richard Strauss

"Macbeth," Tone poem after Shakespeare's drama, Opus 23

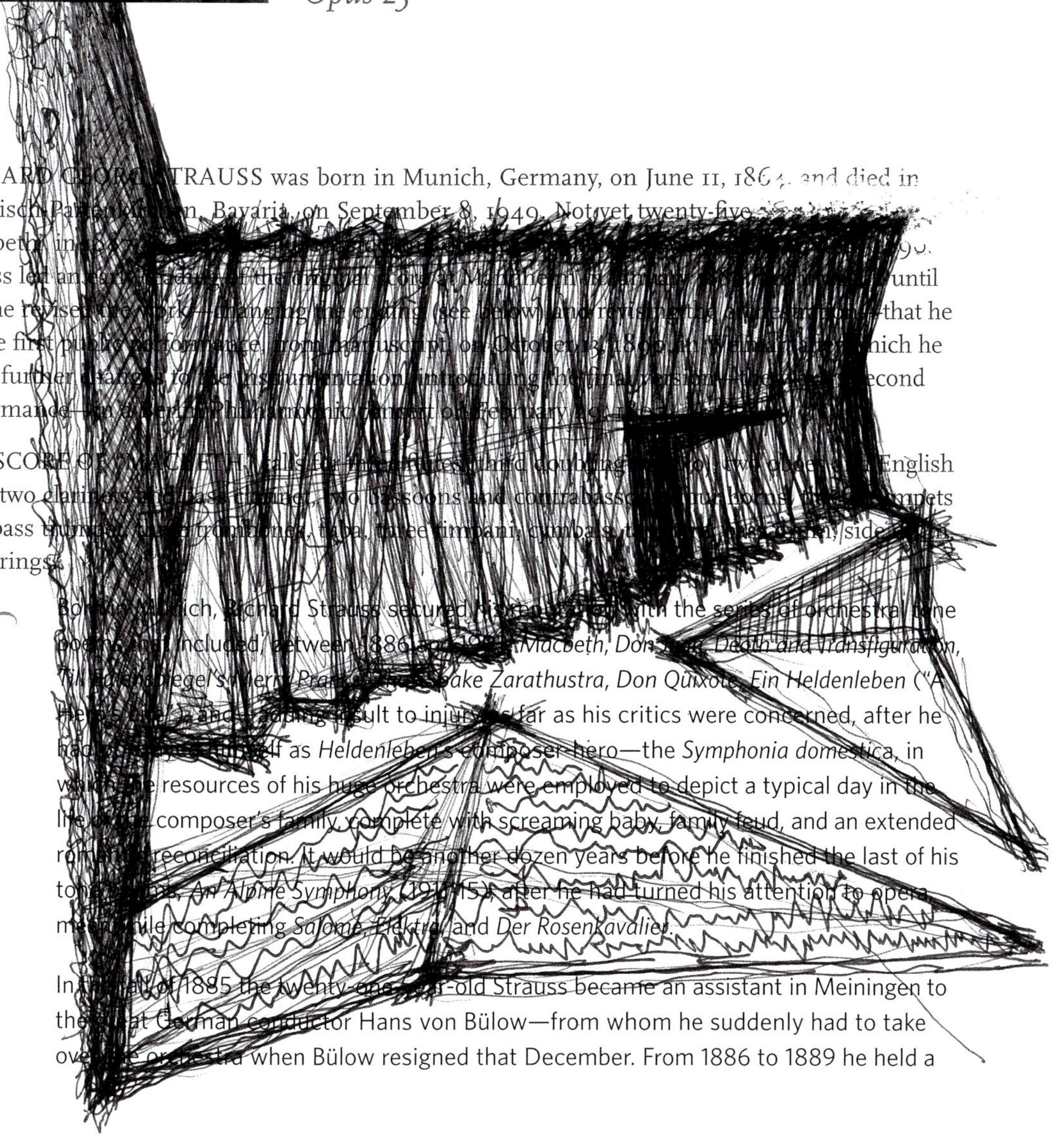

:HAR[illegible]TRAUSS was born in Munich, Germany, on June 11, 1864, and died in misch[illegible]n, Bavaria, on September 8, 1949. Not yet twenty-five [illegible] ıcbeth [illegible] uss led an [illegible] until r he revised [illegible] that he the first [illegible] hich he le further [illegible] econd formance [illegible]

E SCORE OF [illegible] English 1, two [illegible] pets , bass [illegible] side [illegible] strings.

Bo[illegible]ich, [illegible]d Strauss secured [illegible] with the series of orchestral [illegible]ne poem[illegible] included, between 1886 [illegible] *Macbeth, Don* [illegible] *Death and Transfiguration, Till* [illegible]*egel's Merry Pran*[illegible]*ake Zarathustra, Don Quixote, Ein Heldenleben* ("A He[illegible]) and [illegible] insult to injury [illegible] far as his critics were concerned, after he had [illegible]elf as *Heldenleben*'s composer-hero—the *Symphonia domestica*, in wh[illegible] resources of his huge orchestra were employed to depict a typical day in the life [illegible] composer's family, complete with screaming baby, family feud, and an extended rom[illegible] reconciliation. It would be another dozen years before he finished the last of his to[illegible], *An Alpine Symphony* (1911–15), after he had turned his attention to opera, mea[illegible]ile completing *Salome, Elektra*, and *Der Rosenkavalier*.

In [illegible]all of 1885 the twenty-one-[illegible]-old Strauss became an assistant in Meiningen to the [illegible]at German conductor Hans von Bülow—from whom he suddenly had to take ove[illegible] orchestra when Bülow resigned that December. From 1886 to 1889 he held a

National Music Museum - Concept

LIBRARY
CARNEGIE DONATION

Echo

— October 03, 2015

Upon entering Cornell's school of architecture in 1961, I remember seeing an exhibit of Erich Mendelsohn's yellow-trace sketches drawn while he was listening to music.

After that, from time to time, I closed my eyes while listening to see if I could also see music's form. I was surprised that, in my mind's eye, it not only took on form, but color and movement as well, not unlike the aurora borealis that displayed spectacularly one cold night at Cornell. Sometimes I would try to draw what I saw, but like a dream it was hard to catch the moving image. It takes practice, and I've been practicing from time to time ever since.

This "echo" may have been generated by the music that night, or possibly by a house that I was designing, bridging a ravine. —

Exhibition Bridge / Assembly Bridge

— April 05, 2013

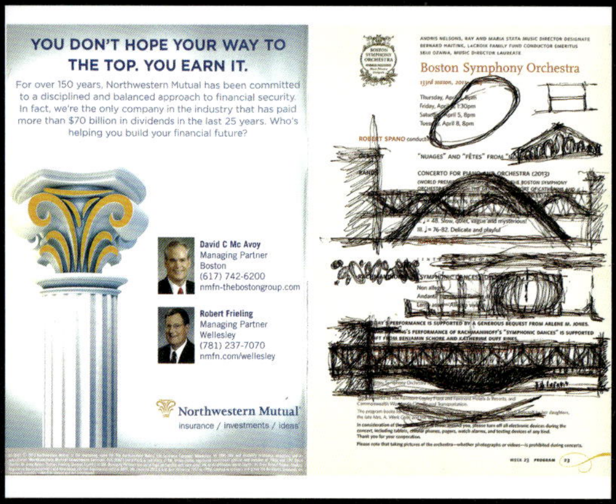

Sketch for an entry pavilion for a construction materials manufacturer, linking two research & development buildings on its corporate campus.

ANDRIS NELSONS, RAY AND MARIA STATA MUSIC DIRECTOR DESIGNATE
BERNARD HAITINK, LACROIX FAMILY FUND CONDUCTOR EMERITUS
SEIJI OZAWA, MUSIC DIRECTOR LAUREATE

Boston Symphony Orchestra

133rd season, 2013–2014

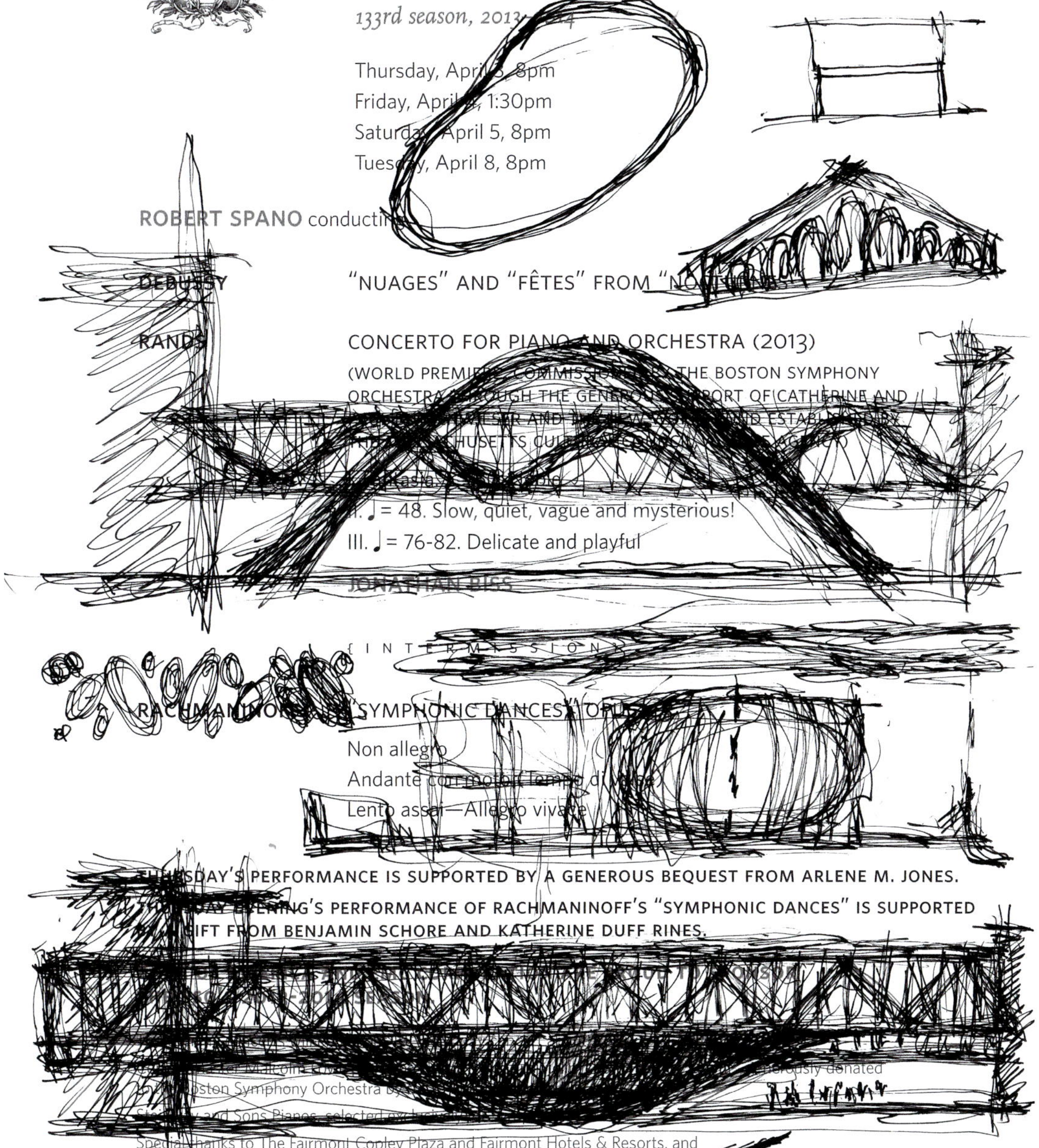

Thursday, April 3, 8pm
Friday, April 4, 1:30pm
Saturday, April 5, 8pm
Tuesday, April 8, 8pm

ROBERT SPANO conducting

DEBUSSY "NUAGES" AND "FÊTES" FROM "NOCTURNES"

RANDS CONCERTO FOR PIANO AND ORCHESTRA (2013)

(WORLD PREMIERE; COMMISSIONED BY THE BOSTON SYMPHONY ORCHESTRA THROUGH THE GENEROUS SUPPORT OF CATHERINE AND [illegible] AND THE NEW WORKS FUND ESTABLISHED BY THE MASSACHUSETTS CULTURAL COUNCIL, A STATE AGENCY)

[illegible]
II. ♩ = 48. Slow, quiet, vague and mysterious!
III. ♩ = 76-82. Delicate and playful

JONATHAN BISS

{ I N T E R M I S S I O N }

RACHMANINOFF "SYMPHONIC DANCES," OP. 45

Non allegro
Andante con moto (Tempo di valse)
Lento assai—Allegro vivace

THURSDAY'S PERFORMANCE IS SUPPORTED BY A GENEROUS BEQUEST FROM ARLENE M. JONES.

[illegible] EVENING'S PERFORMANCE OF RACHMANINOFF'S "SYMPHONIC DANCES" IS SUPPORTED BY A GIFT FROM BENJAMIN SCHORE AND KATHERINE DUFF RINES.

[illegible]

[illegible] generously donated to the Boston Symphony Orchestra by [illegible]

[illegible] and Sons Pianos, selected by [illegible]

Special thanks to The Fairmont Copley Plaza and Fairmont Hotels & Resorts, and Commonwealth Worldwide Chauffeured Transportation.

The program books for the Friday series are given in loving memory of Mrs. Hugh Bancroft by her daughters, the late Mrs. A. Werk Cook and the late Mrs. William [illegible]

In consideration of the performers and those around you, please turn off all electronic devices during the concert, including tablets, cellular phones, pagers, watch alarms, and texting devices of any kind. Thank you for your cooperation.

Please note that taking pictures of the orchestra—whether photographs or videos—is prohibited during concerts.

Music and Architecture seem to have an inverse relationship. They are often described in each other's terms. One is weightless; the other is material. Each has qualities of the other. Music has size, color, form. Architecture is rhythmic, poetic, lyrical. Music can transform environment. Architect Erich Mendelsohn sketched buildings to music, referring to his sketches as "musical compositions". —

A 37 Story Building

— January 31, 1998

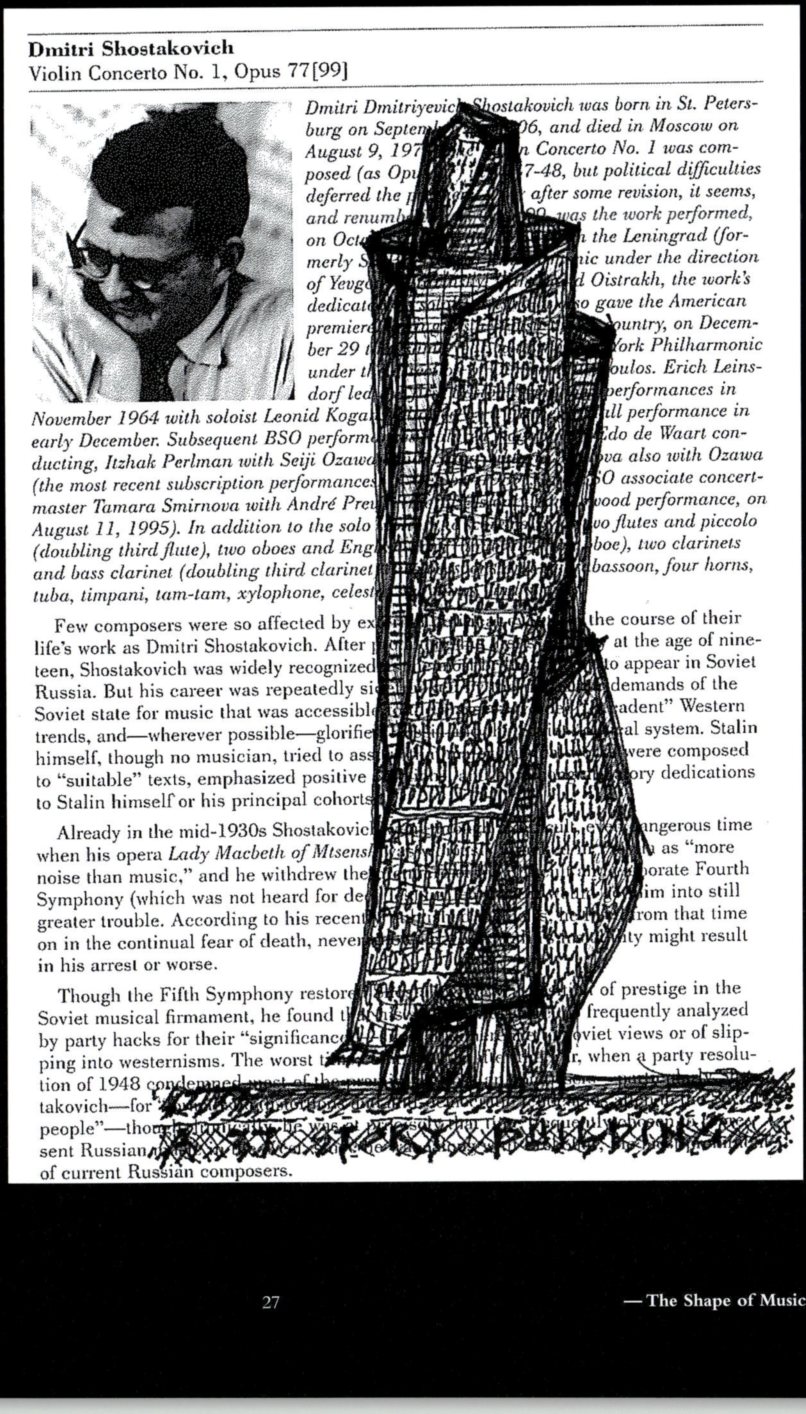

Dmitri Shostakovich
Violin Concerto No. 1, Opus 77[99]

Dmitri Dmitriyevich Shostakovich was born in St. Peters-
burg on Septem ... 06, and died in Moscow on
August 9, 197 ... n Concerto No. 1 was com-
posed (as Op ... 7-48, but political difficulties
deferred the ... after some revision, it seems,
and renumb ... was the work performed,
on Oct ... n the Leningrad (for-
merly S ... nic under the direction
of Yevg ... d Oistrakh, the work's
dedicat ... so gave the American
premiere ... ountry, on Decem-
ber 29 ... York Philharmonic
under t ... oulos. Erich Leins-
dorf le ... performances in
November 1964 with soloist Leonid Koga ... ll performance in
early December. Subsequent BSO perform ... Edo de Waart con-
ducting, Itzhak Perlman with Seiji Ozaw ... va also with Ozawa
(the most recent subscription performance ... O associate concert-
master Tamara Smirnova with André Pre ... wood performance, on
August 11, 1995). In addition to the solo ... wo flutes and piccolo
(doubling third flute), two oboes and Eng ... boe), two clarinets
and bass clarinet (doubling third clarinet ... bassoon, four horns,
tuba, timpani, tam-tam, xylophone, celest

Few composers were so affected by ex ... the course of their
life's work as Dmitri Shostakovich. After ... at the age of nine-
teen, Shostakovich was widely recognized ... to appear in Soviet
Russia. But his career was repeatedly si ... demands of the
Soviet state for music that was accessibl ... adent" Western
trends, and—wherever possible—glorifie ... al system. Stalin
himself, though no musician, tried to ass ... were composed
to "suitable" texts, emphasized positive ... ory dedications
to Stalin himself or his principal cohorts

Already in the mid-1930s Shostakovic ... angerous time
when his opera *Lady Macbeth of Mtsens* ... as "more
noise than music," and he withdrew the ... orate Fourth
Symphony (which was not heard for de ... im into still
greater trouble. According to his recent ... rom that time
on in the continual fear of death, never ... ty might result
in his arrest or worse.

Though the Fifth Symphony restore ... of prestige in the
Soviet musical firmament, he found t ... frequently analyzed
by party hacks for their "significance ... viet views or of slip-
ping into westernisms. The worst t ... r, when a party resolu-
tion of 1948
takovich—for
people"—tho
sent Russian
of current Russian composers.

Bach Hall, Leipzig

— August 01, 2010

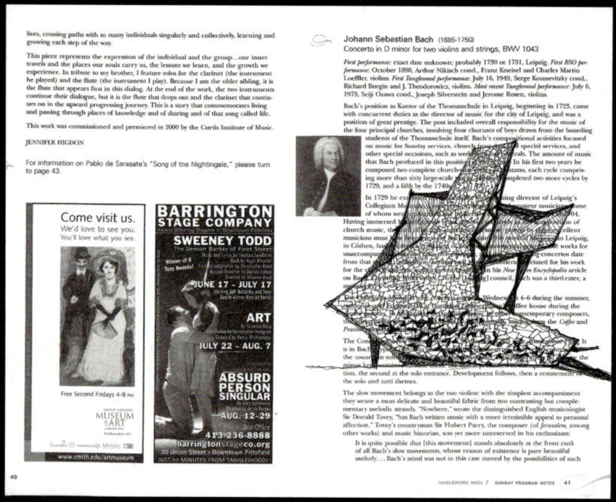

In 1980 I met Sheila Fiekowsky, a violinist, and was drawn into her world of music - that of the Boston Symphony Orchestra. In 1983 I began making sketches in symphony programs before the orchestra began to play. Later, the sketches became part of my listening.

Johann Sebastian Bach (1685-1750)

Concerto in D minor for two violins and strings, BWV 1043

First performance: exact date unknown; probably 1730 or 1731, Leipzig. *First BSO performance*: October 1890, Arthur Nikisch cond., Franz Kneisel and Charles Martin Loeffler, violins. *First Tanglewood performance*: July 16, 1949, Serge Koussevitzky cond., Richard Burgin and J. Theodorowicz, violins. *Most recent Tanglewood performance*: July 6, 1973, Seiji Ozawa cond., Joseph Silverstein and Jerome Rosen, violins.

Bach's position as Kantor of the Thomasschule in Leipzig, beginning in 1723, came with concurrent duties as the director of music for the city of Leipzig, and was a position of great prestige. The post included overall responsibility for the music of the four principal churches, involving four choruses of boys drawn from the boarding

students of the Thomasschule itself. Bach's compositional activities focused on music for Sunday services, church feast days and special services, and other special occasions, such as weddings and funerals. The amount of music that Bach produced in this position is staggering. In his first two years he composed two complete church-year cycles of cantatas, each cycle comprising more than sixty large-scale works. He had completed two more cycles by 1729, and a fifth by the 1740s.

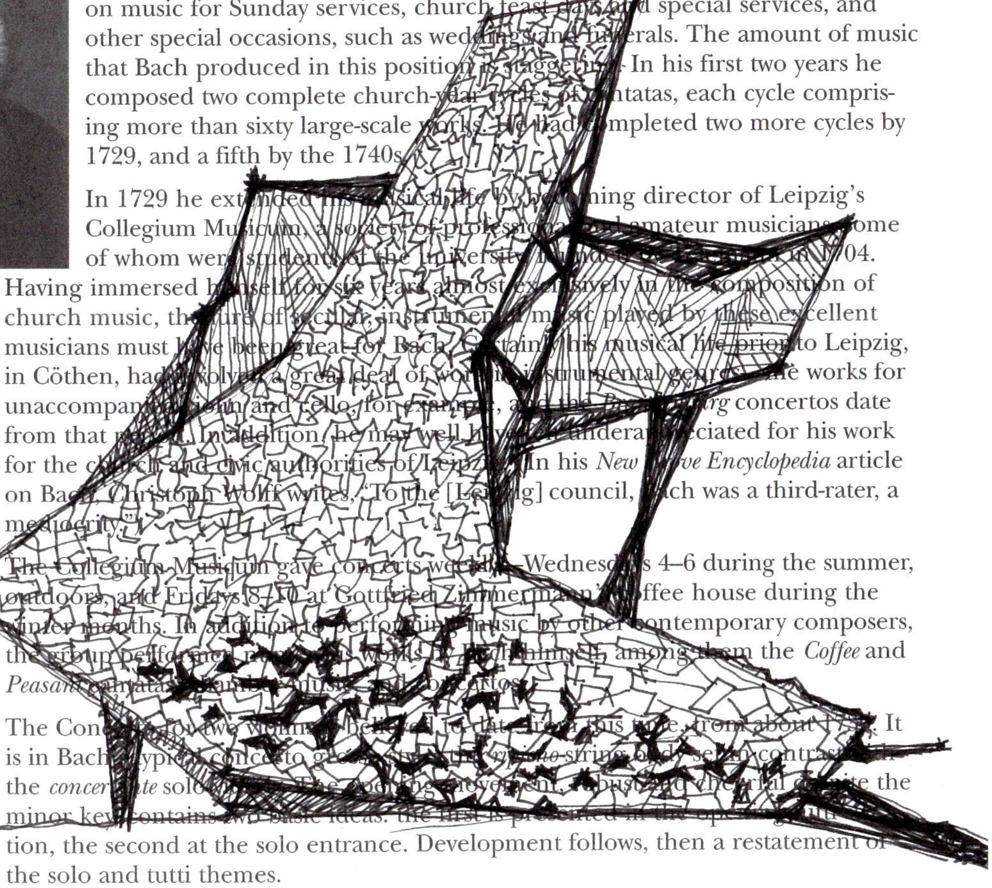

In 1729 he extended his musical life by becoming director of Leipzig's Collegium Musicum, a society of professional and amateur musicians, some of whom were students of the university, founded [illegible] in 1704. Having immersed himself for six years almost exclusively in the composition of church music, the lure of secular, instrumental music played by these excellent musicians must have been great for Bach. Certainly his musical life prior to Leipzig, in Cöthen, had involved a great deal of work in instrumental genres: the works for unaccompanied violin and cello, for example, and the *Brandenburg* concertos date from that period. In addition, he may well have felt underappreciated for his work for the church and civic authorities of Leipzig. In his *New Grove Encyclopedia* article on Bach, Christoph Wolff writes, "To the [Leipzig] council, Bach was a third-rater, a mediocrity."

The Collegium Musicum gave concerts weekly—Wednesdays 4–6 during the summer, outdoors, and Fridays 8–10 at Gottfried Zimmermann's coffee house during the winter months. In addition to performing music by other contemporary composers, the group performed [illegible] works by Bach himself, among them the *Coffee* and *Peasant* cantatas, [illegible] music, and concertos.

The Concerto for two violins [illegible] believed to date from this time, from about [illegible]. It is in Bach's typical concerto grosso style, the *ripieno* string body set in contrast with the *concertante* soloists. The opening movement, robust and cheerful despite the minor key, contains two basic ideas: the first is presented in the opening [illegible] tion, the second at the solo entrance. Development follows, then a restatement of the solo and tutti themes.

The slow movement belongs to the two violins: with the simplest accompaniment they weave a most delicate and beautiful fabric from two contrasting but complementary melodic strands. "Nowhere," wrote the distinguished English musicologist Sir Donald Tovey, "has Bach written music with a more irresistible appeal to personal affection." Tovey's countryman Sir Hubert Parry, the composer (of *Jerusalem*, among other works) and music historian, was yet more unreserved in his enthusiasm:

> It is quite possible that [this movement] stands absolutely at the front rank of all Bach's slow movements, whose reason of existence is pure beautiful melody.... Bach's mind was not in this case moved by the possibilities of such

Each week I have looked forward to listening and drawing what I hear (and see in my mind's eye). I think the best sketches are those that are drawn from the music alone. Sometimes the music is in the background when I'm thinking about an actual design problem, but that rarely produces the best sketch. —

New England Aquarium

COASTAL RHYTHMS
AQUARIUM
GIFT SHOP

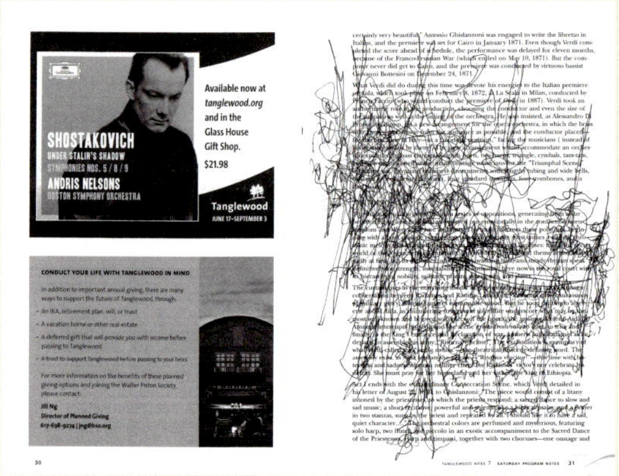

Retractable Canopy supported by masts and cables attached to the Tanglewood Music Shed — August 20, 2016

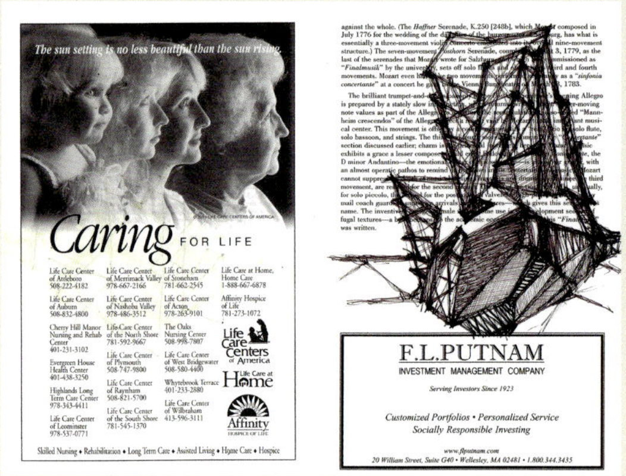

Candy Factory Visitor Center — October 29, 2005

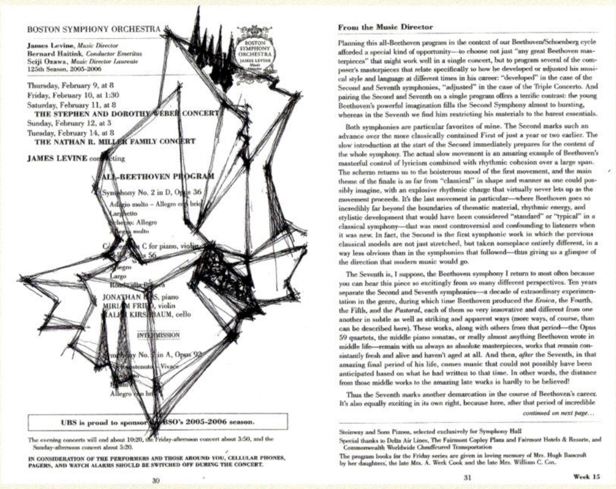

Opus — February 11, 2006

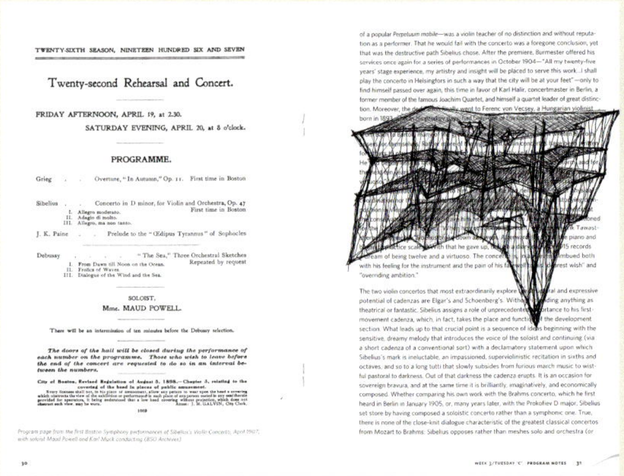

Concept - House — October 16, 2021

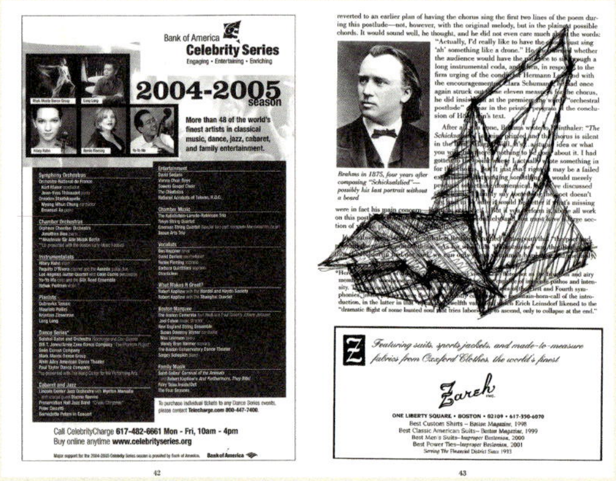

Chapel — February 5, 2005

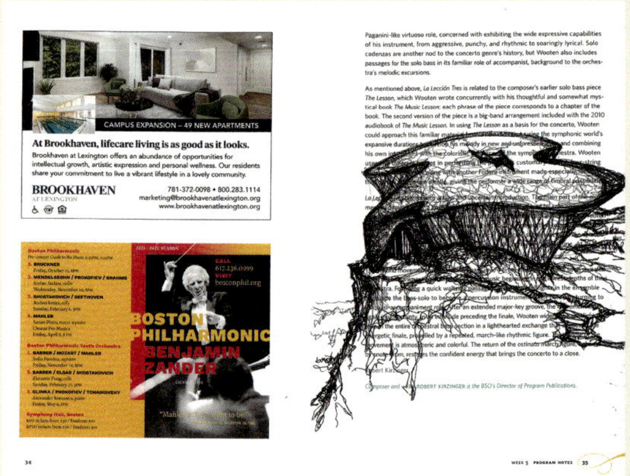

Mews — October 30, 2021

Concept - Housing — October 22, 2005

House for Two Archers — October 02, 2004

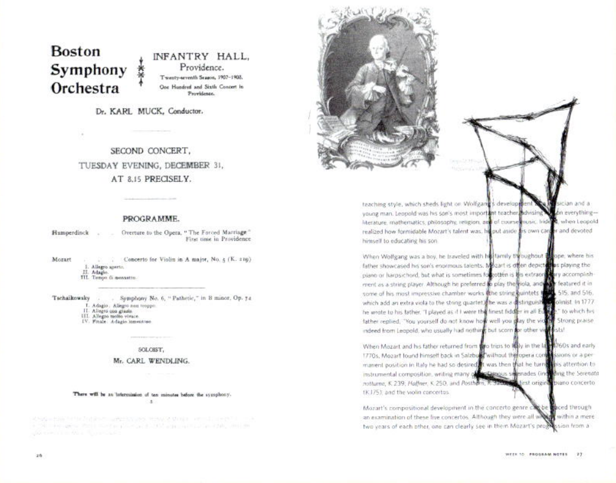

Concept - Air Traffic Control Tower
— January 8, 2022

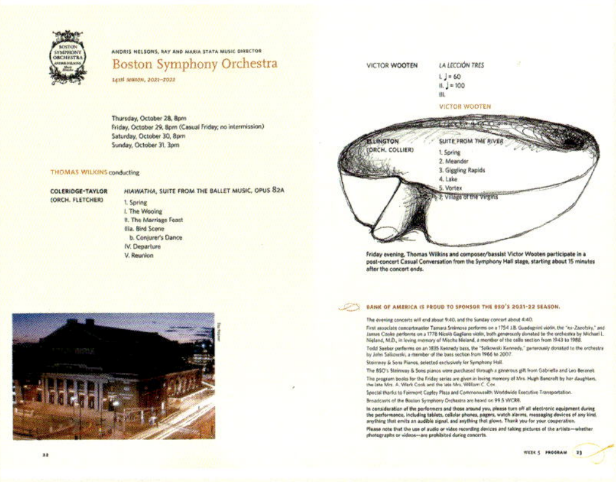

Mushroom Farm — October 30, 2021

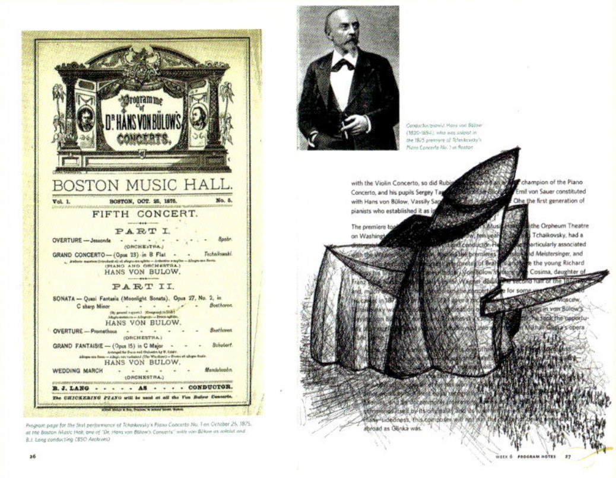

Church of the Autostrada — November 06, 2021

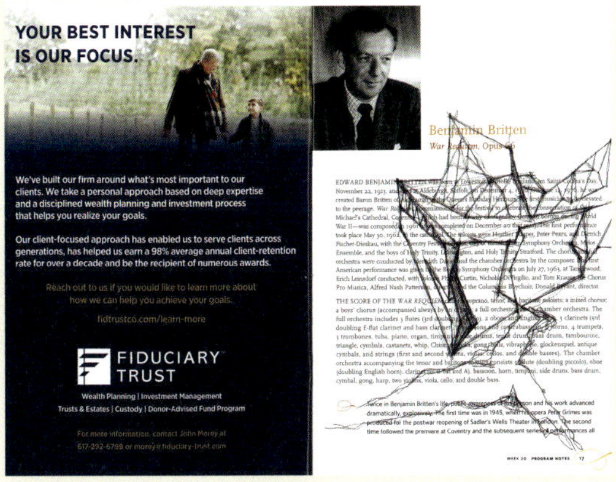

Natural History Museum — April 12, 2022

Treehouse

— March 23, 2019

there is also a cool passion all Stenhammar's own, and the way the solo clarinet cantilena slowly emerges from the background again invokes the play of distant sound on a warm spring evening. The central section's sustained horns and glockenspiel seem to recollect cooler climes.

Writing about the Scherzo, which follows without pause, Stenhammar conceded that "Intermezzo fantastico" or "selvaggio" (literally, "savage") would have been just as appropriate titles, and it is here that the Serenade's Dionysian impulse is given freest rein in music of considerable rhythmic abandon. A brief oasis of *molto sostenuto* strings offers respite from the breathless atmosphere, exemplifying what Robert Quist describes as the Serenade's tendency to interleave moments of "Nordic, contemplative stillness in the context of southern expressions of joy." Upon its reappearance, the scherzo's bacchic frenzy is redoubled, though the movement eventually dissolves into nothingness, sustained strings again leading directly into the Notturno.

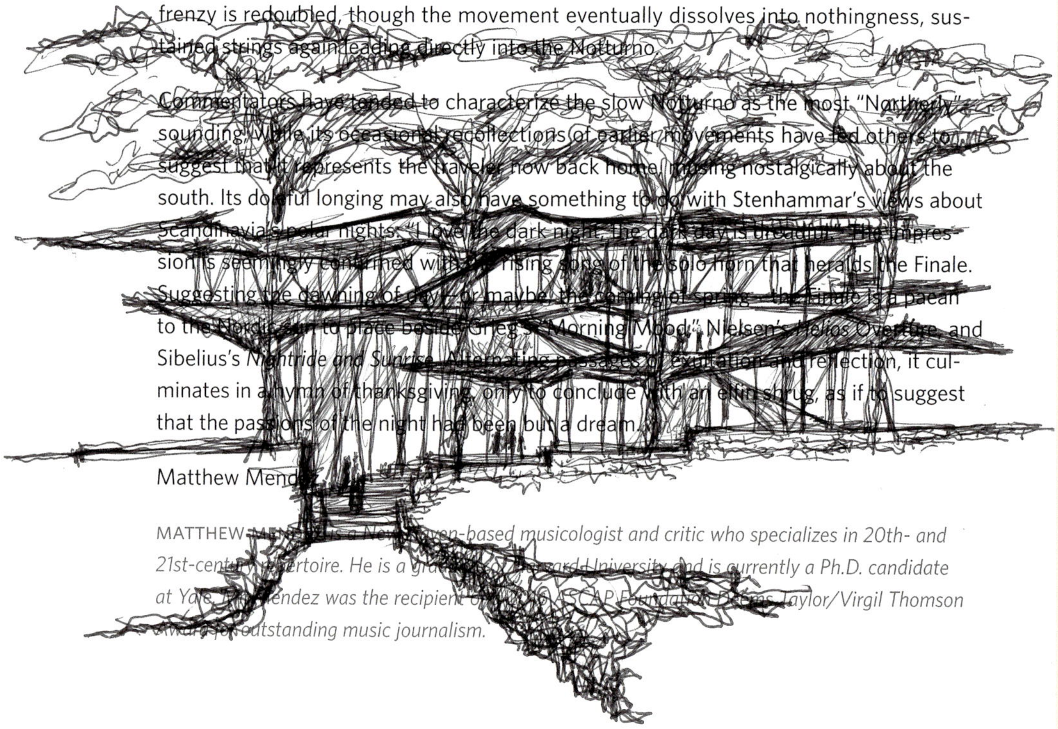

Commentators have tended to characterize the slow Notturno as the most "Northerly"-sounding, while its occasional recollections of earlier movements have led others to suggest that it represents the traveler now back home, musing nostalgically about the south. Its doleful longing may also have something to do with Stenhammar's views about Scandinavia's polar nights: "I love the dark night, the dark day is dreadful." The impression is seemingly confirmed with the rising song of the solo horn that heralds the Finale. Suggesting the dawning of day—or maybe, the coming of spring—the Finale is a paean to the Nordic sun to place beside Grieg's "Morning Mood," Nielsen's *Helios* Overture, and Sibelius's *Nightride and Sunrise*. Alternating passages of exultation and reflection, it culminates in a hymn of thanksgiving, only to conclude with an elfin shrug, as if to suggest that the passions of the night had been but a dream.

Matthew Mendez

MATTHEW MENDEZ *is a New Haven-based musicologist and critic who specializes in 20th- and 21st-century repertoire. He is a graduate of Harvard University and is currently a Ph.D. candidate at Yale. Mr. Mendez was the recipient of a* [illegible] *ASCAP Foundation Deems Taylor/Virgil Thomson Award for outstanding music journalism.*

THE ONLY PREVIOUS BSO PERFORMANCE *of Stenhammar's Serenade in F was given at Tanglewood on August 1, 2021, under Alan Gilbert's direction.*

The Moon

— March 2, 2019

A Building for Performance

— August 22, 1998

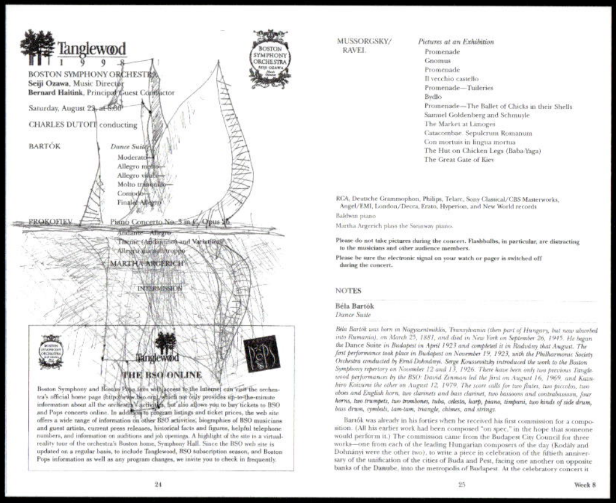
Tanglewood 1998

BOSTON SYMPHONY ORCHESTRA
Seiji Ozawa, Music Director
Bernard Haitink, Principal Guest Conductor

Saturday, August 22, at 8:30

CHARLES DUTOIT conducting

BARTÓK — *Dance Suite*
Moderato—
Allegro molto—
Allegro vivace—
Molto tranquillo—
Comodo—
Finale: Allegro

PROKOFIEV — Piano Concerto No. 3 in C, Opus 26
Andante—Allegro
Theme (Andantino) and Variations
Allegro ma non troppo

MARTHA ARGERICH

INTERMISSION

MUSSORGSKY/RAVEL — *Pictures at an Exhibition*
Promenade
Gnomus
Promenade
Il vecchio castello
Promenade—Tuileries
Bydlo
Promenade—The Ballet of Chicks in their Shells
Samuel Goldenberg and Schmuyle
The Market at Limoges
Catacombae. Sepulcrum Romanum
Con mortuis in lingua mortua
The Hut on Chicken Legs (Baba-Yaga)
The Great Gate of Kiev

RCA, Deutsche Grammophon, Philips, Telarc, Sony Classical/CBS Masterworks, Angel/EMI, London/Decca, Erato, Hyperion, and New World records

Baldwin piano

Martha Argerich plays the Steinway piano.

Please do not take pictures during the concert. Flashbulbs, in particular, are distracting to the musicians and other audience members.

Please be sure the electronic signal on your watch or pager is switched off during the concert.

THE BSO ONLINE

Boston Symphony and Boston Pops fans with access to the Internet can visit the orchestra's official home page (http://www.bso.org), which not only provides up-to-the-minute information about all the orchestra's activities, but also allows you to buy tickets to BSO and Pops concerts online. In addition to program listings and ticket prices, the web site offers a wide range of information on other BSO activities, biographies of BSO musicians and guest artists, current press releases, historical facts and figures, helpful telephone numbers, and information on auditions and job openings. A highlight of the site is a virtual-reality tour of the orchestra's Boston home, Symphony Hall. Since the BSO web site is updated on a regular basis, to include Tanglewood, BSO subscription season, and Boston Pops information as well as any program changes, we invite you to check in frequently.

24

NOTES

Béla Bartók
Dance Suite

Béla Bartók was born in Nagyszentmiklós, Transylvania (then part of Hungary, but now absorbed into Rumania), on March 25, 1881, and died in New York on September 26, 1945. He began the Dance Suite *in Budapest in April 1923 and completed it in Radvány that August. The first performance took place in Budapest on November 19, 1923, with the Philharmonic Society Orchestra conducted by Ernő Dohnányi. Serge Koussevitzky introduced the work to the Boston Symphony repertory on November 12 and 13, 1926. There have been only two previous Tanglewood performances by the BSO: David Zinman led the first on August 16, 1969, and Kazuhiro Koizumi the other on August 12, 1979. The score calls for two flutes, two piccolos, two oboes and English horn, two clarinets and bass clarinet, two bassoons and contrabassoon, four horns, two trumpets, two trombones, tuba, celesta, harp, piano, timpani, two kinds of side drum, bass drum, cymbals, tam-tam, triangle, chimes, and strings.*

Bartók was already in his forties when he received his first commission for a composition. (All his earlier work had been composed "on spec," in the hope that someone would perform it.) The commission came from the Budapest City Council for three works—one from each of the leading Hungarian composers of the day (Kodály and Dohnányi were the other two), to write a piece in celebration of the fiftieth anniversary of the unification of the cities of Buda and Pest, facing one another on opposite banks of the Danube, into the metropolis of Budapest. At the celebratory concert it

25 Week 8

Concept sketch inspired by Bartok's Dance Suite

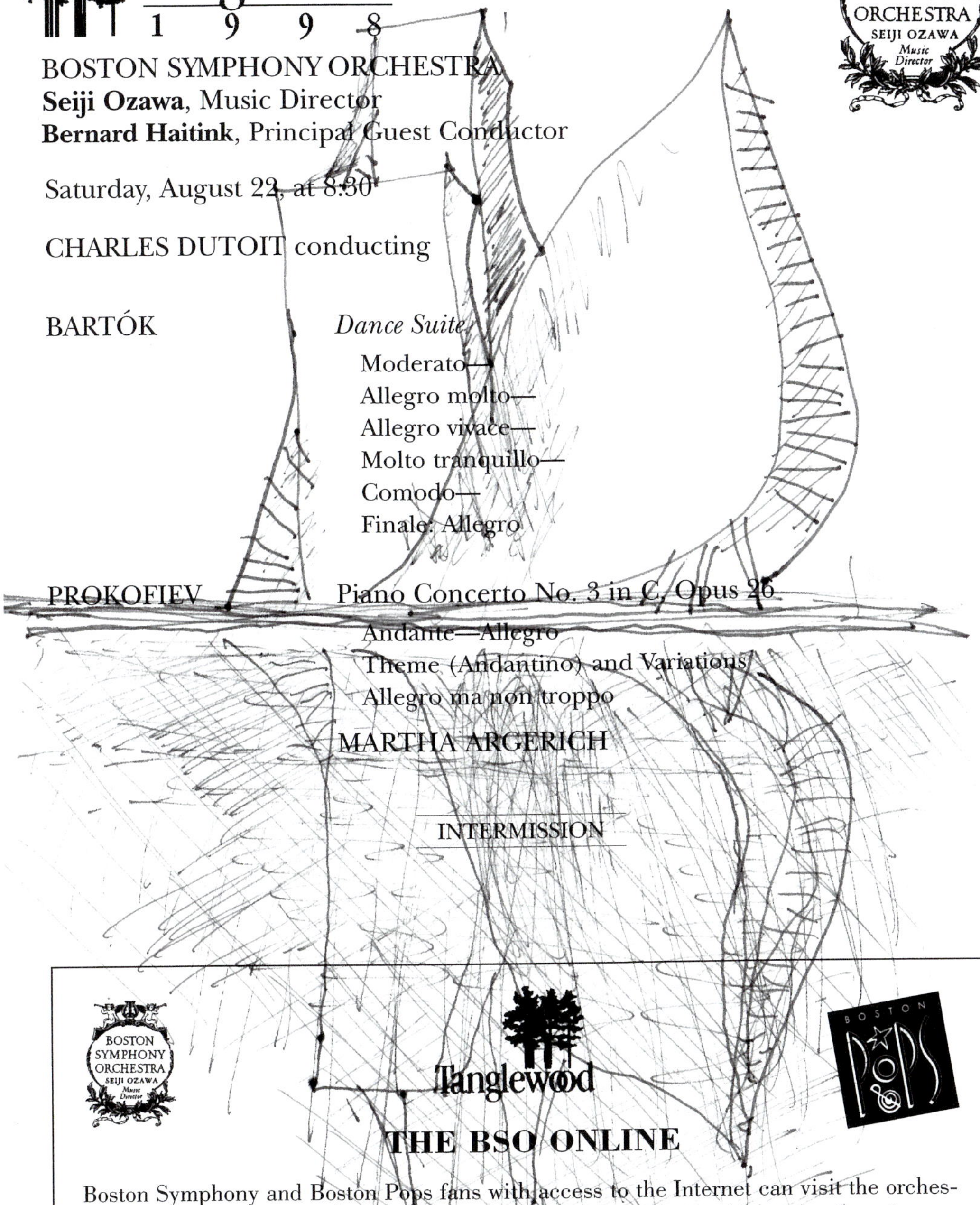

Tanglewood
1 9 9 8

BOSTON SYMPHONY ORCHESTRA
Seiji Ozawa, Music Director
Bernard Haitink, Principal Guest Conductor

Saturday, August 22, at 8:30

CHARLES DUTOIT conducting

BARTÓK *Dance Suite*

Moderato—
Allegro molto—
Allegro vivace—
Molto tranquillo—
Comodo—
Finale: Allegro

PROKOFIEV Piano Concerto No. 3 in C, Opus 26

Andante—Allegro
Theme (Andantino) and Variations
Allegro ma non troppo

MARTHA ARGERICH

INTERMISSION

Tanglewood

THE BSO ONLINE

Boston Symphony and Boston Pops fans with access to the Internet can visit the orchestra's official home page (http://www.bso.org), which not only provides up-to-the-minute information about all the orchestra's activities, but also allows you to buy tickets to BSO and Pops concerts online. In addition to program listings and ticket prices, the web site offers a wide range of information on other BSO activities, biographies of BSO musicians and guest artists, current press releases, historical facts and figures, helpful telephone numbers, and information on auditions and job openings. A highlight of the site is a virtual-reality tour of the orchestra's Boston home, Symphony Hall. Since the BSO web site is updated on a regular basis, to include Tanglewood, BSO subscription season, and Boston Pops information as well as any program changes, we invite you to check in frequently.

94

Red Rocks Resort

— August 20, 2004

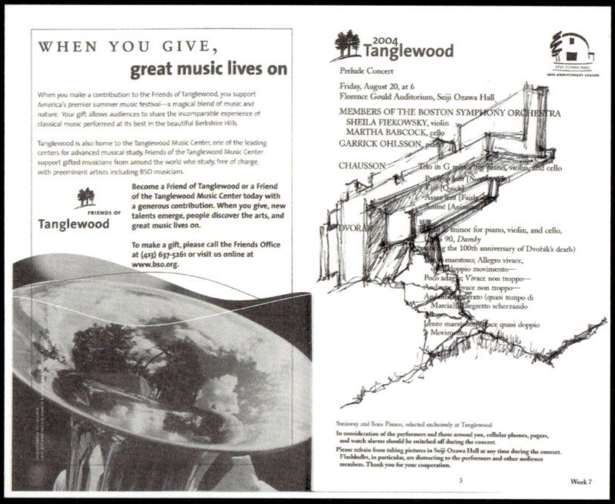

Concept sketch

2004 Tanglewood

SEIJI OZAWA HALL
10th ANNIVERSARY SEASON

Prelude Concert

Friday, August 20, at 6
Florence Gould Auditorium, Seiji Ozawa Hall

MEMBERS OF THE BOSTON SYMPHONY ORCHESTRA
SHEILA FIEKOWSKY, violin
MARTHA BABCOCK, cello
GARRICK OHLSSON, piano

CHAUSSON — Trio in G minor for piano, violin, and cello

- Pas trop lent [Not too slow]
- Vite [Quick]
- Assez lent [Fairly slow]
- Animé [Animated]

DVOŘÁK — Trio in E minor for piano, violin, and cello, Opus 90, *Dumky*
(marking the 100th anniversary of Dvořák's death)

- Lento maestoso; Allegro vivace, quasi doppio movimento—
- Poco adagio; Vivace non troppo—
- Andante; Vivace non troppo—
- Andante moderato (quasi tempo di Marcia); Allegretto scherzando
- Allegro
- Lento maestoso; Vivace quasi doppio Movimento

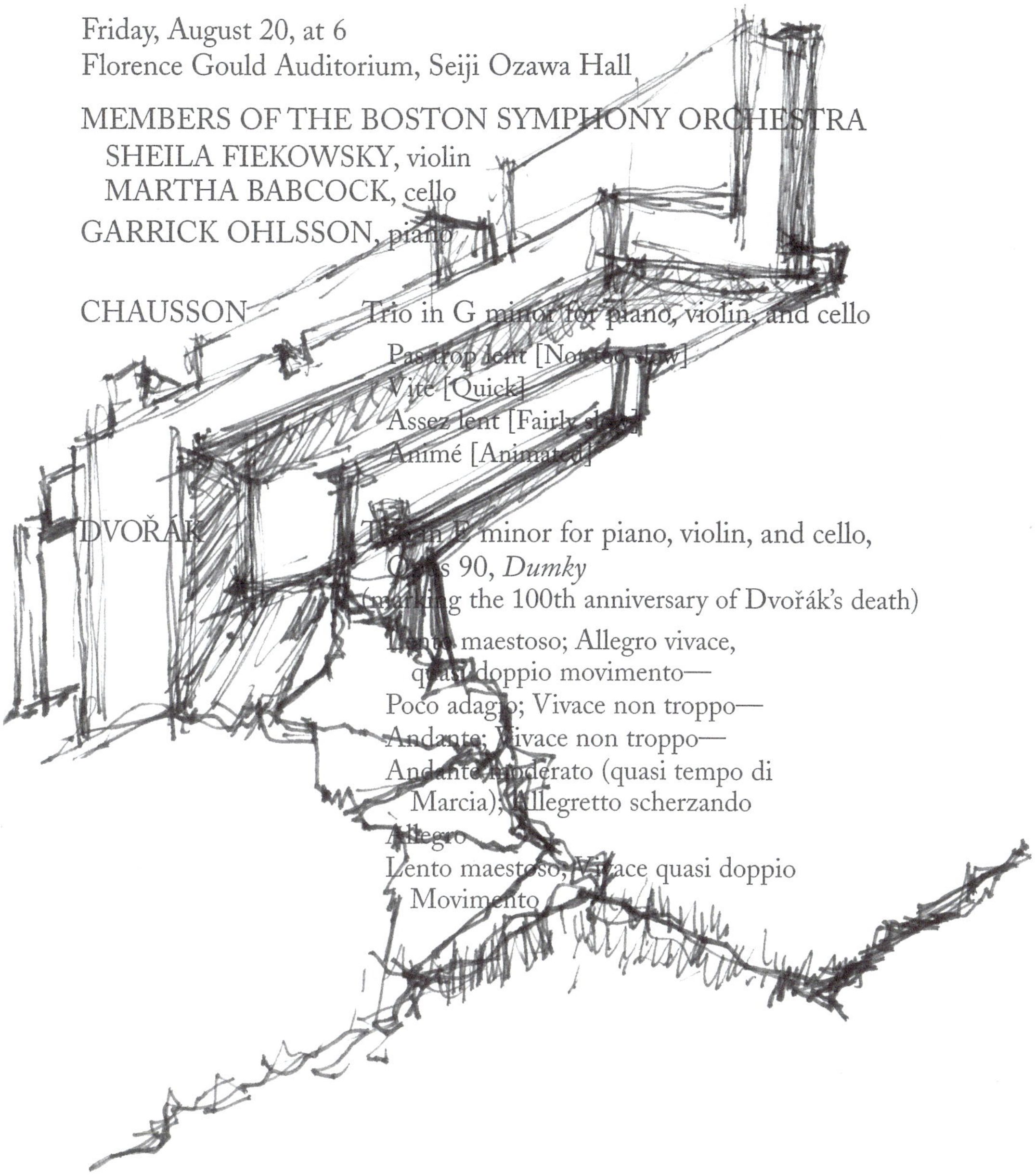

Steinway and Sons Pianos, selected exclusively at Tanglewood

In consideration of the performers and those around you, cellular phones, pagers, and watch alarms should be switched off during the concert.

Please refrain from taking pictures in Seiji Ozawa Hall at any time during the concert. Flashbulbs, in particular, are distracting to the performers and other audience members. Thank you for your cooperation.

Chamber Hall, Moscow

— November 21, 2015

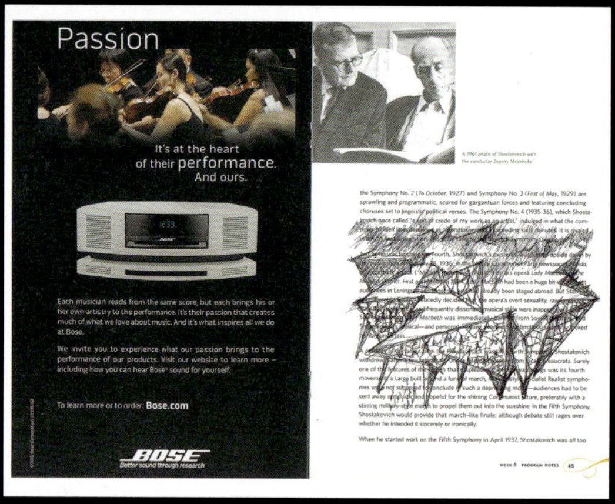

Sited at the edge of a clearing in an urban park, this concept for a Chamber Hall reflects Shostakovich's artistic journey towards Soviet political redemption.

choruses set to jingoistic political verses. The Symphony No. 4 (1935-36), which Shostakovich once called "a sort of credo of my work as an artist," indulged in what the composer himself later described as "grandiosomania." Exceeding sixty minutes, it is rivaled in length, instrumentation, and scale only by the Seventh Symphony (*Leningrad*).

Just as he was finishing the Fourth, Shostakovich's existence was turned upside down by the publication on January 28, 1936, in the official Communist Party newspaper *Pravda*, of a scathing attack ("Muddle Instead of Music") on his opera *Lady Macbeth of the Mtsensk District*. First performed in 1934, *Lady Macbeth* had been a huge hit with Soviet audiences in Leningrad and Moscow, and had already been staged abroad. But Stalin and his cultural advisers belatedly decided that the opera's overt sexuality, raw language, slapstick irreverence, and frequently dissonant musical style were inappropriate for the Soviet audience. *Lady Macbeth* was immediately banned from Soviet theaters, and Shostakovich's musical—and personal—future, previously so limitless, suddenly looked terribly uncertain.

A casualty of the fallout from the *Pravda* attack was the Fourth Symphony. Shostakovich withdrew it after a few rehearsals under intense pressure from local bureaucrats. Surely one of the features of the Fourth that displeased the Party watchdogs was its fourth movement, a Largo built around a funeral march, Mahler-style. Socialist Realist symphonies were not supposed to conclude in such a depressing mood—audiences had to be sent away optimistic and hopeful for the shining Communist future, preferably with a stirring military-style march to propel them out into the sunshine. In the Fifth Symphony,

Hero's Tower

— October 29, 2011

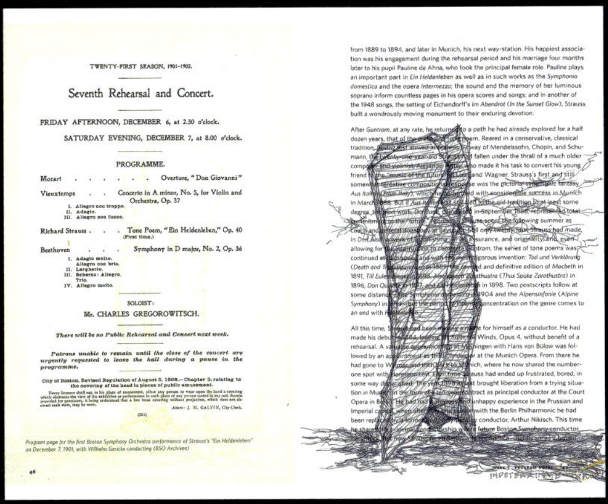

Ein Heldenleben ~ Neither the music nor this sketch represent any particular hero - only the persistence of grace through strength won after many defeats.

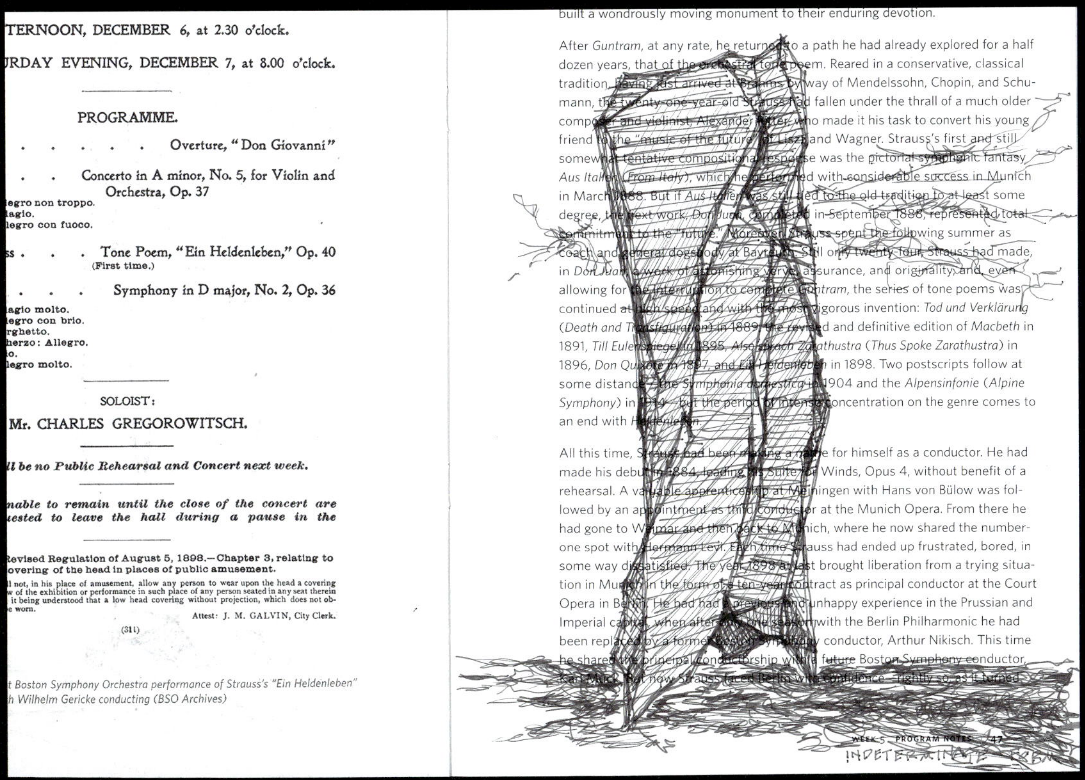

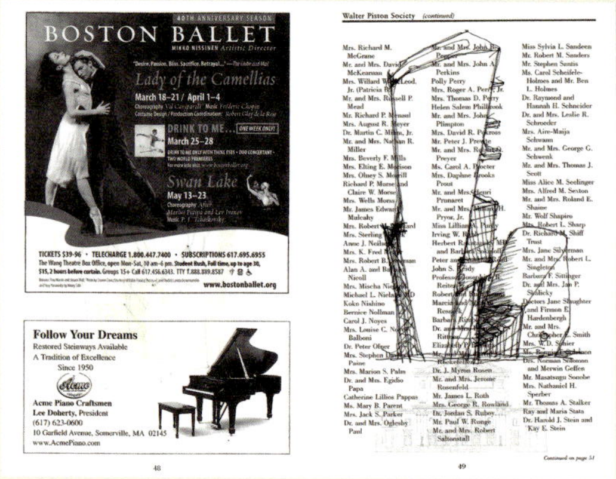

Concept - Tower/Hall — February 14, 2004

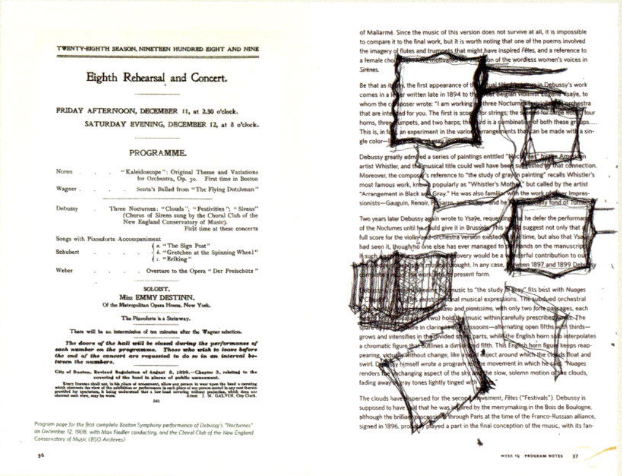

Concepts - Toledo Courthouse — March 18, 2019

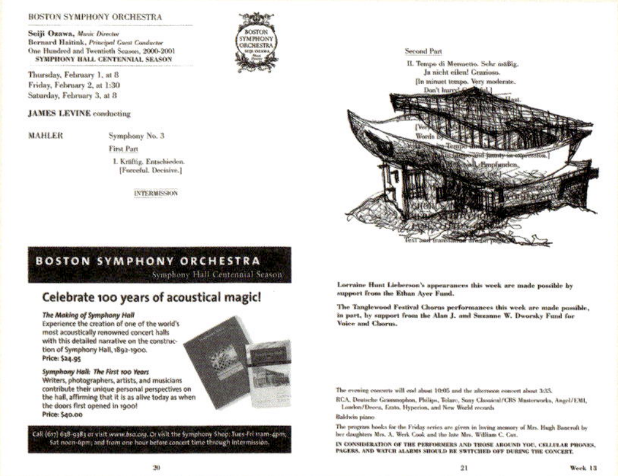

House with Indoor Pool — February 3, 2001

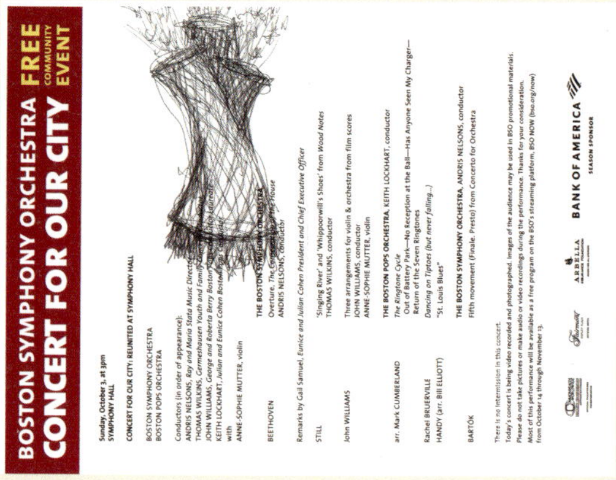

Calliope — October 03, 2021

Energy Foundation — July 24, 2009

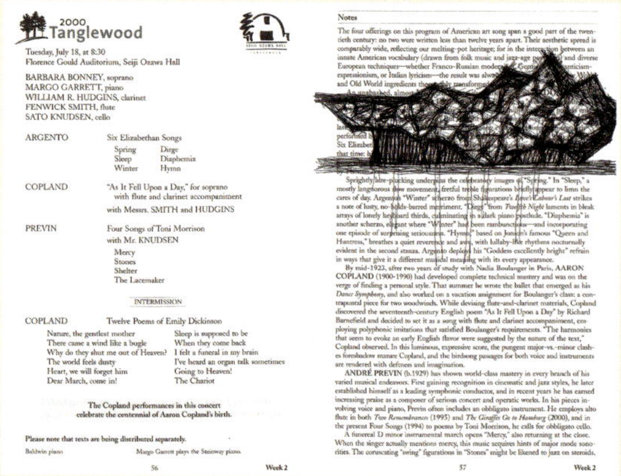

Concert Hall — July 18, 2000

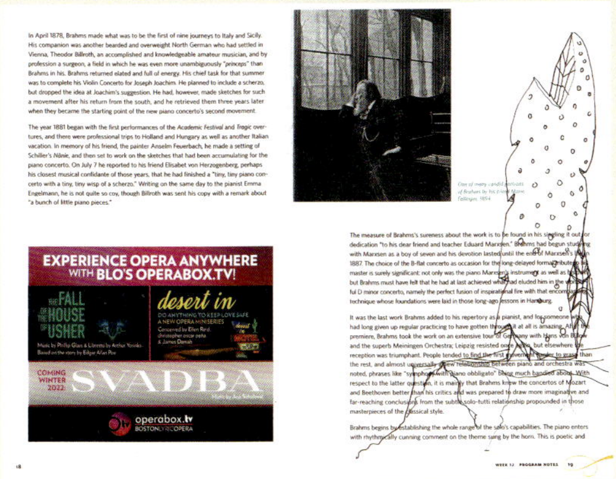

Hotel - Desert Fantasy — January 22, 2022

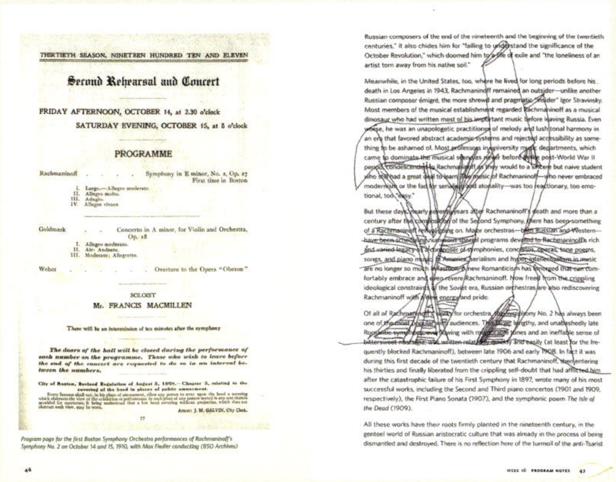

Desert Fantasy — February 11, 2012

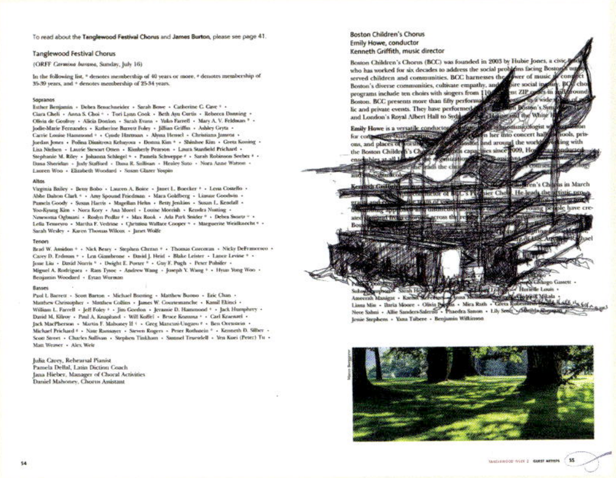

Plein Air Art School — July 16, 2023

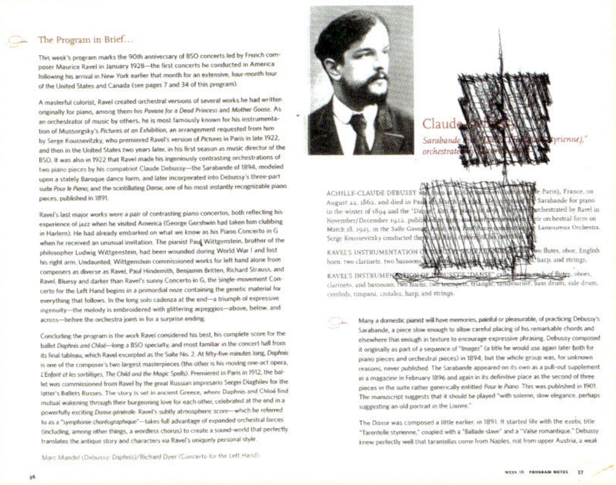

Concept - Toledo Courthouse — February 19, 2018

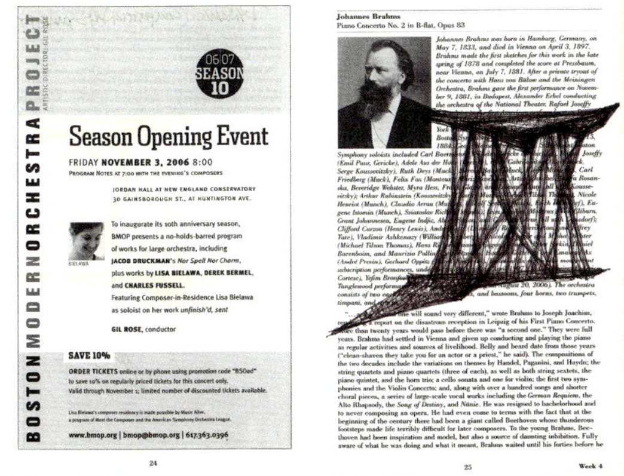

Butterfly House — October 21, 2006

Residential Tower — January 13, 2001

Study - Brattleboro Museum

— March 23, 2019

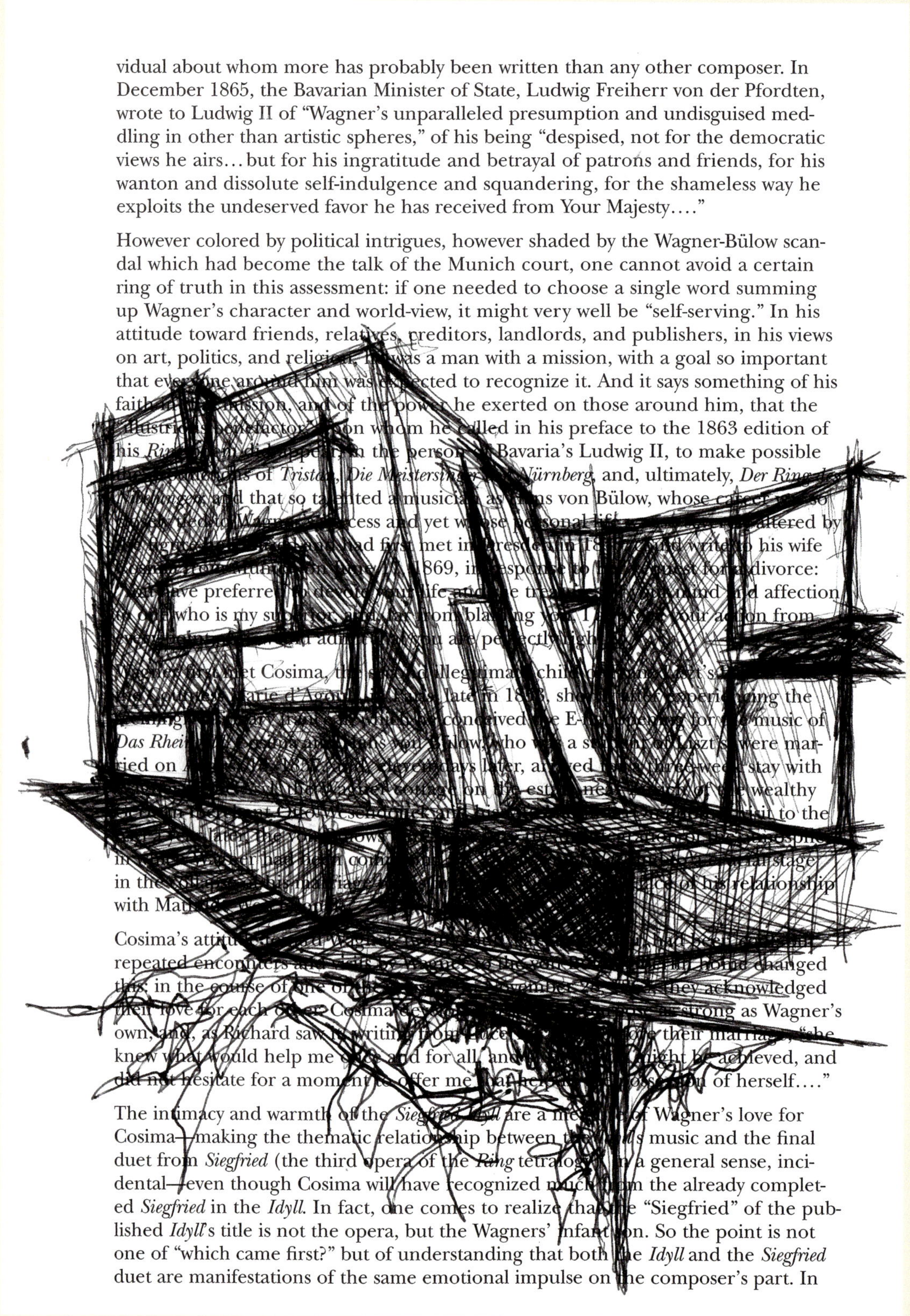

vidual about whom more has probably been written than any other composer. In December 1865, the Bavarian Minister of State, Ludwig Freiherr von der Pfordten, wrote to Ludwig II of "Wagner's unparalleled presumption and undisguised meddling in other than artistic spheres," of his being "despised, not for the democratic views he airs... but for his ingratitude and betrayal of patrons and friends, for his wanton and dissolute self-indulgence and squandering, for the shameless way he exploits the undeserved favor he has received from Your Majesty...."

However colored by political intrigues, however shaded by the Wagner-Bülow scandal which had become the talk of the Munich court, one cannot avoid a certain ring of truth in this assessment: if one needed to choose a single word summing up Wagner's character and world-view, it might very well be "self-serving." In his attitude toward friends, relatives, creditors, landlords, and publishers, in his views on art, politics, and religion, [illegible] was a man with a mission, with a goal so important that [illegible] was expected to recognize it. And it says something of his faith [illegible] the power he exerted on those around him, that the [illegible] whom he called in his preface to the 1863 edition of his [illegible] Bavaria's Ludwig II, to make possible [illegible] *Tristan*, *Die Meistersinger* [illegible] *Nürnberg*, and, ultimately, *Der Ring* [illegible] and that so talented a musician as [illegible] von Bülow, whose [illegible]

[illegible]

The intimacy and warmth of the *Siegfried Idyll* are a [illegible] Wagner's love for Cosima—making the thematic relationship between the [illegible] music and the final duet from *Siegfried* (the third opera of the *Ring* tetralogy) in a general sense, incidental—even though Cosima will have recognized [illegible] the already completed *Siegfried* in the *Idyll*. In fact, one comes to realize that the "Siegfried" of the published *Idyll*'s title is not the opera, but the Wagners' infant son. So the point is not one of "which came first?" but of understanding that both the *Idyll* and the *Siegfried* duet are manifestations of the same emotional impulse on the composer's part. In

Chisel

— July 15, 2018

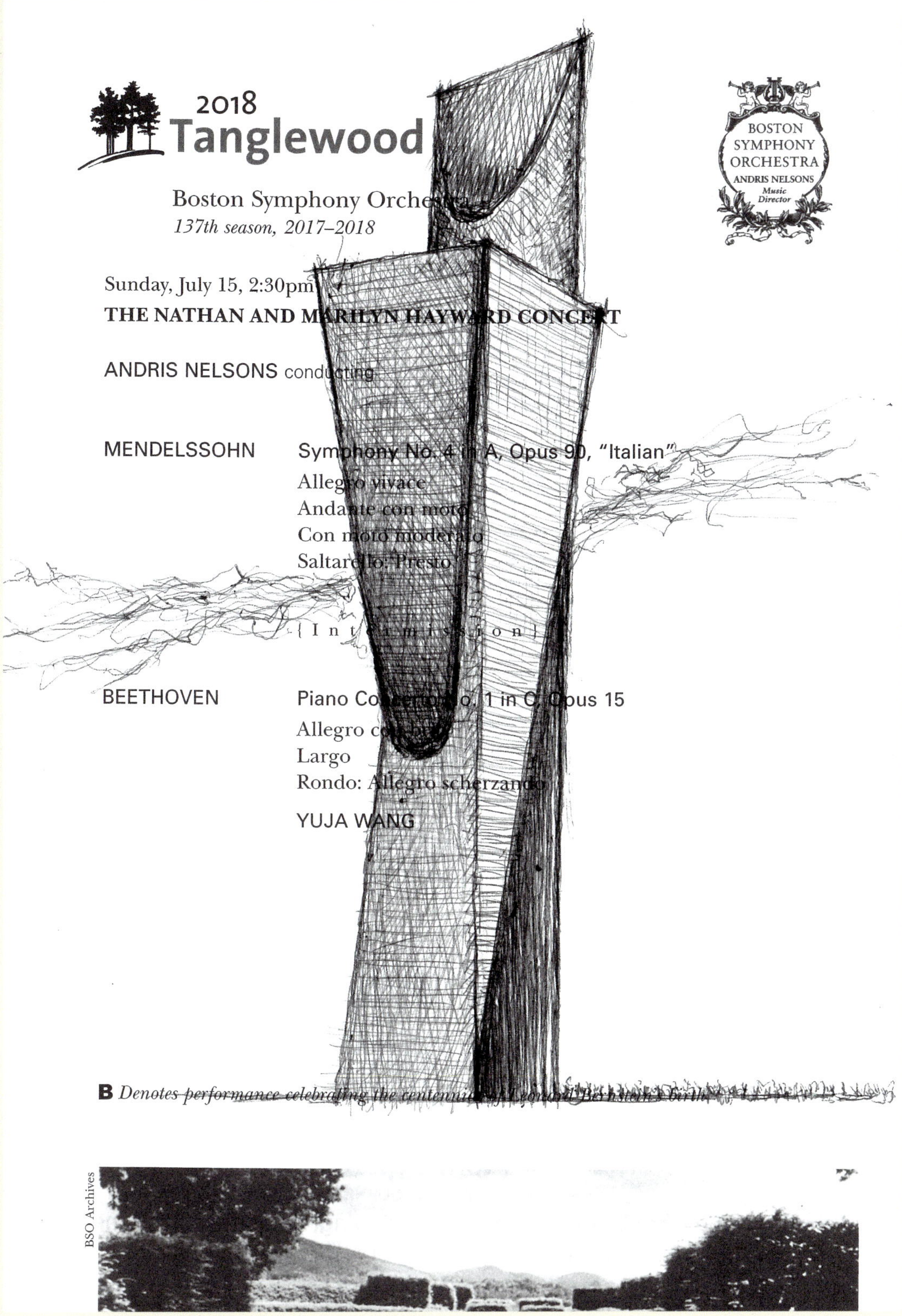

Mozartæum, Salzberg

— January 27, 2001

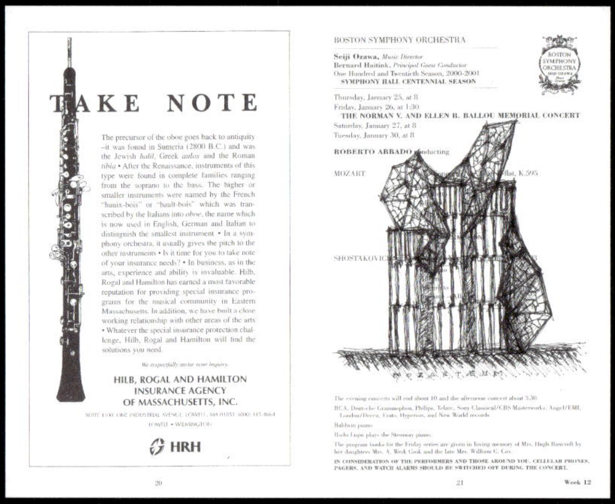

A library/chamber hall for study and performance of Mozart's musical manuscripts 245 years after his birth.

BOSTON SYMPHONY ORCHESTRA

Seiji Ozawa, *Music Director*
Bernard Haitink, *Principal Guest Conductor*
One Hundred and Twentieth Season, 2000-2001
SYMPHONY HALL CENTENNIAL SEASON

Thursday, January 25, at 8
Friday, January 26, at 1:30
THE NORMAN V. AND ELLEN B. BALLOU MEMORIAL CONCERT
Saturday, January 27, at 8
Tuesday, January 30, at 8

ROBERTO ABBADO conducting

MOZART — Piano Concerto No. 27 in B-flat, K.595
Allegro
Larghetto
Allegro
RADU LUPU

INTERMISSION

SHOSTAKOVICH — Symphony No. 10 in E minor, Op. 93
Moderato
Allegro
Allegretto
Andante—Allegro

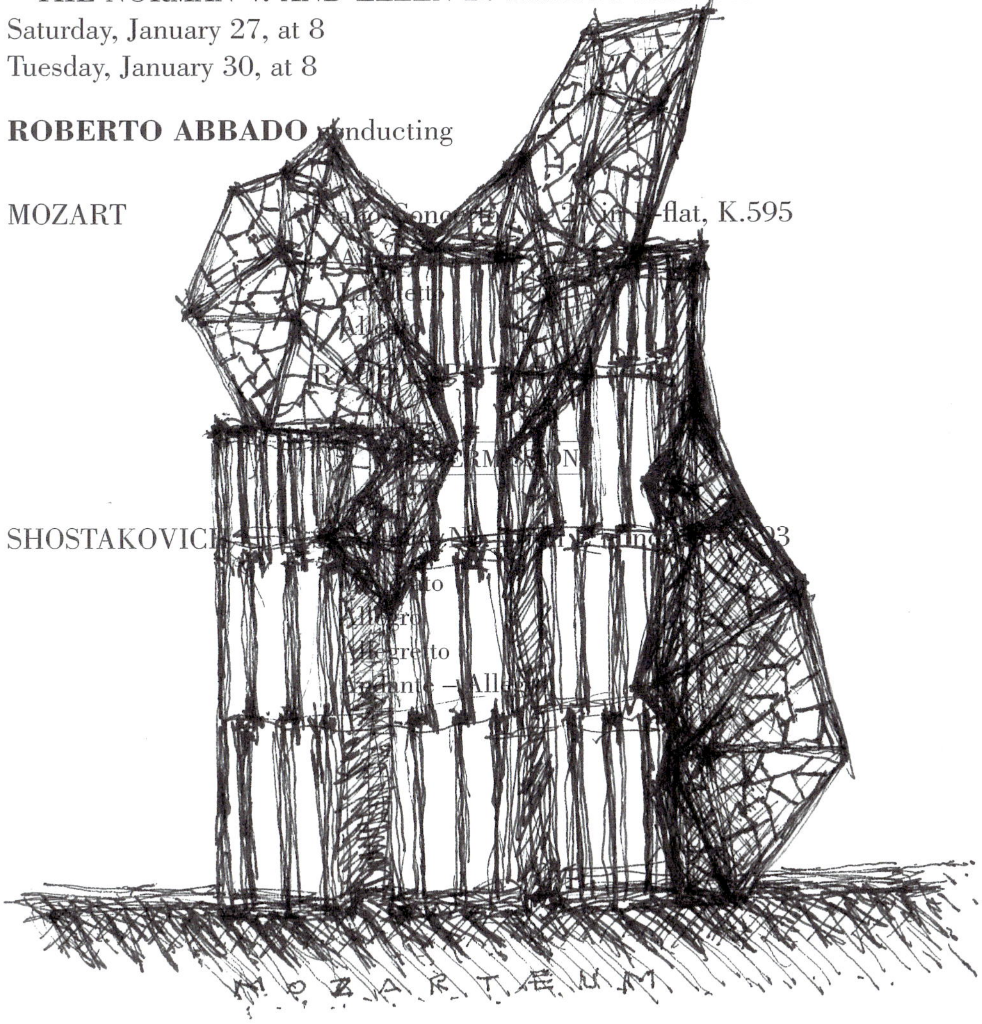

The evening concerts will end about 10 and the afternoon concert about 3:30.

RCA, Deutsche Grammophon, Philips, Telarc, Sony Classical/CBS Masterworks, Angel/EMI, London/Decca, Erato, Hyperion, and New World records

Baldwin piano

Radu Lupu plays the Steinway piano.

The program books for the Friday series are given in loving memory of Mrs. Hugh Bancroft by her daughters Mrs. A. Werk Cook and the late Mrs. William C. Cox.

IN CONSIDERATION OF THE PERFORMERS AND THOSE AROUND YOU, CELLULAR PHONES, PAGERS, AND WATCH ALARMS SHOULD BE SWITCHED OFF DURING THE CONCERT.

21 **Week 12**

Apartments, Hudson, NY

— May 07, 2017

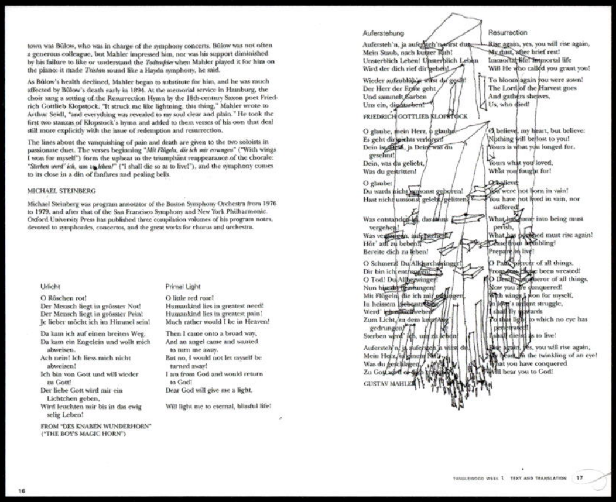

In this case a 9-story apartment building is scaled as if it were taller and denser by exaggerating the slenderness and number of verticals. Multiple balconies amplify scale as do the building's illusory multiple entrances. Filling the corner site at S 5th St & Warren St, it sustains Hudson's ongoing resurrection.

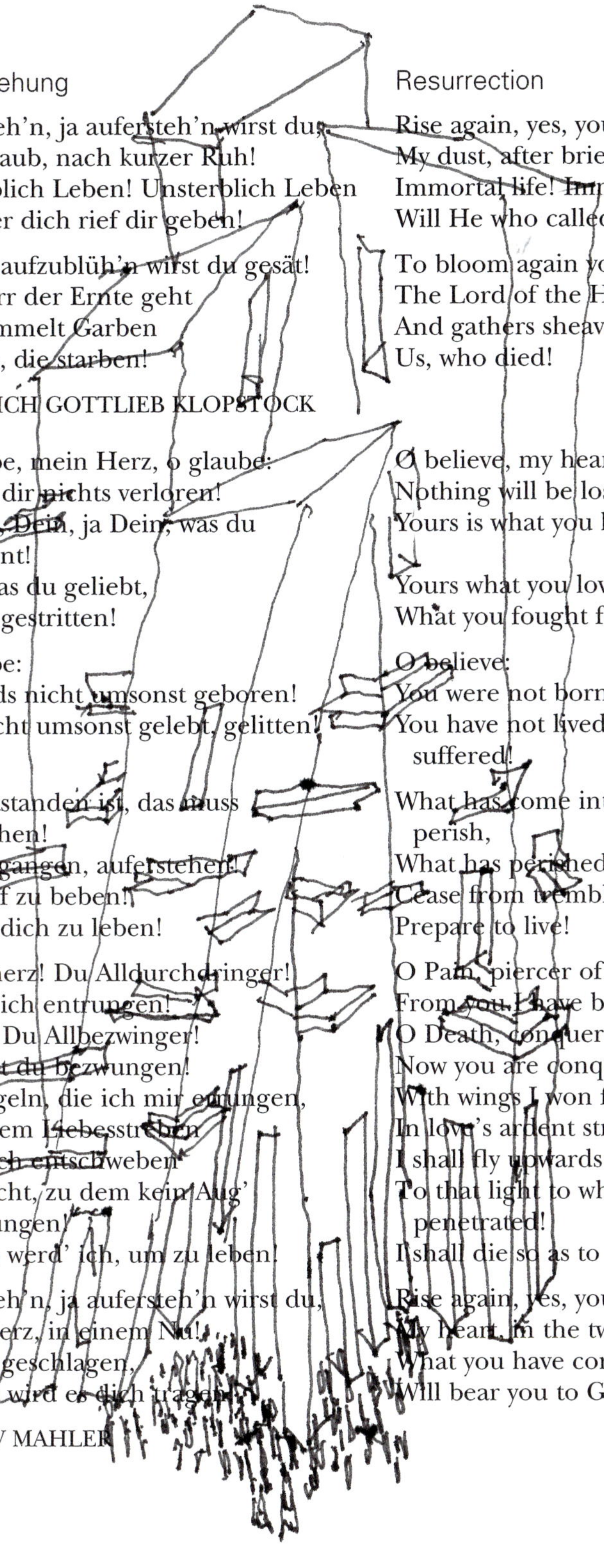

Auferstehung

Aufersteh'n, ja aufersteh'n wirst du,
Mein Staub, nach kurzer Ruh!
Unsterblich Leben! Unsterblich Leben
Wird der dich rief dir geben!

Wieder aufzublüh'n wirst du gesät!
Der Herr der Ernte geht
Und sammelt Garben
Uns ein, die starben!

FRIEDRICH GOTTLIEB KLOPSTOCK

O glaube, mein Herz, o glaube:
Es geht dir nichts verloren!
Dein ist, Dein, ja Dein, was du
gesehnt!
Dein, was du geliebt,
Was du gestritten!

O glaube:
Du wards nicht umsonst geboren!
Hast nicht umsonst gelebt, gelitten!

Was entstanden ist, das muss
vergehen!
Was vergangen, auferstehen!
Hör' auf zu beben!
Bereite dich zu leben!

O Schmerz! Du Alldurchdringer!
Dir bin ich entrungen!
O Tod! Du Allbezwinger!
Nun bist du bezwungen!
Mit Flügeln, die ich mir errungen,
In heissem Liebesstreben
Werd' ich entschweben
Zum Licht, zu dem kein Aug'
gedrungen!
Sterben werd' ich, um zu leben!

Aufersteh'n, ja aufersteh'n wirst du,
Mein Herz, in einem Nu!
Was du geschlagen,
Zu Gott wird es dich tragen!

GUSTAV MAHLER

Resurrection

Rise again, yes, you will rise again,
My dust, after brief rest!
Immortal life! Immortal life
Will He who called you grant you!

To bloom again you were sown!
The Lord of the Harvest goes
And gathers sheaves,
Us, who died!

O believe, my heart, but believe:
Nothing will be lost to you!
Yours is what you longed for,
Yours what you loved,
What you fought for!

O believe:
You were not born in vain!
You have not lived in vain, nor
suffered!

What has come into being must
perish,
What has perished must rise again!
Cease from trembling!
Prepare to live!

O Pain, piercer of all things,
From you, I have been wrested!
O Death, conqueror of all things,
Now you are conquered!
With wings I won for myself,
In love's ardent struggle,
I shall fly upwards
To that light to which no eye has
penetrated!
I shall die so as to live!

Rise again, yes, you will rise again,
My heart, in the twinkling of an eye!
What you have conquered
Will bear you to God!

Three Musicians

— August 20, 2004

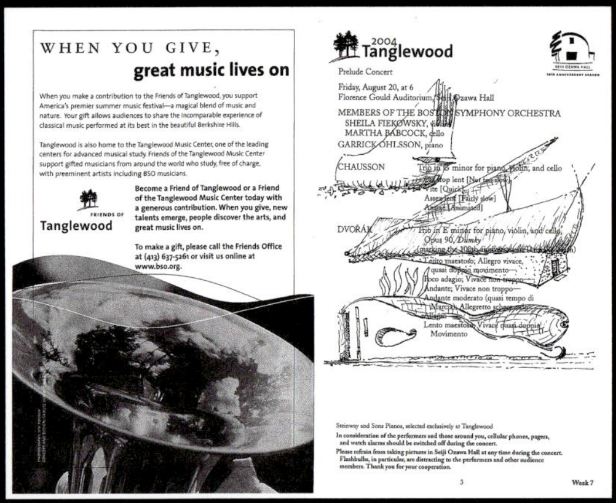

At a prelude concert before the evening program the players had the kind of presence I ordinarily associate only with buildings. Thus each musician is characterized by his or her imagined architectural form. From top to bottom: Sheila Fiekowsky, Violin; Garrick Ohlsson, Piano; Martha Babcock, Cello.

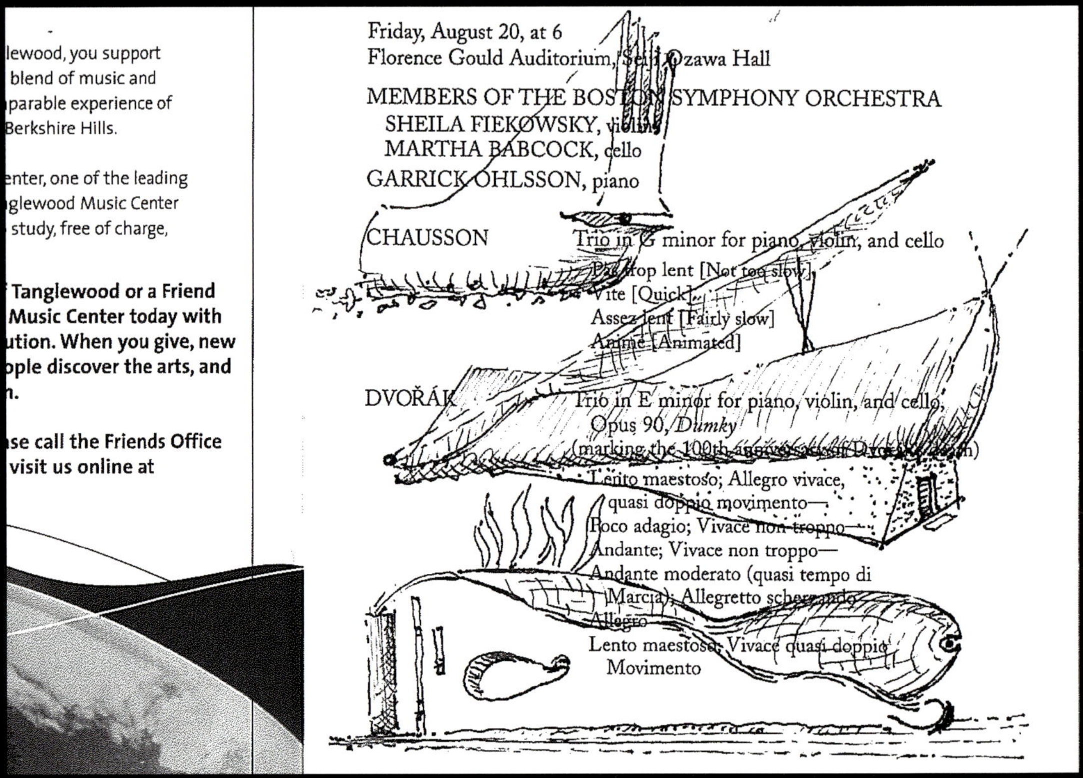

Hotel Casino, Iberian Peninsula

— February11, 2012

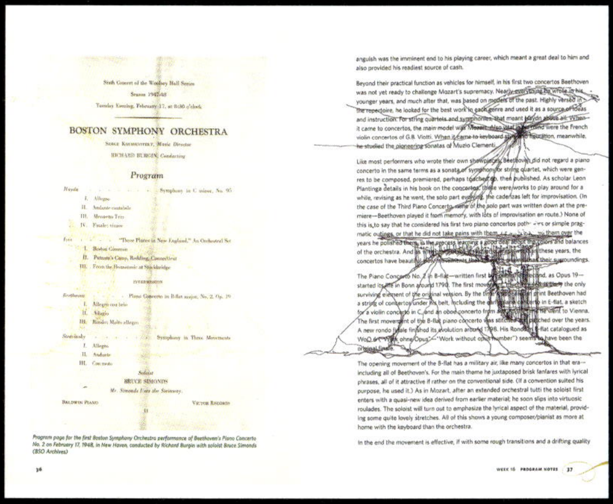

Wide terraces shade uninterrupted views of the large coastal rocks into one of which the casino is carved.

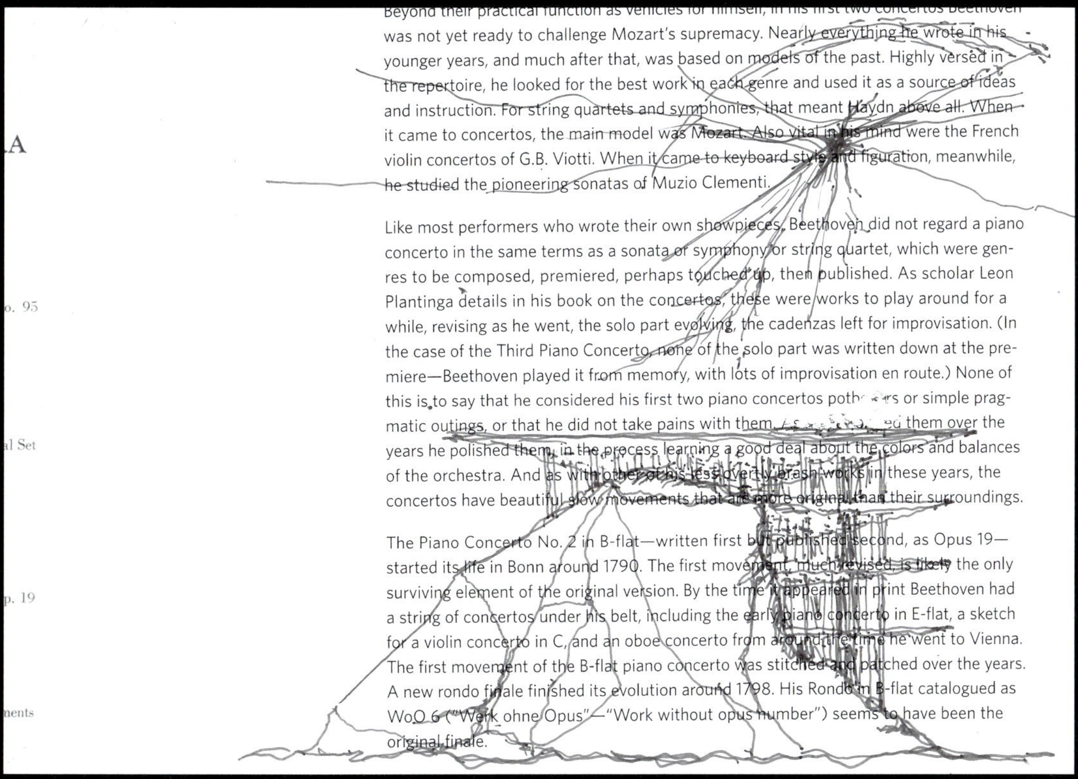
was not yet ready to challenge Mozart's supremacy. Nearly everything he wrote in his younger years, and much after that, was based on models of the past. Highly versed in the repertoire, he looked for the best work in each genre and used it as a source of ideas and instruction. For string quartets and symphonies, that meant Haydn above all. When it came to concertos, the main model was Mozart. Also vital in his mind were the French violin concertos of G.B. Viotti. When it came to keyboard style and figuration, meanwhile, he studied the pioneering sonatas of Muzio Clementi.

Like most performers who wrote their own showpieces, Beethoven did not regard a piano concerto in the same terms as a sonata or symphony or string quartet, which were genres to be composed, premiered, perhaps touched up, then published. As scholar Leon Plantinga details in his book on the concertos, these were works to play around for a while, revising as he went, the solo part evolving, the cadenzas left for improvisation. (In the case of the Third Piano Concerto, none of the solo part was written down at the premiere—Beethoven played it from memory, with lots of improvisation en route.) None of this is to say that he considered his first two piano concertos [illegible] or simple pragmatic outings, or that he did not take pains with them [illegible] them over the years he polished them, in the process learning a good deal about the colors and balances of the orchestra. And as with other of his less overtly brash works in these years, the concertos have beautiful slow movements that are more original than their surroundings.

The Piano Concerto No. 2 in B-flat—written first but published second, as Opus 19—started its life in Bonn around 1790. The first movement, much revised, is likely the only surviving element of the original version. By the time it appeared in print Beethoven had a string of concertos under his belt, including the early piano concerto in E-flat, a sketch for a violin concerto in C, and an oboe concerto from around the time he went to Vienna. The first movement of the B-flat piano concerto was stitched and patched over the years. A new rondo finale finished its evolution around 1798. His Rondo in B-flat catalogued as WoO 6 ("Werk ohne Opus"—"Work without opus number") seems to have been the original finale.

Viewing Tower, Kobe

— July 11, 2010

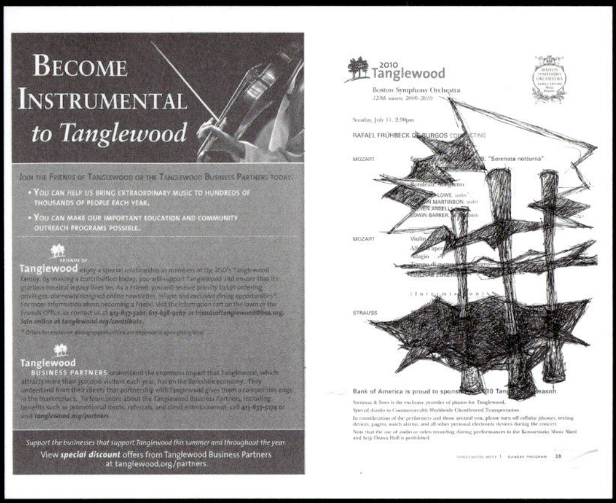

Thunderstorms on the Tanglewood grounds during the afternoon concert sparked a fantasy of this viewing tower far away from here.

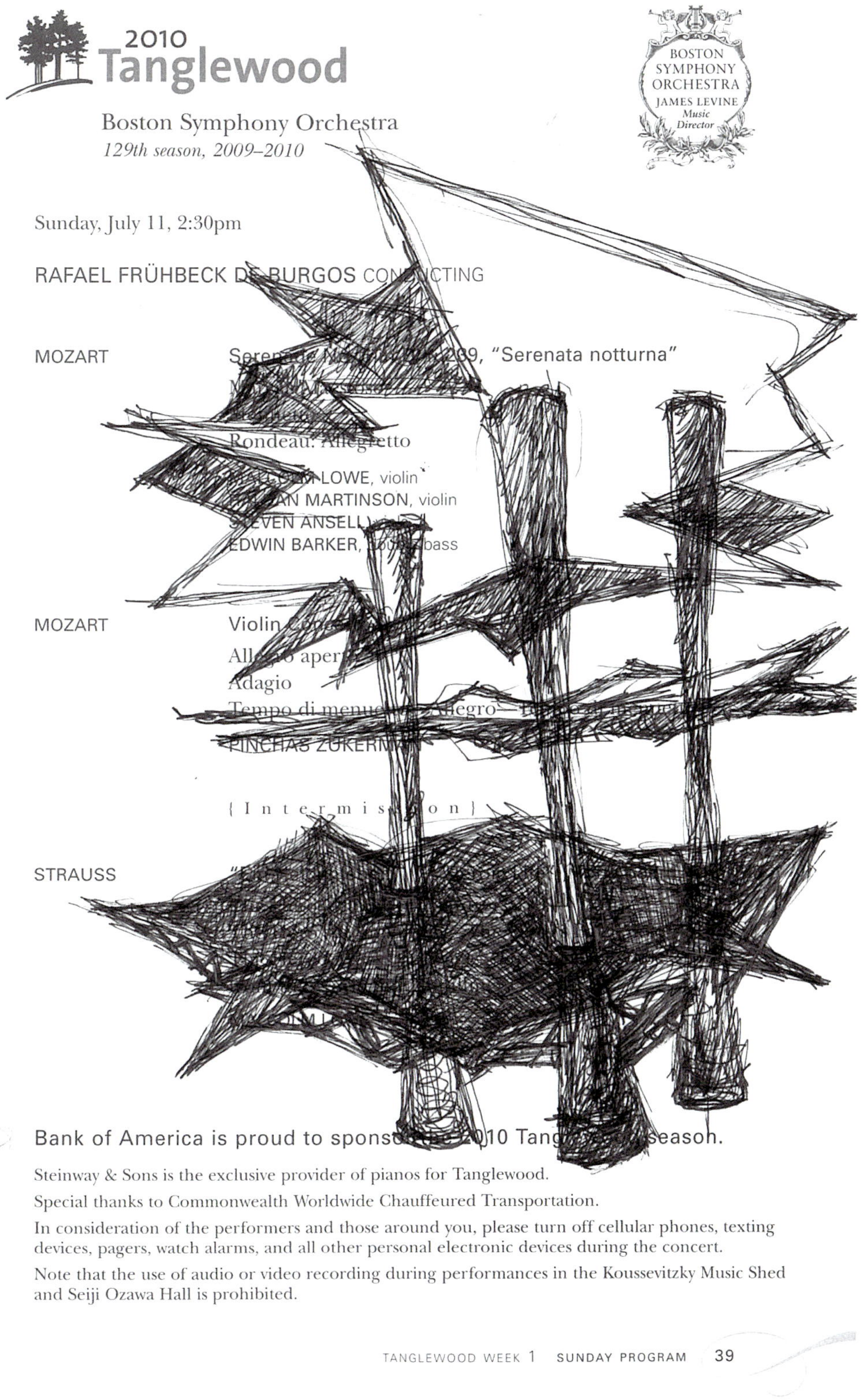

2010 Tanglewood

Boston Symphony Orchestra
129th season, 2009–2010

BOSTON SYMPHONY ORCHESTRA JAMES LEVINE Music Director

Sunday, July 11, 2:30pm

RAFAEL FRÜHBECK DE BURGOS CONDUCTING

MOZART — …9, "Serenata notturna"
Rondeau: Allegretto
…LOWE, violin
…N MARTINSON, violin
…EVEN ANSELL…
EDWIN BARKER, …bass

MOZART — Violin…
All… aper…
Adagio
Tempo di menu…
PINCHAS ZUKERM…

{ I n t e r m i s … o n }

STRAUSS

Bank of America is proud to spons… 2010 Tang… season.

Steinway & Sons is the exclusive provider of pianos for Tanglewood.

Special thanks to Commonwealth Worldwide Chauffeured Transportation.

In consideration of the performers and those around you, please turn off cellular phones, texting devices, pagers, watch alarms, and all other personal electronic devices during the concert.

Note that the use of audio or video recording during performances in the Koussevitzky Music Shed and Seiji Ozawa Hall is prohibited.

TANGLEWOOD WEEK 1 SUNDAY PROGRAM 39

River Center Library, Baton Rouge

— October 06, 2012

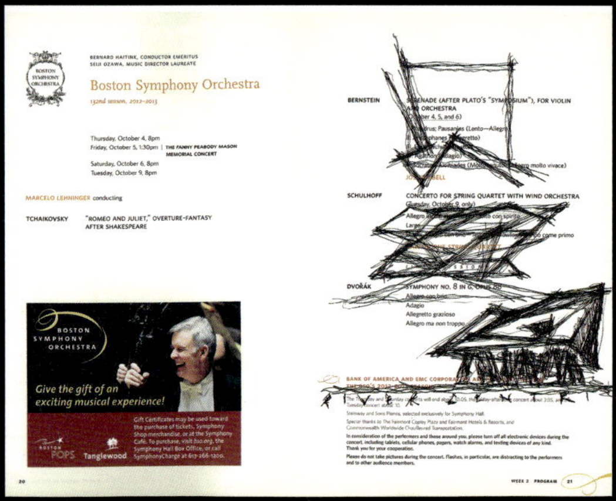

This pre-Concept was drawn very early in the design process with little programmatic content. The site, sketched at the top of page, is basically square, and the building at the bottom depicts a raised structure that provides maximum shade in a hot, sunny and rainy environment. The Library, now under construction, still retains its raised form and sheltering lower floor that provides a canopy above a shaded civic open space.

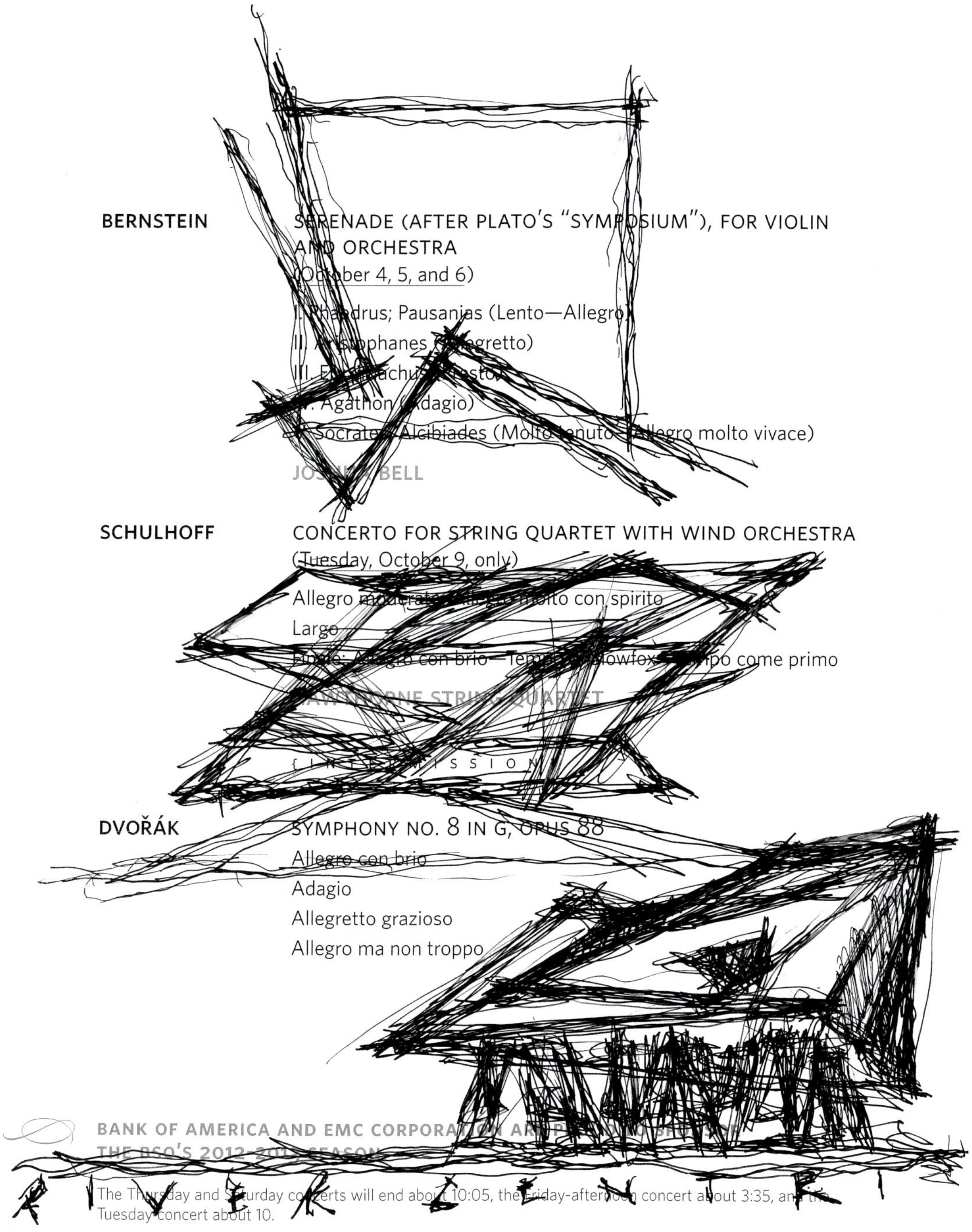

BERNSTEIN SERENADE (AFTER PLATO'S "SYMPOSIUM"), FOR VIOLIN AND ORCHESTRA
(October 4, 5, and 6)

I. Phaedrus; Pausanias (Lento—Allegro)
II. Aristophanes (Allegretto)
III. Eryximachus (Presto)
IV. Agathon (Adagio)
V. Socrates; Alcibiades (Molto tenuto—Allegro molto vivace)

JOSHUA BELL

SCHULHOFF CONCERTO FOR STRING QUARTET WITH WIND ORCHESTRA
(Tuesday, October 9, only)

Allegro moderato; Allegro molto con spirito
Largo
Finale: Allegro con brio—Tempo di Slowfox—Tempo come primo

HAWTHORNE STRING QUARTET

{INTERMISSION}

DVOŘÁK SYMPHONY NO. 8 IN G, OPUS 88

Allegro con brio
Adagio
Allegretto grazioso
Allegro ma non troppo

BANK OF AMERICA AND EMC CORPORATION ARE PROUD SPONSORS OF THE BSO'S 2012–2013 SEASON

The Thursday and Saturday concerts will end about 10:05, the Friday-afternoon concert about 3:35, and the Tuesday concert about 10.

Steinway and Sons Pianos, selected exclusively for Symphony Hall.

Special thanks to The Fairmont Copley Plaza and Fairmont Hotels & Resorts, and Commonwealth Worldwide Chauffeured Transportation.

In consideration of the performers and those around you, please turn off all electronic devices during the concert, including tablets, cellular phones, pagers, watch alarms, and texting devices of any kind. Thank you for your cooperation.

Please do not take pictures during the concert. Flashes, in particular, are distracting to the performers and to other audience members.

WEEK 2 **PROGRAM** 21

River Center Library, Baton Rouge

Study for Pierre Lassonde Pavilion Competition, Montreal

— April 08, 2006

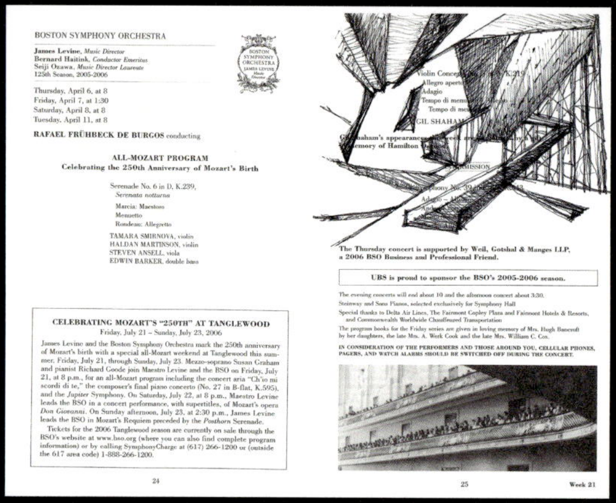

BOSTON SYMPHONY ORCHESTRA

James Levine, *Music Director*
Bernard Haitink, *Conductor Emeritus*
Seiji Ozawa, *Music Director Laureate*
125th Season, 2005-2006

Thursday, April 6, at 8
Friday, April 7, at 1:30
Saturday, April 8, at 8
Tuesday, April 11, at 8

RAFAEL FRÜHBECK DE BURGOS conducting

ALL-MOZART PROGRAM
Celebrating the 250th Anniversary of Mozart's Birth

Serenade No. 6 in D, K.239, *Serenata notturna*
Marcia: Maestoso
Menuetto
Rondeau: Allegretto

TAMARA SMIRNOVA, violin
HALDAN MARTINSON, violin
STEVEN ANSELL, viola
EDWIN BARKER, double bass

CELEBRATING MOZART'S "250TH" AT TANGLEWOOD
Friday, July 21 – Sunday, July 23, 2006

James Levine and the Boston Symphony Orchestra mark the 250th anniversary of Mozart's birth with a special all-Mozart weekend at Tanglewood this summer, Friday, July 21, through Sunday, July 23. Mezzo-soprano Susan Graham and pianist Richard Goode join Maestro Levine and the BSO on Friday, July 21, at 8 p.m., for an all-Mozart program including the concert aria "Ch'io mi scordi di te," the composer's final piano concerto (No. 27 in B-flat, K.595), and the *Jupiter* Symphony. On Saturday, July 22, at 8 p.m., Maestro Levine leads the BSO in a concert performance, with supertitles, of Mozart's opera *Don Giovanni*. On Sunday afternoon, July 23, at 2:30 p.m., James Levine leads the BSO in Mozart's Requiem preceded by the *Posthorn* Serenade.

Tickets for the 2006 Tanglewood season are currently on sale through the BSO's website at www.bso.org (where you can also find complete program information) or by calling SymphonyCharge at (617) 266-1200 or (outside the 617 area code) 1-888-266-1200.

24

Violin Conce...
Allegro aperto
Adagio
Tempo di menu...
Tempo di me...
GIL SHAHAM

...haham's appearance...
...emory of Hamilton...

...MISSION

...phony No. 39...

The Thursday concert is supported by Weil, Gotshal & Manges LLP, a 2006 BSO Business and Professional Friend.

UBS is proud to sponsor the BSO's 2005-2006 season.

The evening concerts will end about 10 and the afternoon concert about 3:30.
Steinway and Sons Pianos, selected exclusively for Symphony Hall
Special thanks to Delta Air Lines, The Fairmont Copley Plaza and Fairmont Hotels & Resorts, and Commonwealth Worldwide Chauffeured Transportation
The program books for the Friday series are given in loving memory of Mrs. Hugh Bancroft by her daughters, the late Mrs. A. Werk Cook and the late Mrs. William C. Cox.

IN CONSIDERATION OF THE PERFORMERS AND THOSE AROUND YOU, CELLULAR PHONES, PAGERS, AND WATCH ALARMS SHOULD BE SWITCHED OFF DURING THE CONCERT.

25 Week 21

Complex program of above and underground connections to a cloister and other existing buildings suggested a multi-level entry with galleries vertically distributed.

Proposed Entrance, Frankfurt International School, Oberursal, Germany

— July 17, 2016

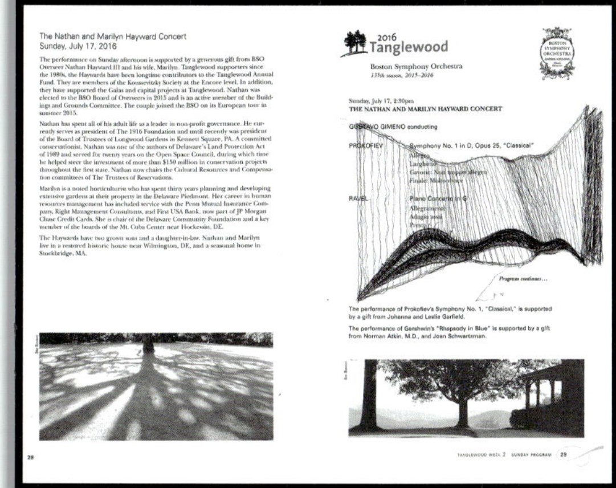

The Nathan and Marilyn Hayward Concert
Sunday, July 17, 2016

The performance on Sunday afternoon is supported by a generous gift from BSO Overseer Nathan Hayward III and his wife, Marilyn. Tanglewood supporters since the 1980s, the Haywards have been longtime contributors to the Tanglewood Annual Fund. They are members of the Koussevitzky Society at the Encore level. In addition, they have supported the Galas and capital projects at Tanglewood. Nathan was elected to the BSO Board of Overseers in 2015 and is an active member of the Buildings and Grounds Committee. The couple joined the BSO on its European tour in summer 2015.

Nathan has spent all of his adult life as a leader in non-profit governance. He currently serves as president of The 1916 Foundation and until recently was president of the Board of Trustees of Longwood Gardens in Kennett Square, PA. A committed conservationist, Nathan was one of the authors of Delaware's Land Protection Act of 1989 and served for twenty years on the Open Space Council, during which time he helped steer the investment of more than $150 million in conservation projects throughout the first state. Nathan now chairs the Cultural Resources and Compensation committees of The Trustees of Reservations.

Marilyn is a noted horticulturist who has spent thirty years planning and developing extensive gardens at their property in the Delaware Piedmont. Her career in human resources management has included service with the Penn Mutual Insurance Company, Right Management Consultants, and First USA Bank, now part of JP Morgan Chase Credit Cards. She is chair of the Delaware Community Foundation and a key member of the boards of the Mt. Cuba Center near Hockessin, DE.

The Haywards have two grown sons and a daughter-in-law. Nathan and Marilyn live in a restored historic house near Wilmington, DE, and a seasonal home in Stockbridge, MA.

2016 Tanglewood

Boston Symphony Orchestra
135th season, 2015–2016

Sunday, July 17, 2:30pm
THE NATHAN AND MARILYN HAYWARD CONCERT

GUSTAVO GIMENO conducting

PROKOFIEV — Symphony No. 1 in D, Opus 25, "Classical"
Allegro
Larghetto
Gavotte: Non troppo allegro
Finale: Molto vivace

RAVEL — Piano Concerto in G
Allegramente
Adagio assai
Presto

Program continues…

The performance of Prokofiev's Symphony No. 1, "Classical," is supported by a gift from Johanna and Leslie Garfield.

The performance of Gershwin's "Rhapsody in Blue" is supported by a gift from Norman Atkin, M.D., and Joan Schwartzman.

TANGLEWOOD WEEK 2 SUNDAY PROGRAM 29

Memories of a recent visit coupled with a recent performance of Prokofiev's Classical Symphony inspired a musical image of arrival to a school of arts and sciences.

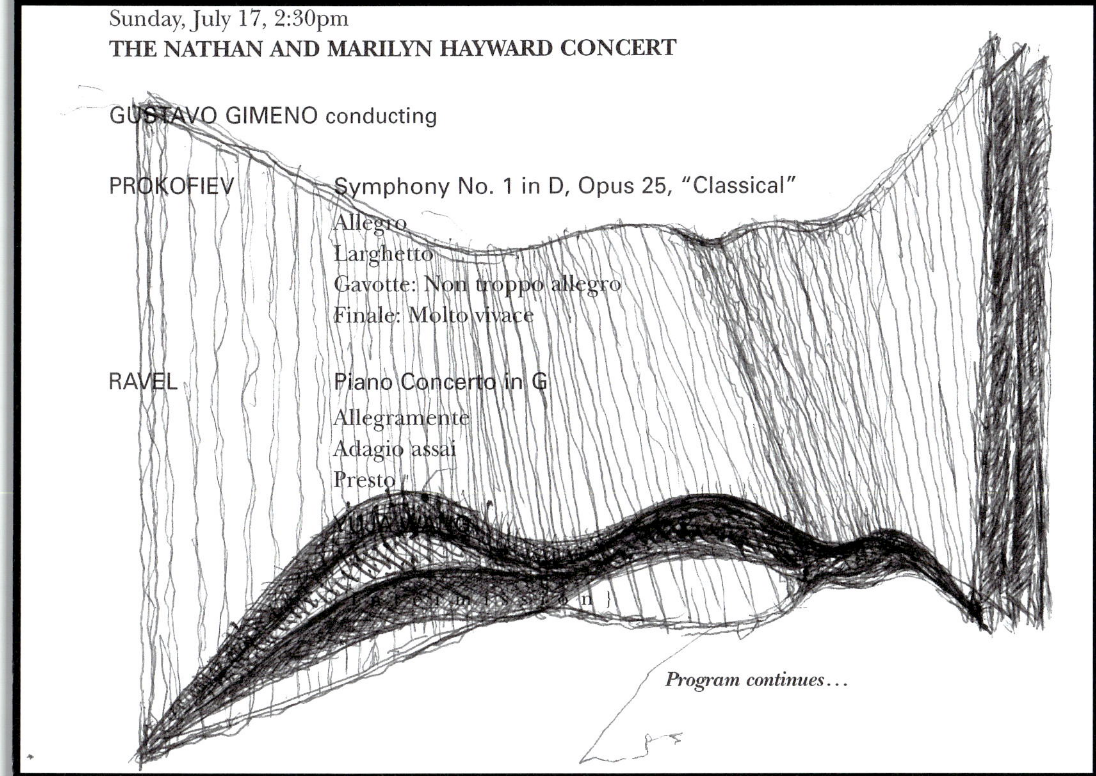

A Small Parisian Tower for a Corner Site

— August, 15, 2010

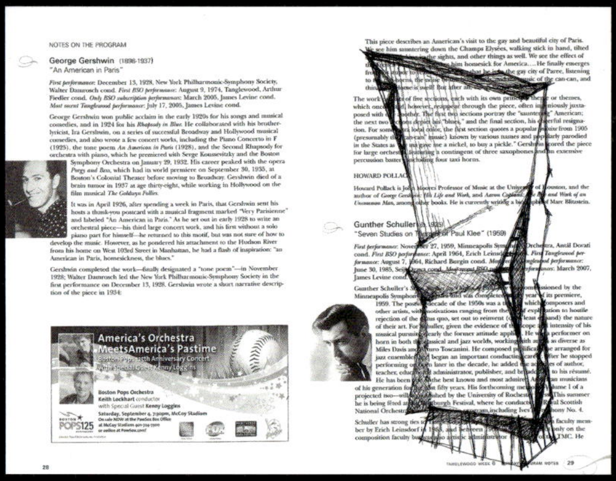

Gershwin's music inspired a tower with human proportions and an American sense of humor.

This piece describes an American's visit to the gay and beautiful city of Paris. We see him sauntering down the Champs Elysées, walking stick in hand, tilted [illegible] the sights, and other things as well. We see the effect of th[illegible] him homesick for America.... He finally emerges fro[illegible] stupor to [illegible] that he is [illegible] the gay city of Paree, listening to t[illegible]-horns, the noise of [illegible] music of the can-can, and thin[illegible] Home is swell! But after all, [illegible]

The work [illegible]ts of five sections, each with its own princ[illegible] theme or themes, which once [illegible]d, however, reappear through the piece, often ing[illegible]niously juxtaposed with o[illegible] another. The first two sections portray the "saunter[illegible]g" American; the next two [illegible]ctions depict his "blues," and the final section, his c[illegible]erful resignation. For some [illegible]tra local color, the first section quotes a popular *m[illegible]xixe* from 1905 (presumably th[illegible] can-can" music) known by various names and p[illegible]pularly parodied in the States as "[illegible] ma gave me a nickel, to buy a pickle." Gershwin scored the piece for large orchest[illegible], featuring a contingent of three saxophones and an extensive percussion batter[illegible] including four taxi horns.

HOWARD POLLACK

Howard Pollack is John Moores Professor of Music at the Unive[illegible] of Houston, and the author of *George Gershwin: His Life and Work*, and *Aaron Copland: [illegible] and Work of an Uncommon Man*, among other books. He is currently writing a bio[illegible]aphy of Marc Blitzstein.

Gunther Schuller (b.1925)

"Seven Studies on Themes of Paul Klee" (1959)

First performance: Nove[illegible]ber 27, 1959, Minneapolis Sym[illegible] Orchestra, Antál Dorati cond. *First BSO perfor[illegible]ance*: April 1964, Erich Leinsd[illegible]. *First Tanglewood performance*: August 7, 1964, Richard Burgin cond. *Most rec[illegible] Tanglewood performance*: June 30, 1985, Seiji Ozawa cond. *Most recent BSO su[illegible] performances*: March 2007, James Levine cond.

Gunther Schuller's *Se[illegible] Studies on Themes of Paul [illegible]* [illegible] commissioned by the Minneapolis Symphony [illegible] and was complete[illegible] year of its premiere, 1959. The postw[illegible] decade of the 1950s was a t[illegible] which composers and other artists, with motivations ranging from the [illegible] of exploration to hostile rejection of the status quo, set out to reinvent ([illegible] least e[illegible]pand) the nature of their art. For Schuller, given the evidence of th[illegible] scope a[illegible] intensity of his musical pursuits, clearly the former attitude appli[illegible]. He w[illegible] a performer on horn in both th[illegible] classical and jazz worlds, working with ar[illegible] as diverse as Miles Davis and Arturo Toscanini. He composed prolifical[illegible] he arranged for jazz ensembles, and began an important conducting care[illegible]. After he stopped performing on horn later in the decade, he added t[illegible]e ac[illegible]es of author, teacher, educ[illegible] administrator, publisher, and br[illegible]adc[illegible] to his résumé. He has been [illegible] the best known and most admire[illegible] A[illegible]an musicians of his generation for the past fifty years. His forthcoming me[illegible]olume I of a projected two—will [illegible] lished by the University of Rochest[illegible]. This summer he is being fêted at [illegible]burgh Festival, where he conducts [illegible] Royal Scottish National Orchestr[illegible] program, including Ives'[illegible] hony No. 4.

Schuller has strong ties t[illegible] a faculty member by Erich Leinsdorf in 1963, and between 19[illegible] only on the composition faculty but was also artistic administrator [illegible] of the TMC. He

TANGLEWOOD WEEK 6 [illegible] PROGRAM NOTES 29

Auroradome; Banff National Park, Alberta, Canada

— April 09, 2011

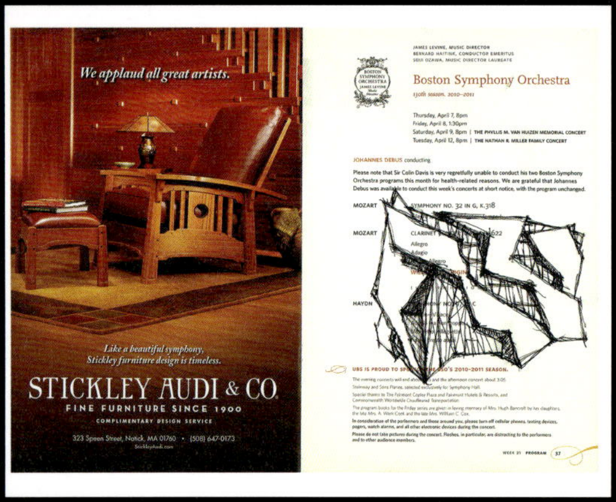

Auroradome Visitor Center on Lake Louise is a restaurant, photograph pavilion and starting point for viewing the Northern Lights.

HESTRA
ES LEVINE
Music
Director

Boston Symphony Orchestra

130th season, 2010–2011

Thursday, April 7, 8pm
Friday, April 8, 1:30pm
Saturday, April 9, 8pm | **THE PHYLLIS M. VAN HUIZEN MEMORIAL CONCERT**
Tuesday, April 12, 8pm | **THE NATHAN R. MILLER FAMILY CONCERT**

NNES DEBUS conducting

: note that Sir Colin Davis is very regretfully unable to conduct his two Boston Symphony
stra programs this month for health-related reasons. We are grateful that Johannes
; was available to conduct this week's concerts at short notice, with the program unchanged.

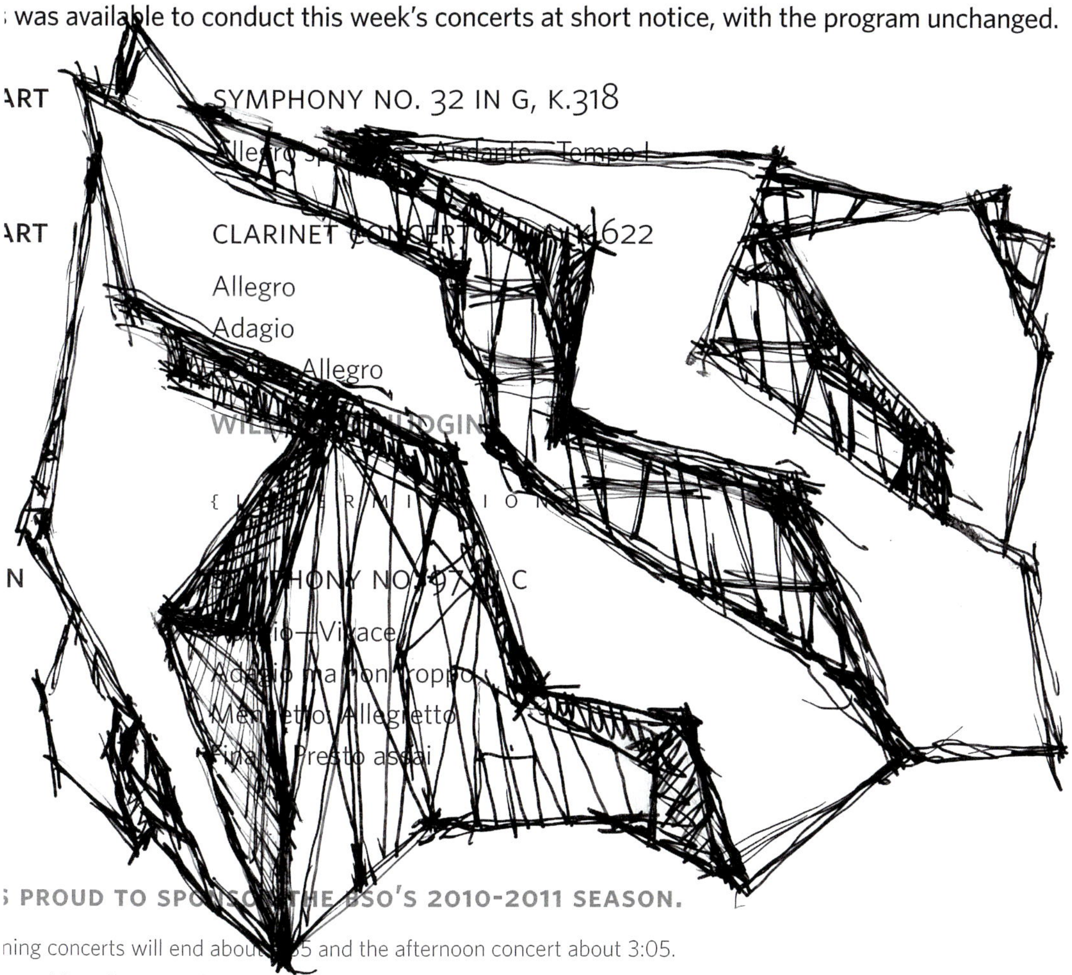

ART — SYMPHONY NO. 32 IN G, K.318

Allegro spiritoso—Andante—Tempo I

ART — CLARINET CONCERTO IN A, K.622

Allegro
Adagio
Rondo: Allegro

WILLIAM HUDGINS

{INTERMISSION}

N — SYMPHONY NO. 97 IN C

Adagio—Vivace
Adagio ma non troppo
Menuetto: Allegretto
Finale: Presto assai

; PROUD TO SPONSOR THE BSO'S 2010-2011 SEASON.

ning concerts will end about 10:05 and the afternoon concert about 3:05.

y and Sons Pianos, selected exclusively for Symphony Hall.

:hanks to The Fairmont Copley Plaza and Fairmont Hotels & Resorts, and
nwealth Worldwide Chauffeured Transportation.

gram books for the Friday series are given in loving memory of Mrs. Hugh Bancroft by her daughters,
Mrs. A. Werk Cook and the late Mrs. William C. Cox.

deration of the performers and those around you, please turn off cellular phones, texting devices,
watch alarms, and all other electronic devices during the concert.

lo not take pictures during the concert. Flashes, in particular, are distracting to the performers
ther audience members.

House on Baldpate Hill

— March 18, 2006

Sited atop a high overlook with expansive views, the professional lives of the clients, painter and real estate developer, are housed in separate wings, one looking north, the other south. Their personal lives meet in a central portion facing west towards the Blue Hills of Massachusetts. The lower site contains a pool.

(Romanian Concerto) in 1951; it was given a rehearsal reading by the orchestra of Hungarian Radio in Budapest the same year (but did not pass the scrutiny of the censors). Thereafter the score was lost, but it was evidently reconstructed from parts in the 1960s, and according to the composer was premiered publicly in Evanston, Illinois, although the details remain elusive. Ligeti's current publisher, Schott International, shows a public premiere date of August 21, 1971, in the Gibraltar School Auditorium as part of the Peninsula Music Festival in Fish Creek, Wisconsin, with Thor Johnson conducting [illegible] Orchestra. Further muddying the waters is recent unconfirmed research by [illegible] Willson, who has located a works list from the early 1950s by Ligeti [illegible] public performances in Hungary between 1951 and 1953. Ligeti revised [illegible] mid-1990s; the current version was published in 1996. These are the [illegible] of Concert Românesc *by the Boston Symphony Orchestra. The score [illegible] (second doubling piccolo), two oboes (second doubling English horn), [illegible] bassoons, three horns (the third being seated apart from the other two [illegible]), two trumpets, percussion (two players [illegible] suspended [illegible] cymbals, snare drum, bass drum), and strings. The piece is about [illegible].*

Ligeti [illegible] father, a bank[illegible] trade, strong[illegible] in 1940, [illegible] prohibited from attending [illegible] conservatory in Cluj, where he studied [illegible] while unofficially attending university [illegible] due to the war. Ligeti's diff[illegible] traveled to Budapest [illegible] the pianist and composer Pál Kadosa.

In 1944 Ligeti, along with many [illegible] lived many more years.)

When "normal" life resumed in war-ravaged Budapest, Ligeti returned there to enroll at the Franz Liszt Academy, where he worked with Sándor Veress and came into contact with Zoltán Kodály, who arranged for him a position as a theory instructor. (Bartók died in New York in 1945 before he could fulfill Hungary's hopes for his return.) He also met the composer and pianist György Kurtág, who became a lifelong friend. As the 1940s continued, the increasing political and military presence of the Soviets became as oppressive in its way as the war had been. Ligeti himself was initially sympathetic to communism, which (in theory) represented a utopian ideal hostile to fascism and anti-Semitism. As Soviet control became more pervasive, however, the differences between the previous occupation and the present one became less clear. Ligeti has commented

27 **Week 19**

Cityhouse, Carrara, Italy

— April 09, 2011

A 5-story residence on a corner site, clad in white Carrara marble.

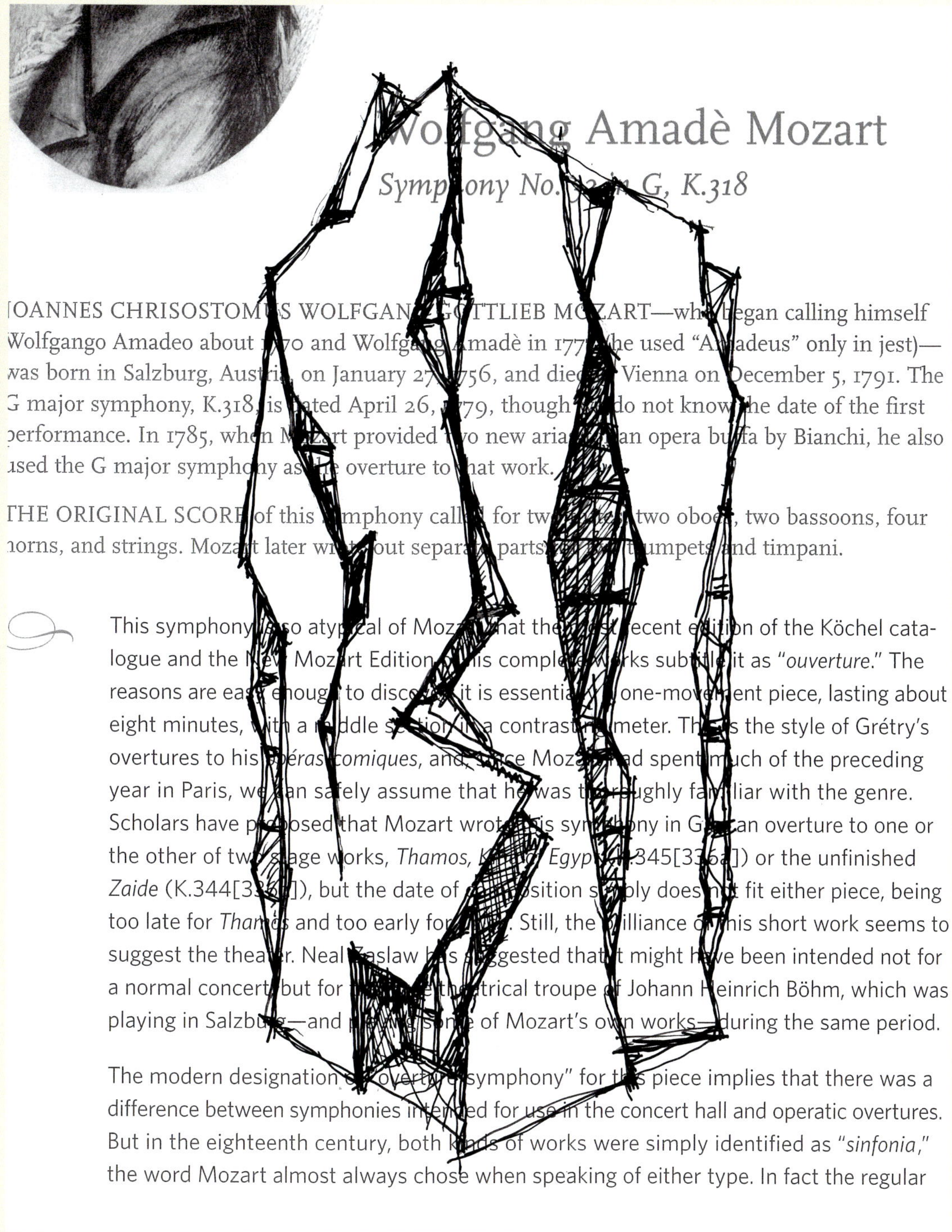

Wolfgang Amadè Mozart

Symphony No. [illegible] in G, K.318

JOANNES CHRISOSTOMUS WOLFGANG GOTTLIEB MOZART—who began calling himself Wolfgango Amadeo about 1770 and Wolfgang Amadè in 1777 (he used "Amadeus" only in jest)—was born in Salzburg, Austria, on January 27, 1756, and died in Vienna on December 5, 1791. The G major symphony, K.318, is dated April 26, 1779, though we do not know the date of the first performance. In 1785, when Mozart provided two new arias for an opera buffa by Bianchi, he also used the G major symphony as the overture to that work.

THE ORIGINAL SCORE of this symphony called for two [illegible], two oboes, two bassoons, four horns, and strings. Mozart later wrote out separate parts [illegible] trumpets and timpani.

This symphony is so atypical of Mozart that the most recent edition of the Köchel catalogue and the New Mozart Edition of his complete works subtitle it as "*ouverture*." The reasons are easy enough to discover: it is essentially a one-movement piece, lasting about eight minutes, with a middle section in a contrasting meter. This is the style of Grétry's overtures to his *opéras comiques*, and, since Mozart had spent much of the preceding year in Paris, we can safely assume that he was thoroughly familiar with the genre. Scholars have proposed that Mozart wrote this symphony in G as an overture to one or the other of two stage works, *Thamos, King of Egypt* (K.345[336a]) or the unfinished *Zaide* (K.344[336b]), but the date of composition simply does not fit either piece, being too late for *Thamos* and too early for [illegible]. Still, the brilliance of this short work seems to suggest the theater. Neal Zaslaw has suggested that it might have been intended not for a normal concert but for [illegible] theatrical troupe of Johann Heinrich Böhm, which was playing in Salzburg—and [illegible] some of Mozart's own works—during the same period.

The modern designation of "overture-symphony" for this piece implies that there was a difference between symphonies intended for use in the concert hall and operatic overtures. But in the eighteenth century, both kinds of works were simply identified as "*sinfonia*," the word Mozart almost always chose when speaking of either type. In fact the regular

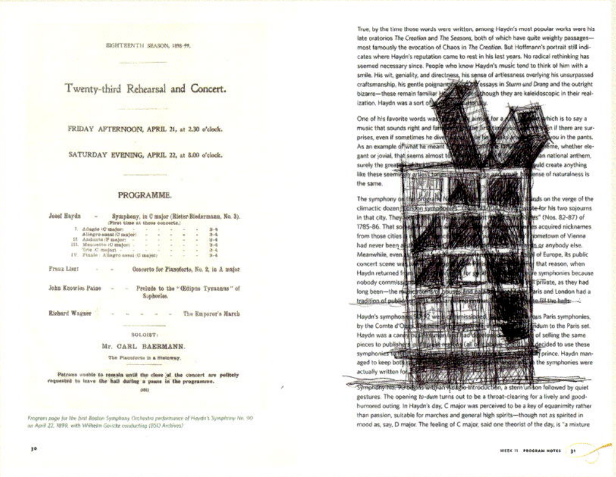

Marshall University Studio Arts, Huntington, WV

Monumental Light Shafts inserted deep into a six-story brick building contain vertical galleries and stairs which redistribute program equally on all floors and revitalize a central section of downtown Huntington.— January 07, 2012

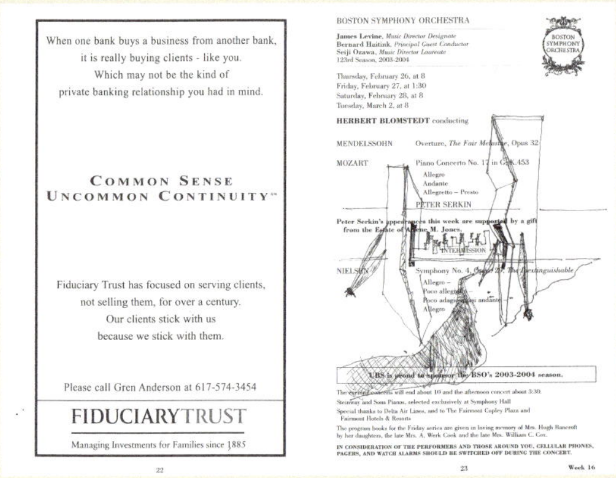

Zephyr Hotel, Butte County, CA

Concept hotel at a crossing of the Feather River Canyon along the historic Union Pacific route, with a future Oroville on the horizon. "Inextinguishable," (Symphony #4) by Carl Neilsen, is played in four connected movements without breaks, referencing the First World War and expressing the "elemental will to live." The Zephyr Hotel is depicted here as one building in two parts echoing the drama of two sets of timpani battling one another in a monumental orchestral landscape. — February 28, 2004

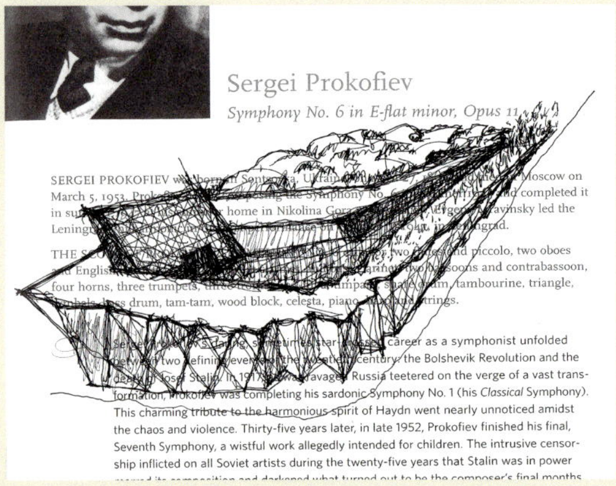

VCU Institute for Contemporary Art

Prior to architect selection this sketch proposed an L-shaped promenade which loops and connects lobby, exhibit galleries, performance space, sculpture terrace, cafe and offices, with access at the corner or from the tree-lined parking court to the roof. Sited at the busiest traffic intersection in Richmond, this building captures the dynamic movement of its historic location and of the University itself.— January 15, 2011

House in the Badlands, SD

Rising above spruce forests, this house is inspired by scenes in the movie "North By Northwest". — November 28, 2003

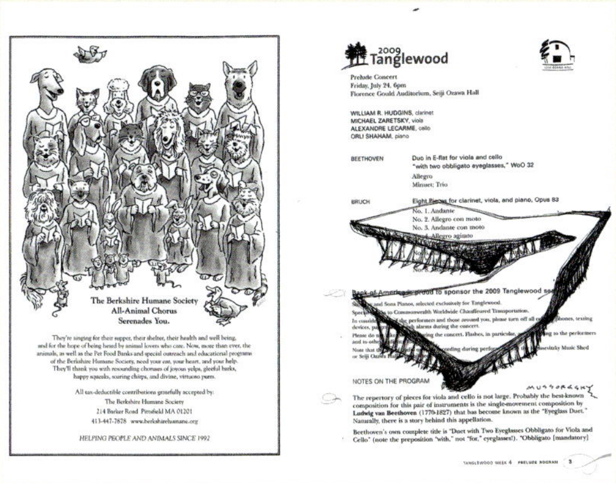

Fiera Internacional Addition, Lisbon, Portugal

Study for a new Exposition Hall, Expo Lisbon, with Grand Plaza entrance. — July 24, 2009

New Concert Hall, Baia Mare, Romania

Proposed for one of the most gently scaled cities in Europe, the new Hall fits, in size and detail, the richness of its urban setting. — November 08, 1997

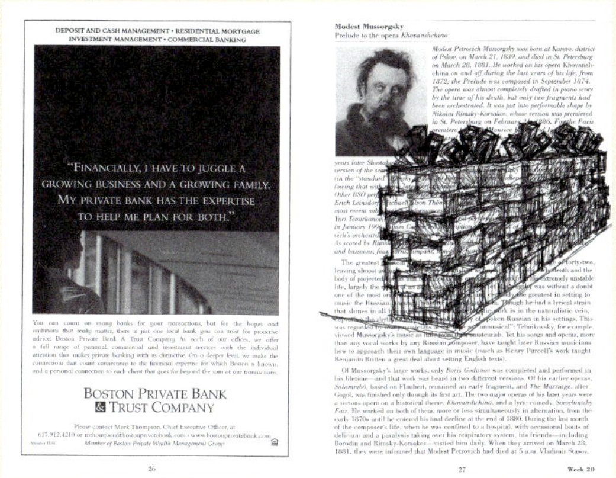

Multi-Family Residential, 196 Orleans St, Boston, MA

Ten years ago this industrial building in East Boston was available for redevelopment. Since then the building across the street has been redesigned for loft living. The concrete structure at 196 Orleans St is re-conceived with multiple bay flats and exuberant rooftop apartments. — April 01, 2006

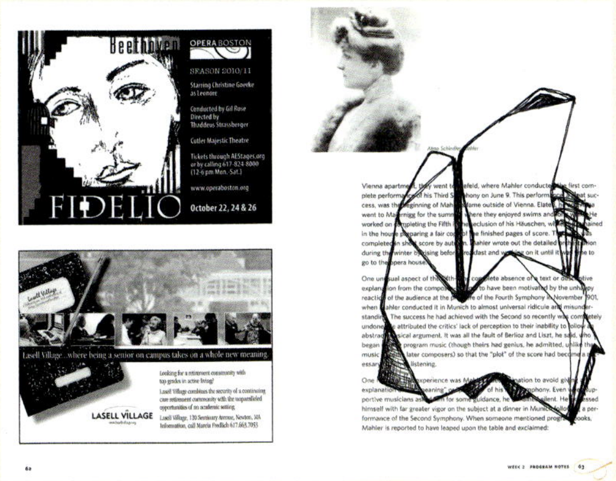

Mahler Musikhauschen, Cologne

Inspired by Mahler's Fifth Symphony Part lll and the expressive architecture of Erich Mendelsohn, this music library would contain Mahler's musical world on the intimate scale in which the composition was written, and a small public performance space on the ground floor. The conclusion of Mahler's Fifth was composed for his new love Alma Schindler who became his wife and his musical inspiration for the rest of his life. The Fifth Symphony's premier performance, which Mahler conducted, was performed in Cologne on October 18, 1904. — October 16, 2010

From a Dream, Mather Point, Grand Canyon National Park

— April 20, 2004

This sketch and three successive sketches track the design of the Tanglewood House.

Remembered from a dream of sunrise over the Grand Canyon, spheres of different sizes roll across the sky flashing their neon colors to the amazement of people standing on the rock jutting from the Canyon wall.

2004 Tanglewood

BOSTON SYMPHONY ORCHESTRA
123rd Season, 2003-2004

Friday, August 20, at 8:30
BERKSHIRE NIGHT
SPONSORED BY BERKSHIRE BANK

ANDREY BOREYKO conducting

Please note that Emmanuel Krivine, originally scheduled to conduct this concert, is unable to be here because of an illness in his family. The originally scheduled program remains unchanged.

MENDELSSOHN — Overture, *The Fair Melusine*, Opus 32

BEETHOVEN — Piano Concerto No. 1 in C, Opus 15
Allegro con brio
Largo
Rondo: Allegro scherzando

LARS VOGT, piano

INTERMISSION

SCHUMANN — Symphony No. 4 in D minor, Opus 120
Ziemlich langsam [Rather slow]—Lebhaft [Lively]
Romanze. Ziemlich langsam
Scherzo. Lebhaft; Trio
Langsam—Lebhaft—Schneller [Faster]—Presto

From a dream.

Earth's Edge, pre-concept for T2, Tanglewood House

— October 30, 2004

The second of 4 sketches depicts a covered viewing platform projecting into the air, looking towards mountains on the horizon. Inspired by a Grand Canyon sunrise years earlier this sketch re-captures the immersive experience of becoming part of the view. Drawn while listening to Schoenberg's "Five Pieces for Orchestra," atmospheric in character, the piece labeled "Things Past" has particular resonance with the earlier Canyon dream.

Arnold Schoenberg

Five Pieces for Orchestra, Opus 16

Arnold Franz Walter Schönberg, who spelled his name Schoenberg after settling in the United States in 1934, was born in Vienna on September 13, 1874, and died in Brentwood, California, on July 13, 1951. He composed the Five Pieces for Orchestra at Steinkirchen, Lower Austria, in June-August 1909. The first, second, and fourth pieces were first heard in an arrangement of disputed authorship (Erwin Stein or Anton von Webern?) for two pianos, eight hands, in Berlin on February 4, 1912. Sir Henry J. Wood conducted the first complete orchestral performance on September 3, 1912, at a Promenade Concert in London. With Frederick Stock conducting, the Chicago Symphony gave the first American performance on October 31, 1913. Schoenberg slightly revised the score in 1922, and in September 1949 reduced the score in the hope of making it more practical for orchestras, but in fact eliminating only six instruments. The original version is used at these concerts. Karl Muck introduced the Five Pieces to the repertoire of the Boston Symphony Orchestra in December 1914, after which they were not heard here again until Richard Burgin conducted them in February/March 1958. Michael Tilson Thomas led performances of the 1949 revised version in Boston, Providence and Cambridge in March 1970, repeated the work in Boston the following October and November, and took them on tour with the orchestra to Washington, D.C., [illegible] City, Germany, and [illegible] 1949 [illegible] in Boston, Baltimore, and Hartford in October 1982, and Simon [illegible] the original version in the BSO's most recent performances, in March 1987. The original score calls for three flutes and piccolo (third flute doubling second piccolo), two oboes and English horn, [illegible] contrabassoon, four horns, three [illegible] tuba, timpani, xylophone, tam-tam, cymbals, bass drum, [illegible] celesta, and strings.

In 1908, Richard Strauss, then conductor of the Berlin Court Orchestra, encouraged Schoenberg to send him some "not too long" pieces to look at. A year later Schoenberg took Strauss up on his offer, writing:

> These are short orchestral pieces (duration from one to three minutes) without cyclic connection.... Since they are not a cycle one could easily perform just three or four. Three I should think would be the minimum for them not just to fizzle. The orchestration does not exceed the customary; the difficulty certainly does.... [I have] tremendous confidence in them, especially with respect to sonority and atmosphere. And that is all they are about—absolutely not symphonic, completely the opposite, no architecture, no structure. Only a kaleidoscopic changing of colors, rhythms, and moods. But—and this is an advantage that might enable you to risk them—*very short*!

While Schoenberg slightly exaggerated the brevity of his pieces, telling Strauss that the shortest ran three-quarters of a minute and the longest less than two minutes, they must have seemed bewilderingly compressed to the composer of *Ein Heldenleben* and the *Symphonia domestica*. They take about fifteen minutes, and it is not by chance that the longest of them is the one titled *Things Past*.

Strauss turned the pieces down, fearing to offer them to "the conservative Berlin audience." Schoenberg had to wait three years for a performance, one he could not even hear since no one had told him it was happening, and he could not manage a trip to London at almost no notice. The audience there hissed. Chicago—and soon after,

Elevation; Earth's Edge

— October 30, 2004

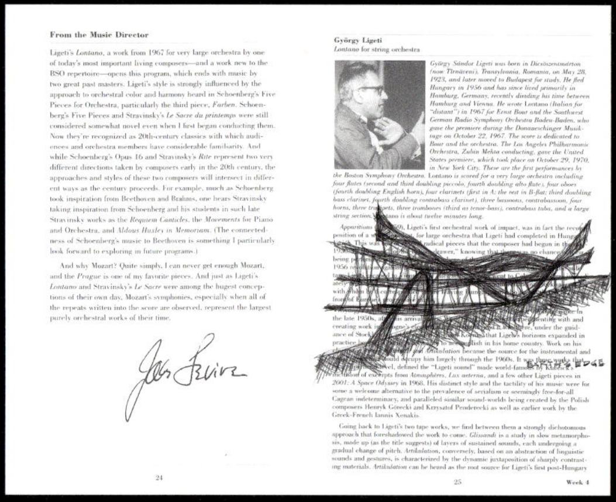

From the Music Director

Ligeti's *Lontano*, a work from 1967 for very large orchestra by one of today's most important living composers—and a work new to the BSO repertoire—opens this program, which ends with music by two great past masters. Ligeti's style is strongly influenced by the approach to orchestral color and harmony heard in Schoenberg's Five Pieces for Orchestra, particularly the third piece, *Farben*. Schoenberg's Five Pieces and Stravinsky's *Le Sacre du printemps* were still considered somewhat novel even when I first began conducting them. Now they're recognized as 20th-century classics with which audiences and orchestra members have considerable familiarity. And while Schoenberg's Opus 16 and Stravinsky's *Rite* represent two very different directions taken by composers early in the 20th century, the approaches and styles of these two composers will intersect in different ways as the century proceeds. For example, much as Schoenberg took inspiration from Beethoven and Brahms, one hears Stravinsky taking inspiration from Schoenberg and his students in such late Stravinsky works as the *Requiem Canticles*, the *Movements* for Piano and Orchestra, and *Aldous Huxley in Memoriam*. (The connectedness of Schoenberg's music to Beethoven is something I particularly look forward to exploring in future programs.)

And why Mozart? Quite simply, I can never get enough Mozart, and the *Prague* is one of my favorite pieces. And just as Ligeti's *Lontano* and Stravinsky's *Le Sacre* were among the hugest conceptions of their own day, Mozart's symphonies, especially when all of the repeats written into the score are observed, represent the largest purely orchestral works of their time.

24

György Ligeti
Lontano for string orchestra

György Sándor Ligeti was born in Dicsöszentmárton (now Tîrnăveni), Transylvania, Romania, on May 28, 1923, and later moved to Budapest for study. He fled Hungary in 1956 and has since lived primarily in Hamburg, Germany, recently dividing his time between Hamburg and Vienna. He wrote Lontano *(Italian for "distant") in 1967 for Ernst Bour and the Southwest German Radio Symphony Orchestra Baden-Baden, who gave the premiere during the Donaueschinger Musiktage on October 22, 1967. The score is dedicated to Bour and the orchestra. The Los Angeles Philharmonic Orchestra, Zubin Mehta conducting, gave the United States premiere, which took place on October 29, 1970, in New York City. These are the first performances by the Boston Symphony Orchestra.* Lontano *is scored for a very large orchestra including four flutes (second and third doubling piccolo, fourth doubling alto flute), four oboes (fourth doubling English horn), four clarinets (first in A; the rest in B-flat; third doubling bass clarinet, fourth doubling contrabass clarinet), three bassoons, contrabassoon, four horns, three trumpets, three trombones (third as tenor-bass), contrabass tuba, and a large string section.* [illegible] *is about twelve minutes long.*

Apparitions [illegible], Ligeti's first orchestral work of impact, was in fact the recomposition of a [illegible] for large orchestra that Ligeti had completed in Hungary [illegible] radical pieces that the composer had begun in the [illegible] drawer," knowing that [illegible] no chance [illegible] [illegible] the late 1950s, [illegible] his arrival [illegible] experimenting with and creating work in [illegible] under the guidance of Stock[illegible] that Ligeti's horizons expanded in practice [illegible] to accomplish in his home country. Work on his [illegible] *Artikulation* became the source for the instrumental and [illegible] would occupy him largely through the 1960s. It was these works that [illegible] level, defined the "Ligeti sound" made world-famous by Kubrick's [illegible] of excerpts from *Atmosphères*, *Lux aeterna*, and a few other Ligeti pieces in *2001: A Space Odyssey* in 1968. His distinct style and the tactility of his music were for some a welcome alternative to the prevalence of serialism or seemingly free-for-all Cagean indeterminacy, and paralleled similar sound-worlds being created by the Polish composers Henryk Górecki and Krzysztof Penderecki as well as earlier work by the Greek-French Iannis Xenakis.

Going back to Ligeti's two tape works, we find between them a strongly dichotomous approach that foreshadowed the work to come. *Glissandi* is a study in slow metamorphosis, made up (as the title suggests) of layers of sustained sounds, each undergoing a gradual change of pitch. *Artikulation*, conversely, based on an abstraction of linguistic sounds and gestures, is characterized by the dynamic juxtaposition of sharply contrasting materials. *Artikulation* can be heard as the root source for Ligeti's first post-Hungary

25 **Week 4**

T2 at Tanglewood went through many iterations. In this sketch the house appears as a wavy 2-story structure sited on a hill. Ligeti's musical influence here is of the atmospheric attempting to move towards greater definition. As Ligeti's "Lotano" was in part inspired by a particular German Renaissance painting, so it is well known that music can inspire architecture. It seems necessary to explore many possibilities on the way to finding something acceptable to build. This sketch is one at the beginning.

György Ligeti
Lontano for string orchestra

György Sándor Ligeti was born in Dicsõszentmárton (now Tîrnäveni), Transylvania, Romania, on May 28, 1923, and later moved to Budapest for study. He fled Hungary in 1956 and has since lived primarily in Hamburg, Germany, recently dividing his time between Hamburg and Vienna. He wrote Lontano *(Italian for "distant") in 1967 for Ernst Bour and the Southwest German Radio Symphony Orchestra Baden-Baden, who gave the premiere during the Donaueschinger Musiktage on October 22, 1967. The score is dedicated to Bour and the orchestra. The Los Angeles Philharmonic Orchestra, Zubin Mehta conducting, gave the United States premiere, which took place on October 29, 1970, in New York City. These are the first performances by the Boston Symphony Orchestra.* Lontano *is scored for a very large orchestra including four flutes (second and third doubling piccolo, fourth doubling alto flute), four oboes (fourth doubling English horn), four clarinets (first in A; the rest in B-flat; third doubling bass clarinet, fourth doubling contrabass clarinet), three bassoons, contrabassoon, four horns, three trumpets, three trombones (third as tenor-bass), contrabass tuba, and a large string section.* [illegible]tano *is about twelve minutes long.*

Apparitions ([illegible]59), Ligeti's first orchestral work of impact, was in fact the recom[illegible] position of a w[illegible], for large orchestra that Ligeti had completed in Hunga[illegible] [illegible]. This was [illegible] radical pieces that the composer had begun in the [illegible] 1950s [illegible] "for the [illegible] drawer," knowing tha[illegible] no chance [illegible] being p[illegible] 1956 re[illegible]volution against [illegible] the mili- tary, Ligeti escaped to Vien[illegible] went to Co[illegible] ately [illegible] with [illegible] with whom he'd co[illegible] leaving Hunga[illegible] front of Europe's progr[illegible]

[illegible] wrote in the late 1950s, aft[illegible] his arrival [illegible] experimenting with and creating work in [illegible]ogne's ele[illegible] and it was there, under the guidance of Stock[illegible] Koenig, that Ligeti's horizons expanded in practice be[illegible] to accomplish in his home country. Work on his ele[illegible] and *Artikulation* became the source for the instrumental and [illegible] would occupy him largely through the 1960s. It was these works that, [illegible] level, defined the "Ligeti sound" made world-famous by Kubrick's inclusion of excerpts from *Atmosphères*, *Lux aeterna*, and a few other Ligeti pieces in *2001: A Space Odyssey* in 1968. His distinct style and the tactility of his music were for some a welcome alternative to the prevalence of serialism or seemingly free-for-all Cagean indeterminacy, and paralleled similar sound-worlds being created by the Polish composers Henryk Górecki and Krzysztof Penderecki as well as earlier work by the Greek-French Iannis Xenakis.

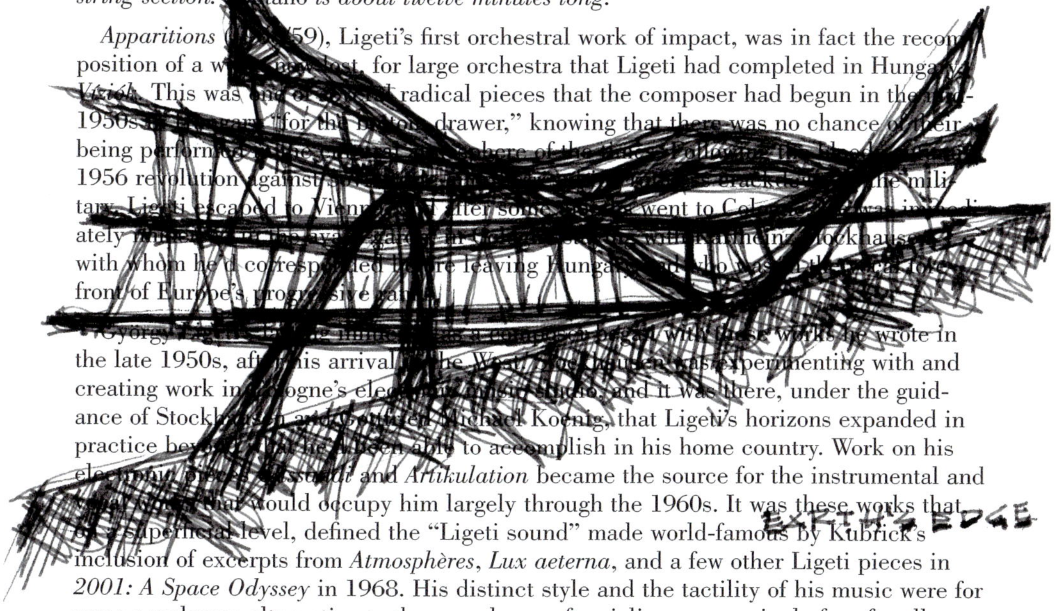

Going back to Ligeti's two tape works, we find between them a strongly dichotomous approach that foreshadowed the work to come. *Glissandi* is a study in slow metamorphosis, made up (as the title suggests) of layers of sustained sounds, each undergoing a gradual change of pitch. *Artikulation*, conversely, based on an abstraction of linguistic sounds and gestures, is characterized by the dynamic juxtaposition of sharply contrasting materials. *Artikulation* can be heard as the root source for Ligeti's first post-Hungary

Tanglewood 2, West Stockbridge, MA

— January 28, 2006

A year later images of the Grand Canyon sunrise merged with the immediacy of designing Tanglewood 2. While listening to Debussy's "Afternoon of a Faun" this sketch previewed the house's main living space.

OSTON SYMPHONY ORCHESTRA

ımes Levine, *Music Director*
ɜrnard Haitink, *Conductor Emeritus*
ɜiji Ozawa, *Music Director Laureate*
:5th Season, 2005-2006

ıursday, January 26, at 8
:iday, January 27, at 1:30
ıturday, January 28, at 8
THE RAYMOND C. AND JOAN C. GREEN CONCERT
ıesday, January 31, at 8

ERNARD HAITINK conducting

AVEL *Alborada del gracioso*

OZART ...concerto No. 23 in A, K.488

GOODE

OUSSEL Symphony No. 3 in G minor, Opus 42
Allegro vivo
Adagio
Vivace
Allegro con spirito

UBS is proud to sponsor the BSO's 2005-2006 season.

ıe evening concerts will end about 9:55 and the afternoon concert about 3:25.

ɜinway and Sons Pianos, selected exclusively for Symphony Hall

Flower Market, Honolulu, Hawaii

— October 23, 2010

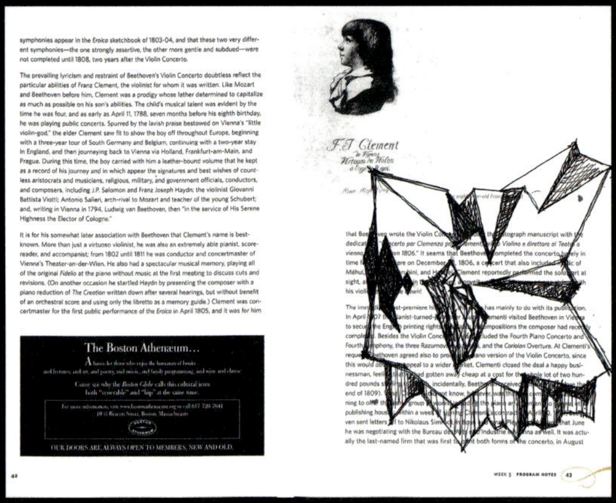

A folded metal roof supported by steel-framed metal screens shelters a small market on a sloping site near the end of the Pali Highway as it descends from the mountains.

[illegible] e eight-year-old Franz [illegible]

that Bee[illegible]ven wrote the Violin Co[illegible] th[illegible]utograph manuscript with the dedicat[illegible] "*[illegible]ncerto par Clemenza po[illegible] Clement, [illegible]o Violino e direttore al Teatro a vienna[illegible]vn 1806.*" It seems that Beethove[illegible] completed the concerto barely in time f[illegible]iere on December [illegible]3, 1806, a concert that also included m[illegible]sic of Méhul, [illegible]rubini, and Ha[illegible]del. Clement reportedly performed the solo part at sight, a[illegible] in t[illegible]am, a novelty [illegible]ith his violi[illegible]e down!

The imm[illegible]di[illegible]ost-premiere hi[illegible] of th[illegible] has mainly to do with its publication. In April 1[illegible]07 th[illegible]ianist-turned-p[illegible]er [illegible]uz[illegible]ementi visited Beethoven in Vienna to secur[illegible] the Eng[illegible]h printing rights t[illegible]atch [illegible]ompositions the composer had recently comple[illegible]. Besides the Violin Conce[illegible]luded the Fourth Piano Concerto and Fourth [illegible]mphony, the three Razumovs[illegible]s, and the *Coriolan* Overture. At Clementi's reque[illegible] Beethoven agreed also to pro[illegible]ano version of the Violin Concerto, since this would ob[illegible]ppeal to a wider [illegible]arket. Clementi closed the deal a happy businessman, feeli[illegible] that [illegible]ad gotten away cheap at a cost for th[illegible]hole lot of two hundred pounds st[illegible]ing [illegible], incidentally, Beeth[illegible]ceived [illegible]fore the end of 1809). [illegible] did not know, however, was tha[illegible] com[illegible]ning to o[illegible]er th[illegible] group [illegible] works, including the piano arrangement to several other publishing hous[illegible] within a week [illegible] signing Clementi's contract [illegible] April [illegible], Beethoven sent letters off to Nikolaus Simrock in Bonn and [illegible] Pley[illegible] that June he was negotiating with the Bureau des Arts et d'Industrie in Vienna as well. It was actually the last-named firm that was first to print both forms of the concerto, in August

Mixed-Use Tower, Back Bay, Boston

— November 05, 1998

A 40-story hotel/residential tower west of the Hynes Auditorium would provide parking, banquet and service functions above a retail arcade. Planned for a triangular site above the Mass Pike, the Tower would look west towards the Blue Hills and north towards the Charles Rive.

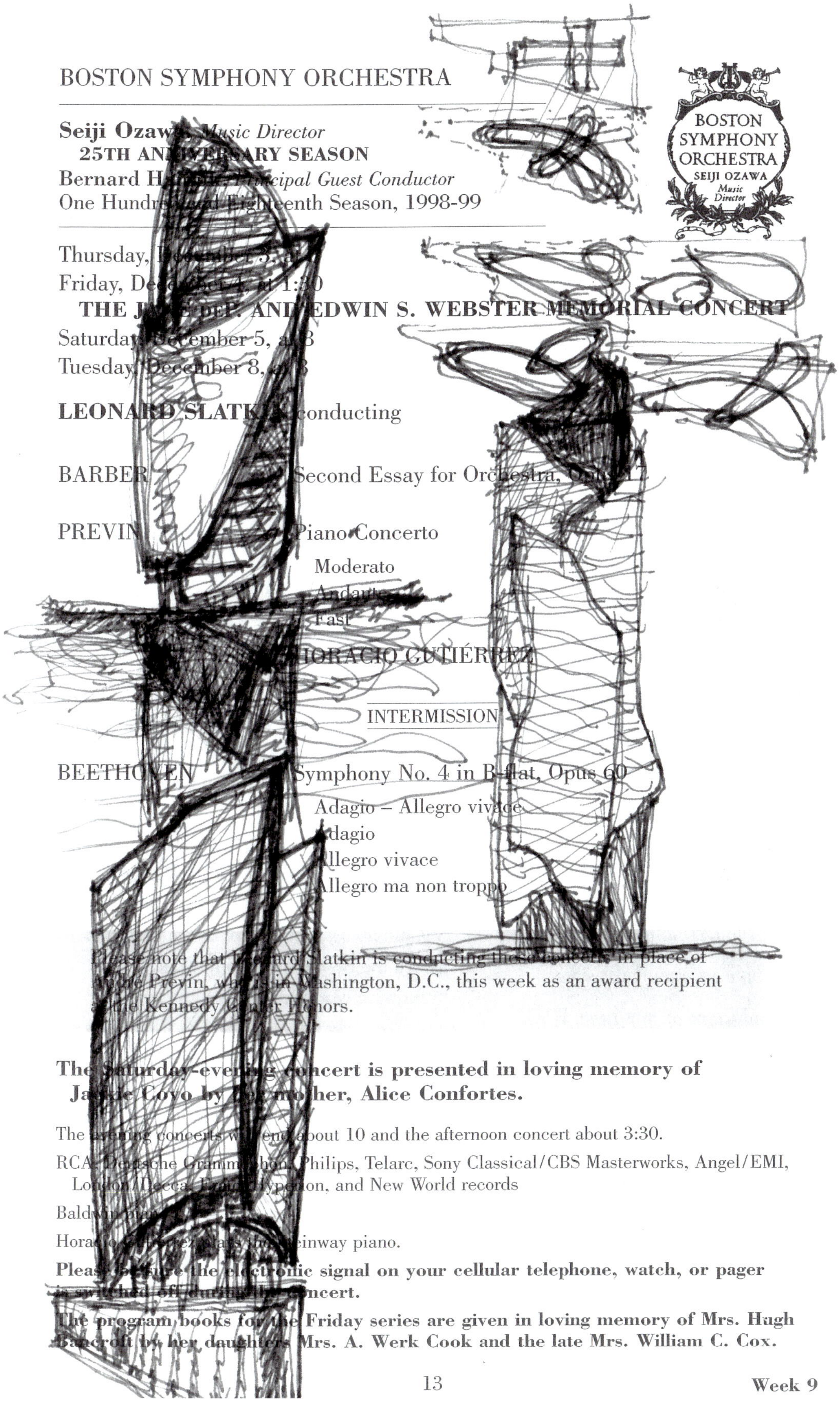
BOSTON SYMPHONY ORCHESTRA

Seiji Ozawa, *Music Director*
25TH ANNIVERSARY SEASON
Bernard H[illegible], *Principal Guest Conductor*
One Hund[illegible] Eighteenth Season, 1998-99

Thursday, [illegible]
Friday, De[illegible] at 1:30
THE [illegible] AND EDWIN S. WEBSTER MEMORIAL CONCERT
Saturday, December 5, at 8
Tuesday, December 8, at 8

LEONARD SLATKIN conducting

BARBER Second Essay for Orchestra, [illegible]

PREVIN Piano Concerto
Moderato
Andante
Fast
HORACIO GUTIÉRREZ

INTERMISSION

BEETHOVEN Symphony No. 4 in B-flat, Opus 60
Adagio – Allegro vivace
Adagio
Allegro vivace
Allegro ma non troppo

[illegible] note that [illegible] Slatkin is conducting these concerts in place of [illegible] Previn, who is in Washington, D.C., this week as an award recipient [illegible] Kennedy Center Honors.

The Saturday-evening concert is presented in loving memory of Jackie Covo by her mother, Alice Confortes.

The evening concerts will end about 10 and the afternoon concert about 3:30.

RCA, Deutsche Grammophon, Philips, Telarc, Sony Classical/CBS Masterworks, Angel/EMI, London/Decca, [illegible], Hyperion, and New World records

Baldwin [illegible]

Hora[illegible] [illegible] Steinway piano.

Please be sure the electronic signal on your cellular telephone, watch, or pager is switched off during the concert.

The program books for the Friday series are given in loving memory of Mrs. Hugh Bancroft by her daughters Mrs. A. Werk Cook and the late Mrs. William C. Cox.

13 **Week 9**

Orange Blossom Hotel, Miami Beach, Florida

— January 03, 1998

As unlikely as it was, Sinfonia da Requiem brought a reminder of the tropical fragrance of orange blossoms I knew growing up. However, this idea for a hotel is inspired as much by the photograph below the sketch as the music I was hearing.

as premiered with great success in Britain, then given its first American
Tanglewood on August 6, 1946, under Koussevitzky's protégé Leonard

It is possible that Britten and Koussevitzky took [illegible] occasion of the cor
nce at Tanglewood to [illegible] the question [illegible] whether he would now com
nony for Boston. The [illegible] suggesting that such a discussion
ace comes fr[illegible] following year, but [illegible] e way Bri
s comments that 'the Symphony [illegible] as been ta
efore. The composer wrote to Koussevitzky [illegible] 1947, to tel
unding of the English Opera Group [illegible] organize
rs, and to explain that he [illegible] (which hap
s third, *Albert Herring*; the second [illegible] already be
e preceding year):

> ... [illegible] ly. As you
> des[illegible] ing ideas
> all [illegible] my bigg
> pie[illegible] et down
> pho[illegible] shire Festi
> poss[illegible] if not, as
> parti[illegible] ink the b
> to let [illegible] our plans
> By-the-[illegible] I am planning it [illegible] nk you w
> is a real Symphony (the emphasis is [illegible] sequentl
> Latin wor[illegible]

The last sentence comes as a surprise! [illegible] as it stan
sh words, and although the orchestra pla[illegible] part throughout
ir to say that the emphasis is on the voices [illegible] Britten did not
ork in time for the 1947 Berkshire Festival—his estimate was off by a go
art of the delay may well have come from what was evidently a change o
ad actually begun putting together a collection of Medieval Latin poems f
out a re-reading of much English lyric verse and a particularly lovely Sp

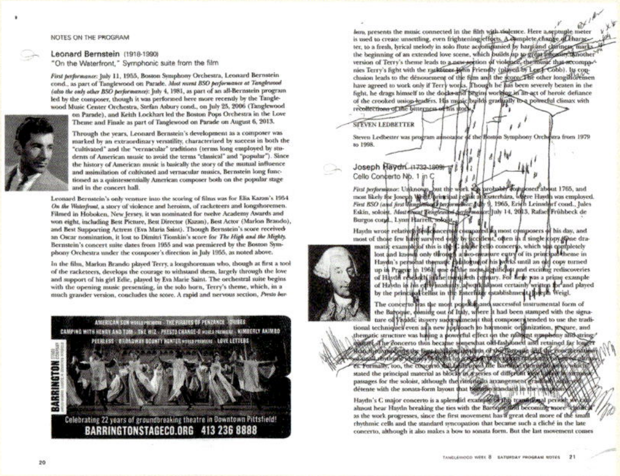

Haydn Fantasy — August 29, 2016

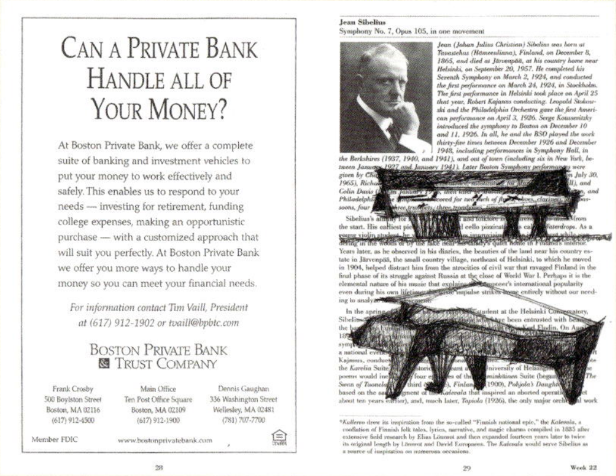

Piano Factory — April 14, 2001

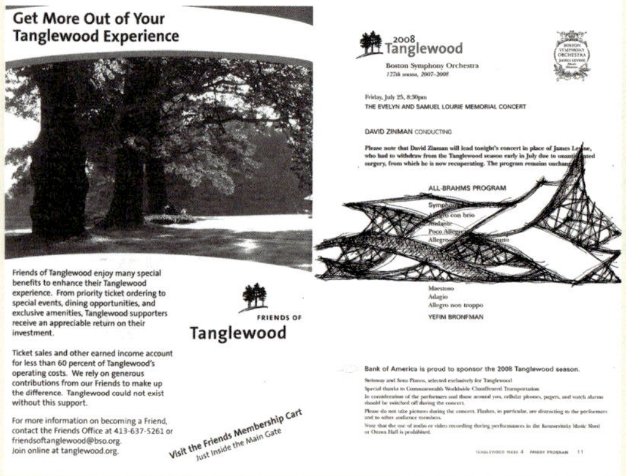

Goat Island Yacht Club, Newport, Rhode Island — July 25, 2008

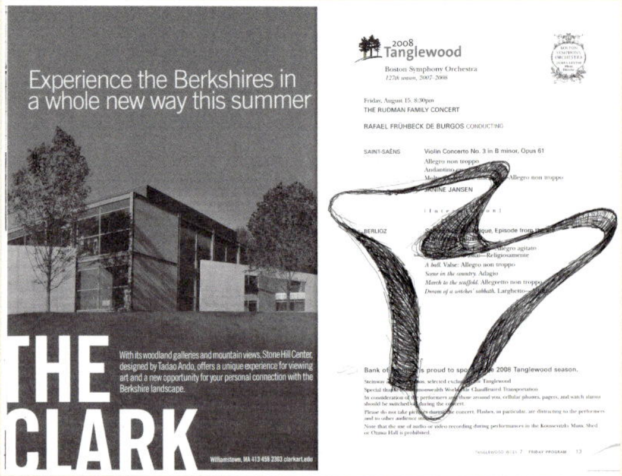

Soundscape — August 15, 2008

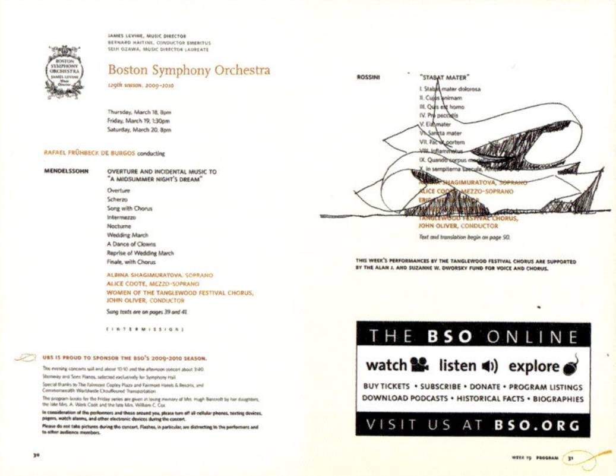

Soundscape — March 20, 2010

Institut La Mer — November 19, 2005

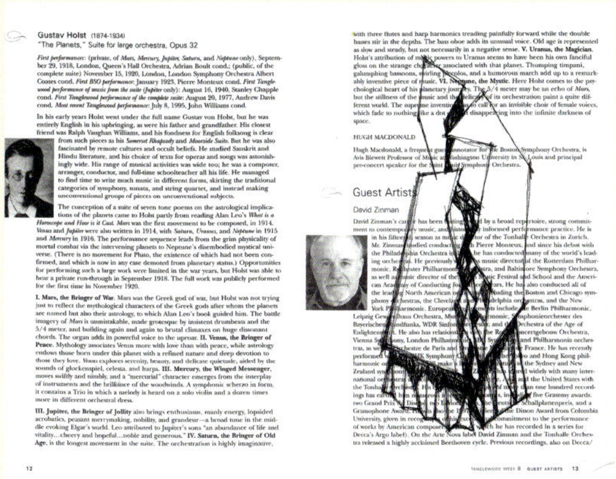

Study - Tower — August 29, 2016

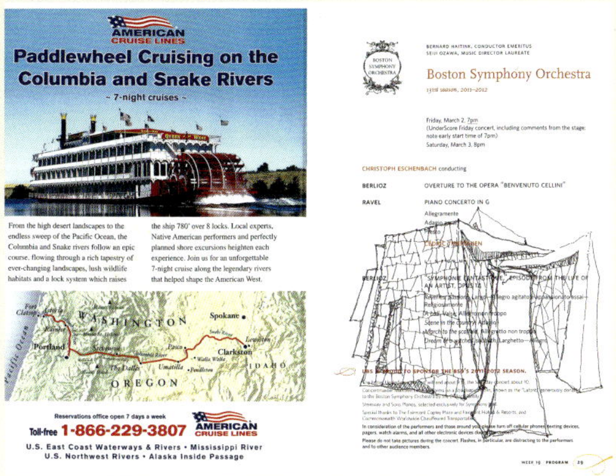

Theme - Berlioz — March 03, 2012

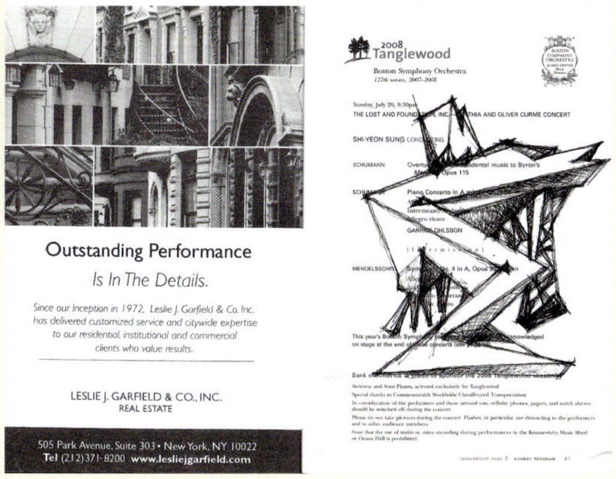

Monument — September 20, 2008

Fairy House — March 28, 2009

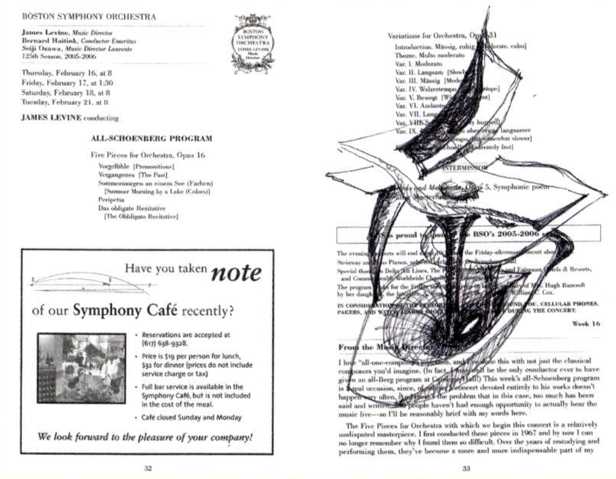

Orchid House — February 18, 2006

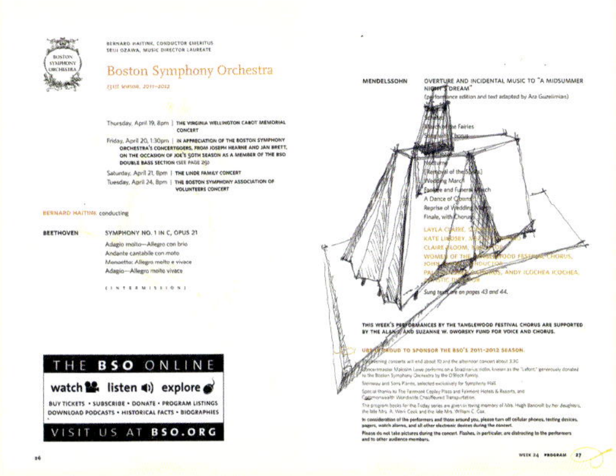

Fabric Chapel — April 21, 2012

Sound Study

— April 15, 2023

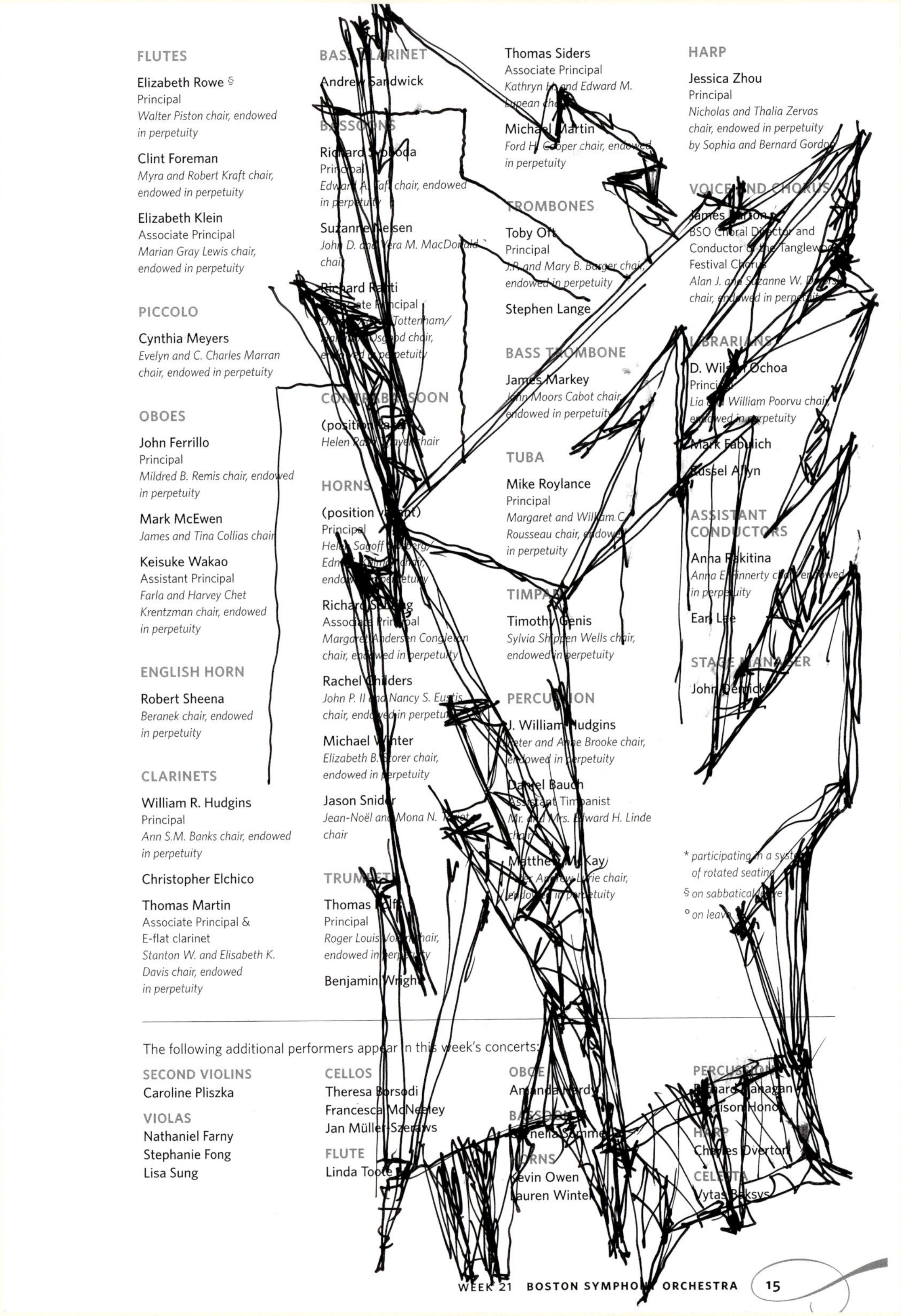

FLUTES
Elizabeth Rowe §
Principal
Walter Piston chair, endowed in perpetuity
Clint Foreman
Myra and Robert Kraft chair, endowed in perpetuity
Elizabeth Klein
Associate Principal
Marian Gray Lewis chair, endowed in perpetuity

PICCOLO
Cynthia Meyers
Evelyn and C. Charles Marran chair, endowed in perpetuity

OBOES
John Ferrillo
Principal
Mildred B. Remis chair, endowed in perpetuity
Mark McEwen
James and Tina Collias chair
Keisuke Wakao
Assistant Principal
Farla and Harvey Chet Krentzman chair, endowed in perpetuity

ENGLISH HORN
Robert Sheena
Beranek chair, endowed in perpetuity

CLARINETS
William R. Hudgins
Principal
Ann S.M. Banks chair, endowed in perpetuity
Christopher Elchico
Thomas Martin
Associate Principal & E-flat clarinet
Stanton W. and Elisabeth K. Davis chair, endowed in perpetuity

BASS CLARINET
Andrew Sandwick

BASSOONS
Richard Svoboda
Principal
Edward A. Taft chair, endowed in perpetuity
Suzanne Nelsen
John D. and Vera M. MacDonald chair
Richard Ranti
Associate Principal
Diana Osgood Tottenham/ Hamilton Osgood chair, endowed in perpetuity

CONTRABASSOON
(position vacant)
Helen Rand Thayer chair

HORNS
(position vacant)
Principal
Helen Sagoff Slosberg/ Edna S. Kalman chair, endowed in perpetuity
Richard Sebring
Associate Principal
Margaret Andersen Congleton chair, endowed in perpetuity
Rachel Childers
John P. II and Nancy S. Eustis chair, endowed in perpetuity
Michael Winter
Elizabeth B. Storer chair, endowed in perpetuity
Jason Snider
Jean-Noël and Mona N. Tariot chair

TRUMPETS
Thomas Rolfs
Principal
Roger Louis Voisin chair, endowed in perpetuity
Benjamin Wright

Thomas Siders
Associate Principal
Kathryn H. and Edward M. Lupean chair
Michael Martin
Ford H. Cooper chair, endowed in perpetuity

TROMBONES
Toby Oft
Principal
J.P. and Mary B. Barger chair, endowed in perpetuity
Stephen Lange

BASS TROMBONE
James Markey
John Moors Cabot chair, endowed in perpetuity

TUBA
Mike Roylance
Principal
Margaret and William C. Rousseau chair, endowed in perpetuity

TIMPANI
Timothy Genis
Sylvia Shippen Wells chair, endowed in perpetuity

PERCUSSION
J. William Hudgins
Peter and Anne Brooke chair, endowed in perpetuity
Daniel Bauch
Assistant Timpanist
Mr. and Mrs. Edward H. Linde chair
Matthew McKay
Peter Andrew Lurie chair, endowed in perpetuity

HARP
Jessica Zhou
Principal
Nicholas and Thalia Zervas chair, endowed in perpetuity by Sophia and Bernard Gordon

VOICE AND CHORUS
James Burton
BSO Choral Director and Conductor of the Tanglewood Festival Chorus
Alan J. and Suzanne W. Dworsky chair, endowed in perpetuity

LIBRARIANS
D. Wilson Ochoa
Principal
Lia and William Poorvu chair, endowed in perpetuity
Mark Fabulich
Russel Allyn

ASSISTANT CONDUCTORS
Anna Rakitina
Anna E. Finnerty chair, endowed in perpetuity
Earl Lee

STAGE MANAGER
John Demick

* participating in a system of rotated seating
§ on sabbatical leave
° on leave

The following additional performers appear in this week's concerts:

SECOND VIOLINS
Caroline Pliszka

VIOLAS
Nathaniel Farny
Stephanie Fong
Lisa Sung

CELLOS
Theresa Borsodi
Francesca McNeeley
Jan Müller-Szeraws

FLUTE
Linda Toote

OBOE
Amanda Hardy

BASSOON
Cornelia Sommer

HORNS
Kevin Owen
Lauren Winter

PERCUSSION
Richard Flanagan
Harrison Honor

HARP
Charles Overton

CELESTA
Vytas Baksys

WEEK 21 BOSTON SYMPHONY ORCHESTRA 15

Evening Tower

— April 5, 2023

Maurice Rav[illegible]

Alborada del gracios[illegible]

JOSEPH MA[illegible]ICE RAVEL was born in Ciboure near Saint-[illegible]ean-de-Luz, Bas[illegible]-Pyrénées[illegible] the Basque regio[illegible] of France just a short distance from the S[illegible]anish border, [illegible] March 7, 187[illegible] and died in Paris [illegible]ecember 28, [illegible]937. He composed *Alborada del gracio*[illegible] as a piano pie[illegible] in 1905, orchestrating [illegible] in 1918. [illegible]emiere of the orc[illegible]stra version was given in Paris [illegible] May 17, 1919, Rhené-[illegible]

THE SCORE FOR *Albor*[illegible] calls [illegible], 2 oboes, English horn, [illegible]clarinet[illegible] 2 bassoons, contrabassoo[illegible] 4 h[illegible] [illegible]uba, timpani, percussion [illegible] crotales, triangle, cymbal[illegible] [illegible] bass drum), 2 harps, an[illegible] strings (first and second violins, vi[illegible], cellos, [illegible]) [illegible] piece is about 8 minutes [illegible].

In 1905 Ravel com[illegible]osed a set of [illegible] piano [illegible] under the title *M*[illegible]*oirs* (Mi[illegible]). Three of the five in[illegible] works—*U*[illegible]*ne Barq*[illegible]*l'océan, Alborada* [illegible]*el gracioso* [illegible] *Vallée des cloches*—w[illegible]re all la[illegible]er orchestrated. [illegible] most successful [illegible] these re[illegible] pieces is certainly the [illegible]*orada del gracio*[illegible]. In its [illegible]iginal keyboard f[illegible]mat, the piece [illegible] filled with pow[illegible] and impossibly fast re[illegible]ted notes that [illegible]re a challenge to even the most gift[illegible] vir[illegible]. S[illegible]h overwhel[illegible]ing [illegible]chnical d[illegible]man[illegible]s almost cried out to be translated to the [illegible], es[illegible]ially for a comp[illegible]ser li[illegible]e R[illegible]vel, to whom the art of transcribing fr[illegible]m [illegible] orch[illegible]stra was a welcome [illegible]allen[illegible], one that he met repeatedly with remar[illegible] succes[illegible].

The title of the piece is [illegible] a bit mysterious. "Alborad[illegible]s the Spanish equivalent of the French "au[illegible] Italian "alba," and the Germ[illegible] Morgenlied," all of them "dawn songs," a [illegible]eristic genre from the lyric [illegible] the Middle Ages. Generally they are con[illegible] as being sung by a friend [illegible] out for the safety of two illicit lovers. As th[illegible] wanes, the friend, outside th[illegible]oom window, sings that the dawn is appro[illegible] and that it is time for th[illegible] part. (In Act II of [illegible] opera, Wagner employed the same [illegible]re of the [illegible] Brangäne's unheeded

WEEK 21 PROGRAM NOT[illegible]

Li River Hotel, Guilin, China

— November 29, 1997

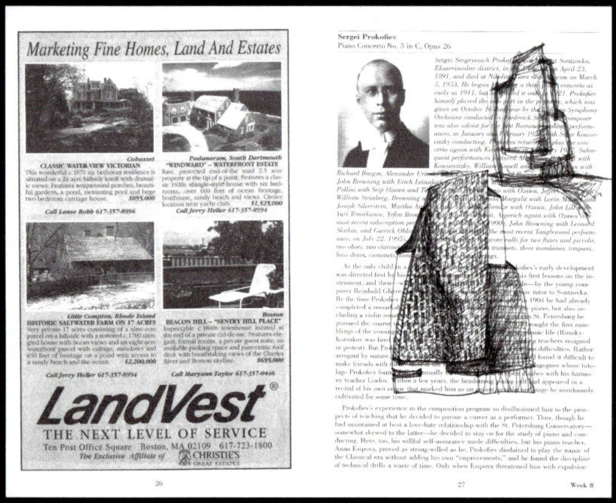

Echoing the spectacular karst formations along the Li River, the 18-story structure would be an embarkation point for travel down-river to Yangshuo. The roughly conical form would spread the building's weight over the weak limestone substructure of the region's site.

ıkofiev

erto No. 3 in C, Opus 26

Sergei Sergeyevich Prokofiev was born at Sontzovka, Ekaterinoslav district, in the Ukraine, on April 23, 1891, and died at Nikolina Gora near Moscow on March 5, 1953. He began planning a third piano concerto as early as 1911, but completed it only in 1921. Prokofiev himself played the solo part in the premiere, which was given on October 16 that year by the Chicago Symphony Orchestra conducted by Frederick Stock. The composer was also soloist for the first Boston Symphony performances, in January and February 1926, with Serge Koussevitzky conducting. Prokofiev returned to play the concerto again with Koussevitzky in February 1937. Subsequent performances featured Alexander Borovsky with Koussevitzky, William Kapell and Gary Graffman with
ʒin, Alexander Urinsky with Charles Munch and Burgin, [illegible] and
ng with Erich Leinsdorf, Graffman with Michael Tilson Thomas, Maurizio
Seiji Ozawa and Tilson Thomas, Byron Janis with Ozawa, Jeffrey Siegel with
ıberg, Browning with Aldo Ceccato, Israela Margalit with Lorin Maazel and
stein, Martha Argerich and Alexander Toradze with Ozawa, John Lill with
nov, Yefim Bronfman with Charles Dutoit, Argerich again with Ozawa (the
ubscription performances, in November 1990), John Browning with Leonard
Garrick Ohlsson with Marek Janowski (the most recent Tanglewood perform-
22, 1995). Besides the solo piano, the score calls for two flutes and piccolo,
o clarinets, two bassoons, four horns, two trumpets, three trombones, timpani,
ıstanets, tambourine, cymbals, and strings.

y child in a cultured and affluent household, Prokofiev's early development
first by his gifted pianist mother, who gave him his first lessons on the in-
d then—when his talent proved to be unmistakable—by the young com-
ıld Glière, who was hired to come as a private music tutor to Sontzovka.
Prokofiev entered the St. Petersburg Conservatory in 1904 he had already
remarkable number of juvenile works, mostly for the piano, but also in-
lin sonata and an opera. During his first four years in St. Petersburg he
course in composition. It was a difficult time: 1905 brought the first rum-
coming revolution, disturbing the tranquillity of academic life (Rimsky-
s fired for anti-government activities, and other leading teachers resigned
ut Prokofiev himself was responsible for most of his own difficulties. Rather
ature, he was also younger than the other students and found it difficult to
with them. Most of his teachers were conservative pedagogues whose tute-
v found dull; eventually he found himself in open clashes with his harmo-
adov. Within a few years, the headstrong young colt had appeared in a
own music that marked him as an *enfant terrible*, an image he assiduously
some time.

experience in the composition program so disillusioned him to the pros-
ıing that he decided to pursue a career as a performer. Thus, though he
ed at best a love-hate relationship with the St. Petersburg Conservatory—

Forest House, Highlands, North Carolina

— November 27, 2010

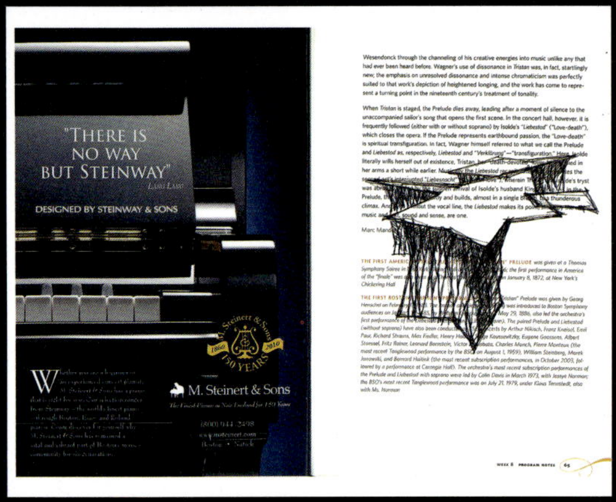

Echoing the trunks and branches of trees, the structure and glazing frames of various laminated thicknesses surround and enclose three connected pavilions. Steel is inserted into the angular verticals for structural continuity. The house is set at the edge of a steep forest ravine and is entered from above as if entering through the forest canopy.

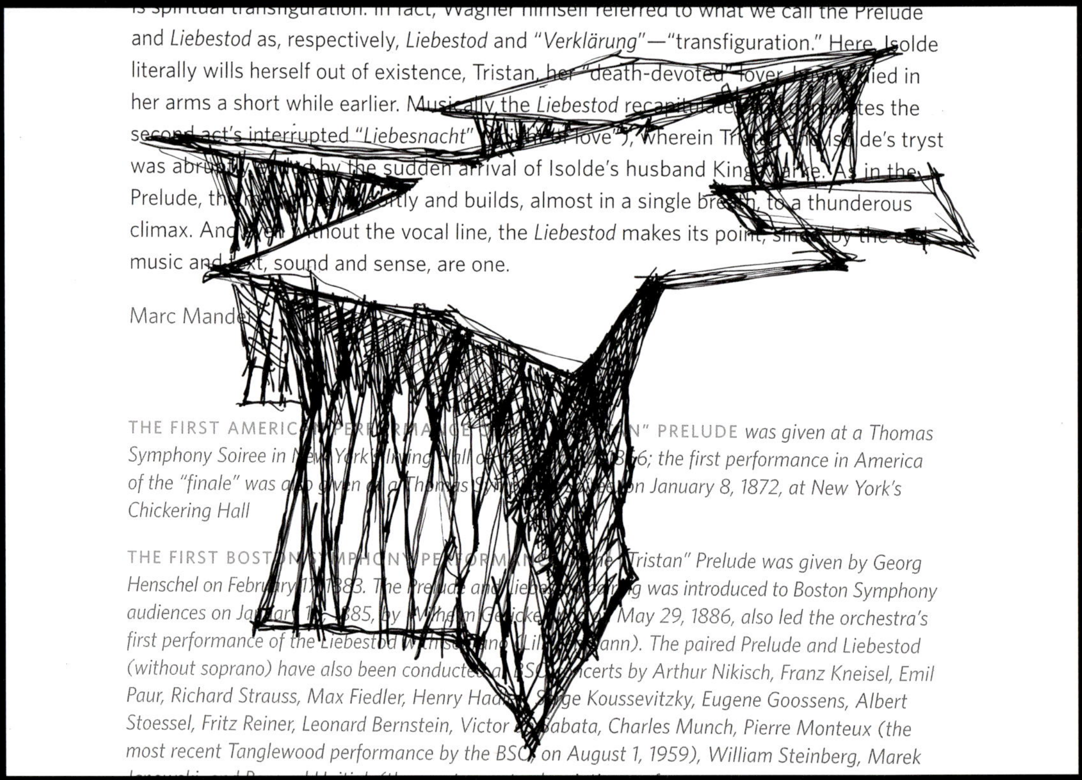

Sanctuary, Island Cemetery, River Styx

— October 10, 2009

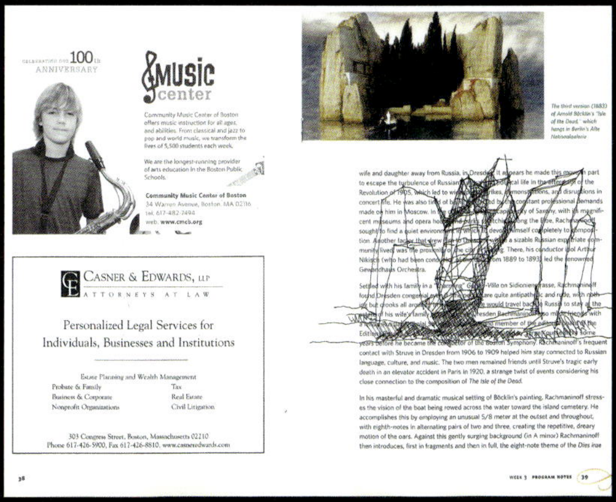

Inspired by Rachmaninoff's symphonic poem "Isle of the Dead", this setting depicts a faceted glass sanctuary which substitutes for the tall cypresses that stand at the center of the fabled island. As in the musical composition, the drawing departs from the painting by introducing a different theme, one which suggests eternal light to undermine eternal darkness.

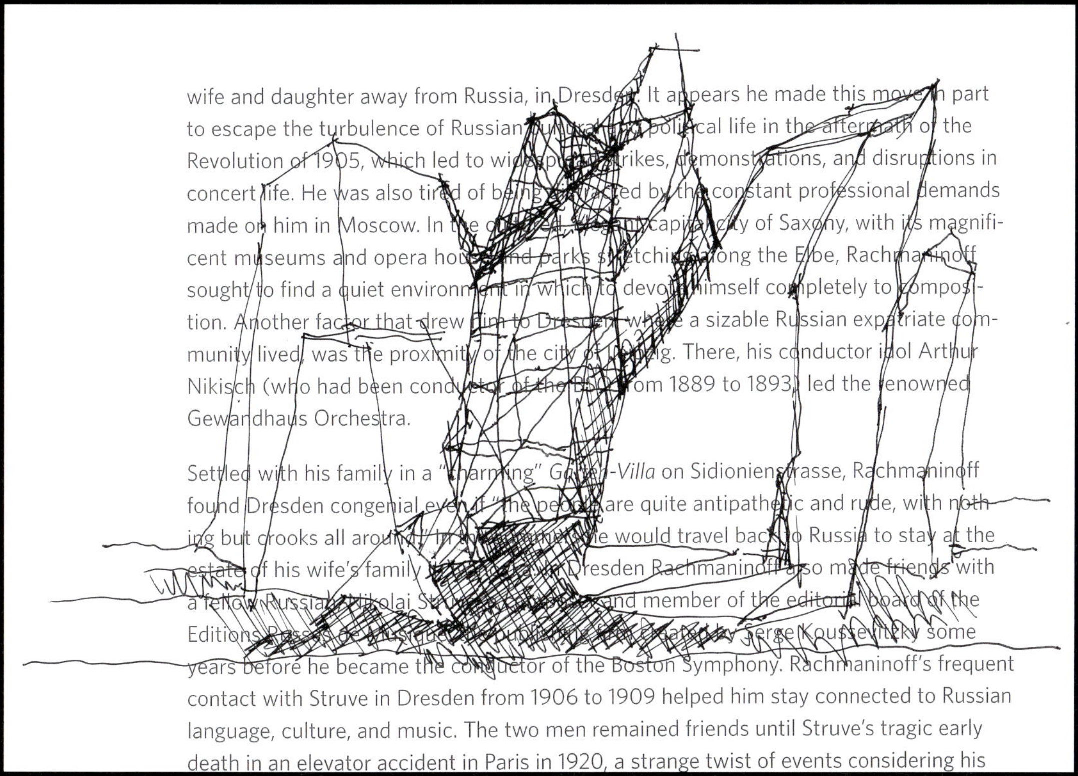

wife and daughter away from Russia, in Dresden. It appears he made this move in part to escape the turbulence of Russian [illegible] political life in the aftermath of the Revolution of 1905, which led to widespread strikes, demonstrations, and disruptions in concert life. He was also tired of being [illegible] by the constant professional demands made on him in Moscow. In the [illegible] capital city of Saxony, with its magnificent museums and opera house and parks stretching along the Elbe, Rachmaninoff sought to find a quiet environment in which to devote himself completely to composition. Another factor that drew him to Dresden, where a sizable Russian expatriate community lived, was the proximity of the city of Leipzig. There, his conductor idol Arthur Nikisch (who had been conductor of the BSO from 1889 to 1893) led the renowned Gewandhaus Orchestra.

Settled with his family in a "charming" *Garten-Villa* on Sidonienstrasse, Rachmaninoff found Dresden congenial even if "the people are quite antipathetic and rude, with nothing but crooks all around." [illegible] he would travel back to Russia to stay at the estate of his wife's family [illegible] Dresden Rachmaninoff also made friends with a fellow Russian, Nikolai Struve, [illegible] and member of the editorial board of the Editions [illegible] Serge Koussevitzky some years before he became the conductor of the Boston Symphony. Rachmaninoff's frequent contact with Struve in Dresden from 1906 to 1909 helped him stay connected to Russian language, culture, and music. The two men remained friends until Struve's tragic early death in an elevator accident in Paris in 1920, a strange twist of events considering his

House on the Border, Tucson, Arizona

— February 25, 2017

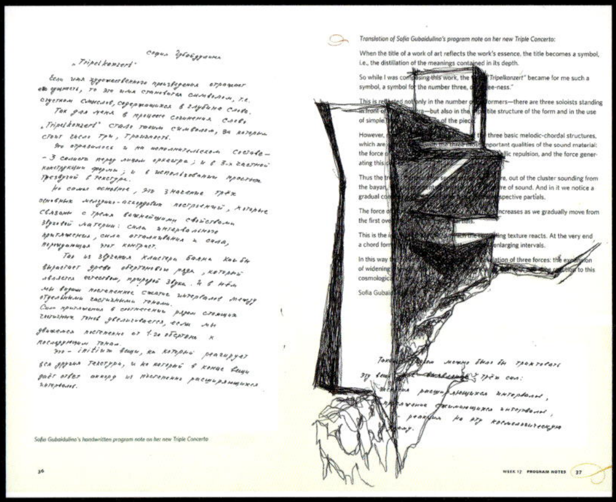

Listening to Gubaidulena's 2017 "Tripelkonzert" is a musically dark experience. From the program ~ "spare, austere passages for the soloist alternate starkly with orchestral passages." This music inspired a brooding house which features a lookout and a pool reflecting a clear blue sky.

Translation of Sofia Gubaidulina's program note on her new Triple Concerto:

When the title of a work of art reflects the work's essence, the title becomes a symbol, i.e., the distillation of the meanings contained in its depth.

So while I was composing this work, the [illegible] *"Tripelkonzert"* became for me such a symbol, a symbol for the number three, o[illegible]ee-ness."

This is reflected not only in the number o[illegible]formers—there are three soloists standing in front of [illegible]tra—but also in the [illegible]tite structure of the form and in the use of simple [illegible] of the piece.

However, [illegible] of the three basic melodic-chordal structures, which are [illegible] with the three most important qualities of the sound material: the force o[illegible]allic repulsion, and the force generating this co[illegible]

Thus the tre[illegible]re, out of the cluster sounding from the bayan, [illegible]re of sound. And in it we notice a gradual co[illegible]spective partials.

The force of [illegible] increases as we gradually move from the first ove[illegible] partials.

This is the *i*[illegible]ing texture reacts. At the very end a chord form[illegible] enlarging intervals.

In this way the [illegible]elation of three forces: the expansion of widening [illegible], and the reaction to this cosmologica[illegible]

Sofia Gubai[illegible]

Таким образом можно было бы трактовать эту вещь как выявление трёх сил: экспансия расширяющихся интервалов, притяжение сжимающихся интервалов, и — реакция на эту космологическую драму.

Yacht Club, Ft Lauderdale, Florida

— October 10, 2009

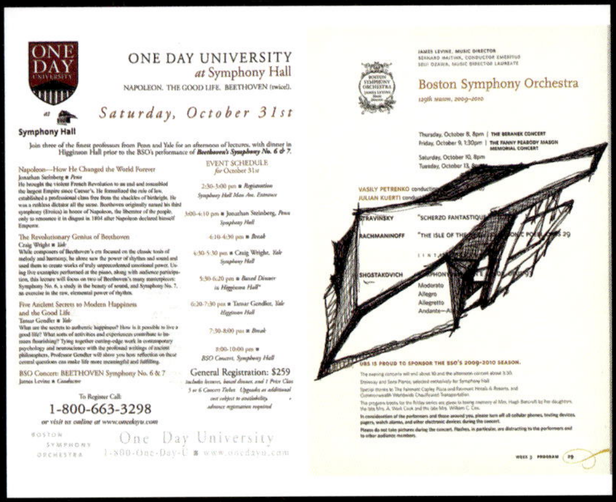

Located on Florida's Inland Waterway, the structure transforms the imagery of yachts into a building. As in "Scherzo Fantastique," which was composed as an abstract work, Stravinsky unwittingly suggested traditional connections to the past.

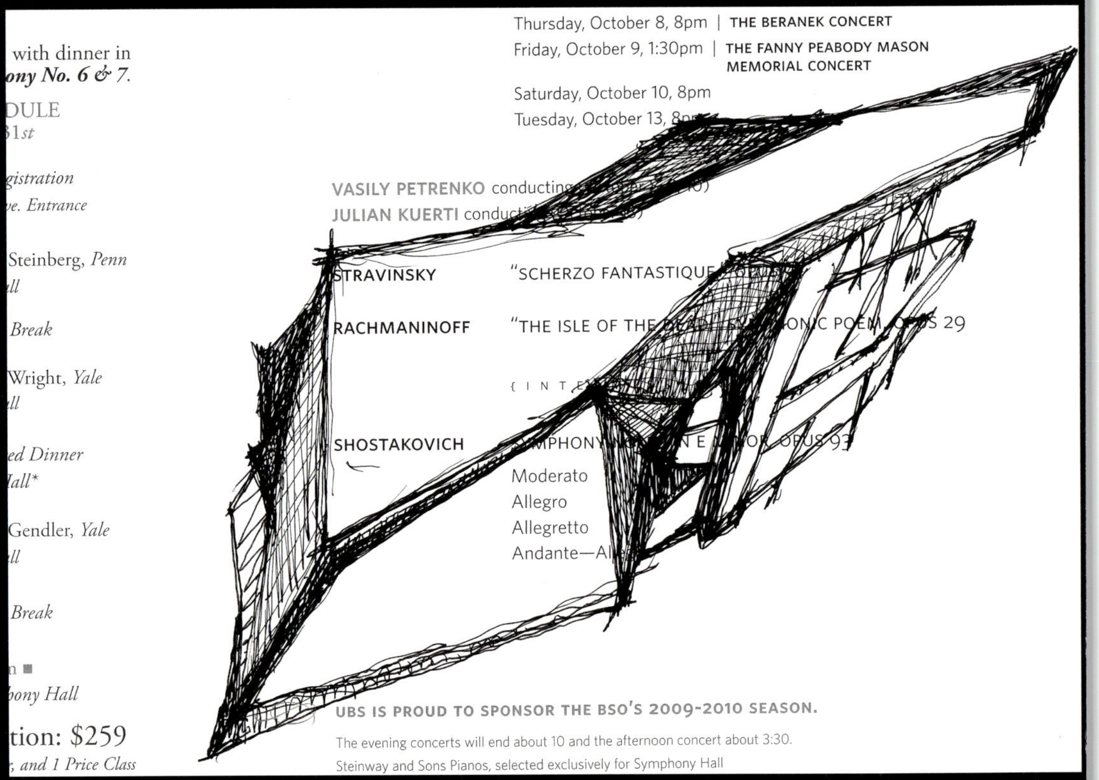

New Philharmonic Hall, Casablanca, Morocco

— February 05, 2005

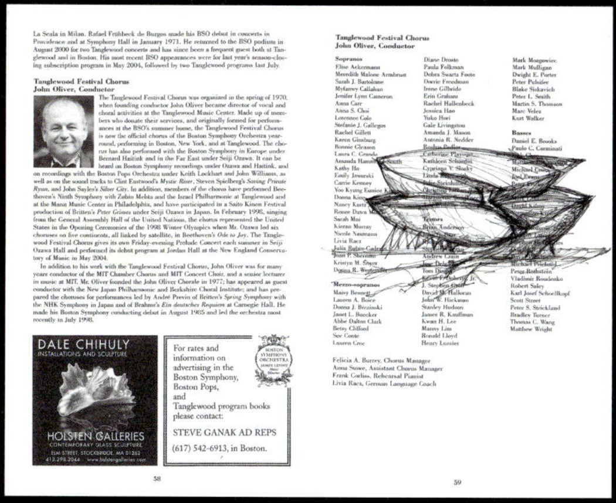

DALE CHIHULY
INSTALLATIONS AND SCULPTURE
HOLSTEN GALLERIES
CONTEMPORARY GLASS SCULPTURE

For rates and information on advertising in the Boston Symphony, Boston Pops, and Tanglewood program books please contact:
STEVE GANAK AD REPS
(617) 542-6913, in Boston.

Located near the City's Atlantic port, the new Hall contains two venues, a main hall seating 2400, and an 800 seat chamber hall for smaller ensembles.

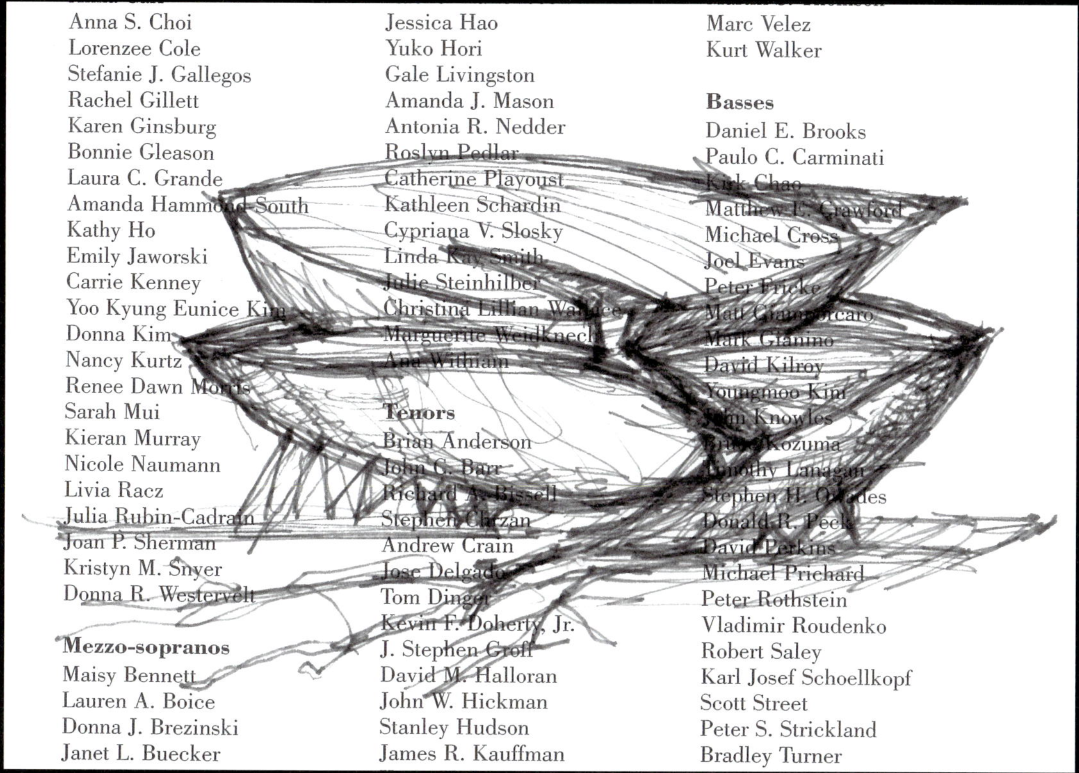

Anna S. Choi
Lorenzee Cole
Stefanie J. Gallegos
Rachel Gillett
Karen Ginsburg
Bonnie Gleason
Laura C. Grande
Amanda Hammond South
Kathy Ho
Emily Jaworski
Carrie Kenney
Yoo Kyung Eunice Kim
Donna Kim
Nancy Kurtz
Renee Dawn Morris
Sarah Mui
Kieran Murray
Nicole Naumann
Livia Racz
Julia Rubin-Cadrain
Joan P. Sherman
Kristyn M. Snyer
Donna R. Westervelt

Mezzo-sopranos
Maisy Bennett
Lauren A. Boice
Donna J. Brezinski
Janet L. Buecker

Jessica Hao
Yuko Hori
Gale Livingston
Amanda J. Mason
Antonia R. Nedder
Roslyn Pedlar
Catherine Playoust
Kathleen Schardin
Cypriana V. Slosky
Linda Kay Smith
Julie Steinhilber
Christina Lillian Wallace
Marguerite Weidknecht
Ana Withiam

Tenors
Brian Anderson
John C. Barr
Richard A. Bissell
Stephen Chrzan
Andrew Crain
Jose Delgado
Tom Dinger
Kevin F. Doherty, Jr.
J. Stephen Groff
David M. Halloran
John W. Hickman
Stanley Hudson
James R. Kauffman

Marc Velez
Kurt Walker

Basses
Daniel E. Brooks
Paulo C. Carminati
Kirk Chao
Matthew E. Crawford
Michael Cross
Joel Evans
Peter Fricke
Matt Giammarcaro
Mark Gianino
David Kilroy
Youngmoo Kim
John Knowles
Bruce Kozuma
Timothy Lanagan
Stephen H. Owades
Donald R. Peck
David Perkins
Michael Prichard
Peter Rothstein
Vladimir Roudenko
Robert Saley
Karl Josef Schoellkopf
Scott Street
Peter S. Strickland
Bradley Turner

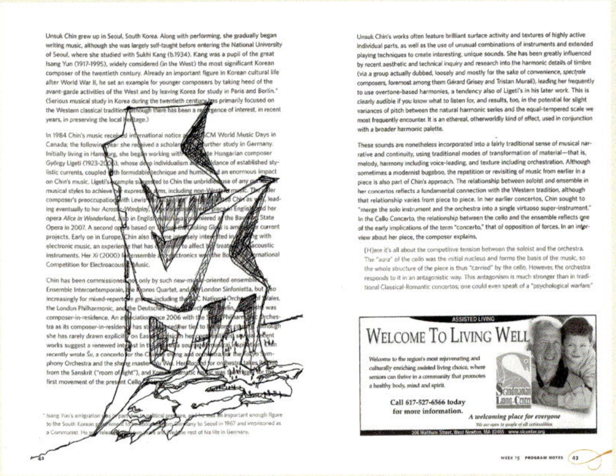

Micomicón, Hollywood, California

When James Levine commissioned Elliot Carter to compose a short introduction to his large work "Symphonia," Carter gave it the form of a brief orchestral fantasy which he named Micomicón, an imaginary fantastical kingdom borrowed from Cervantes's "Don Quixote." The musical imagery of Quixote's quest on horseback inspired this Fun House (Horse) as an adventure ride at Universal Studios. — January 17, 2004

Folded Rock Museum, Sedona AZ

Clad in the red sandstone of its desert setting, the Folded Rock Museum is inspired by Shostakovich's Symphony No. 10, written in response to Stalin's death in 1953 which signaled the beginning of cultural liberation in post-Stalinist USSR. The inward-looking somber mood of the composition broke open the imposition of twenty-five years of communal Social Realism, offering instead an intensely personal response to art. Shostakovich simply stated, "I wanted to express human emotions and passions." The Museum is dedicated to the theme of individuality. — October 13, 2005

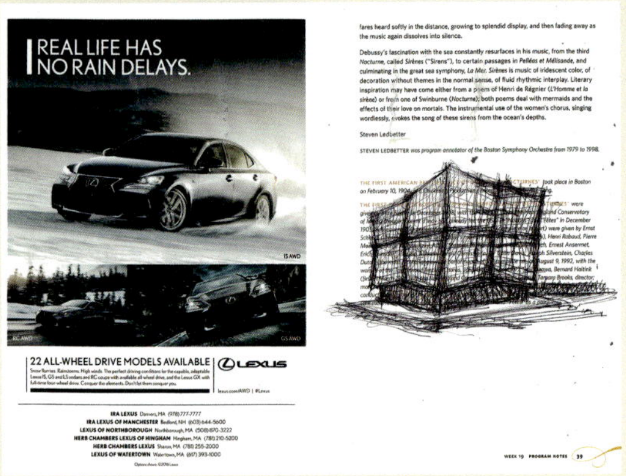

History Faculty Library, University of Cape Town, South Africa

For the university campus setting near the base of Table Mountain, the library's form is suggested by the persistence of stone and the luminosity of education, not accidentally informed by Gordon Bunshaft's use of translucent veined marble in Yale's Beinecke Library. Sketched during a performance of Haydn's 60th Symphony, I suspect the architecture has something to do with musical precision and light. — March 18, 2017

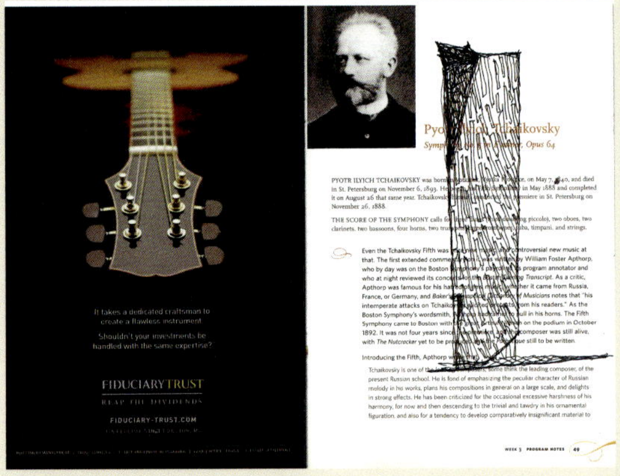

Office Building, Lincoln, NE

Proposed for the quarter block at 13th and L, this high-rise building stands diagonally one block northwest of the state capitol. Rising as a cylinder from the plain like a single grain elevator, openings in the masonry façade spiral upward ignoring expression of the floors from street to sky.
— October 23, 2010

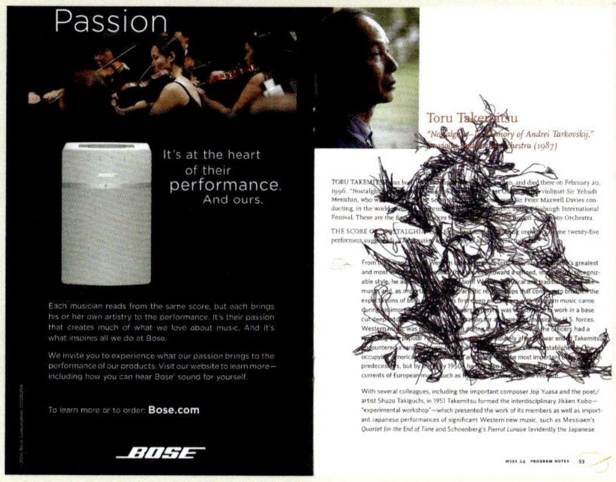

Takemitsu Soundscape — April 29, 2017

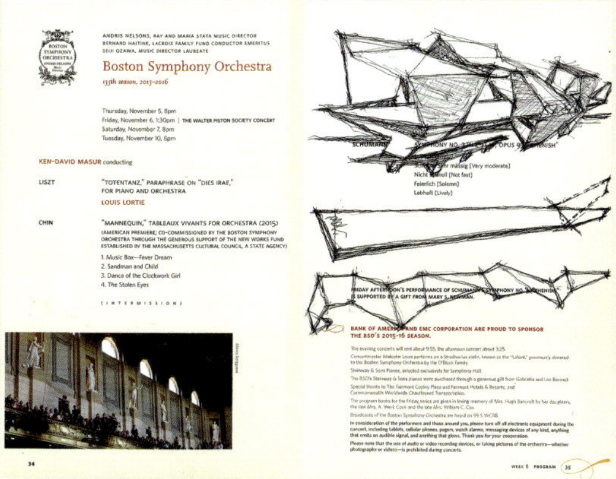

A House Concept, Delhi, New York (homage to Roger Williams)

Memories of a summer visit to Delhi, NY, and sculptor/architect Roger William's studio, were sparked by the Boston Symphony's fall performance of Schumann's "Rhenish Symphony." The house, conceived as a 100' long concrete platform, is raised 14' above grade on a high meadow and wrapped in a folded spiral of Corten steel. Interior surfaces are heavily insulated, finished in unpainted hard-troweled white plaster, and enclosed in low-iron insulating glass. — November 07, 2015

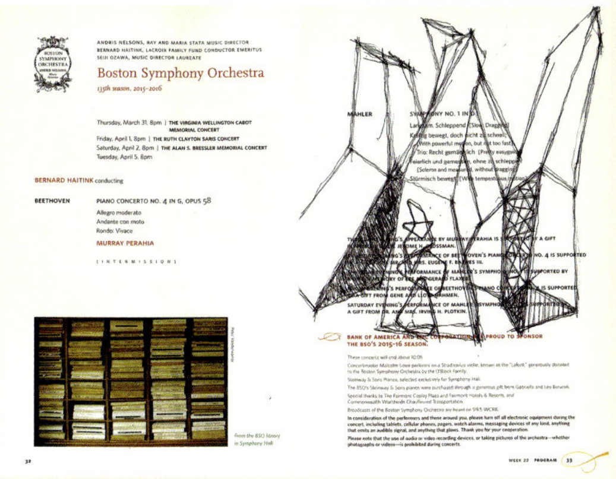

TeleCity, Beijing

To be located on a superblock near the CCTV Tower, this mixed-use residential grouping seeks to help preserve a dense portion of the area's vibrant historic neighborhood by replacing a 1940's residential block nearby. A percentage set-aside of the profits would fund ongoing preservation/restoration efforts by the city of Beijing. — April 02, 2016

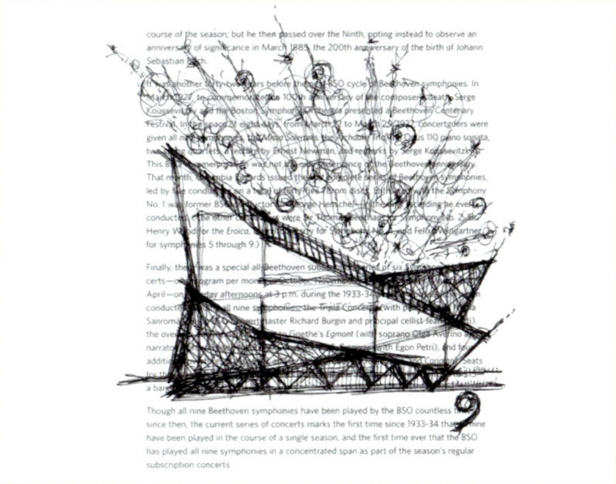

Beethoven Recital Hall, Heiligenstadt, Austria

This 800 seat Music Hall is intentionally small by today's audience standards, and is sited in the Vienna village/suburb where Beethoven composed both his 2nd Symphony and a life-affirming document known as the Heiligenstadt Testament. Although in 1802 his approaching deafness was likely incurable, and this realization brought him to the brink of suicidal despair, he wrote: "Art alone stopped me. It seemed inconceivable that I should leave this world without having produced all that I felt I must. And so I go on leading this miserable life." This resolution of life and art, written before any of his greatest musical achievements, inspired this small Hall, intended for today's composers as well as Beethoven performances. The Hall's glass ceiling and roof offers only views of trees and sky. — November 07, 2009

The Visitor Center previews the experience of space travel through observation as the visitor moves upward through the structure towards a distant star. —

On a hilltop in the coastal city of La Serena is the embarkation point for Las Campanas Observatory where the Giant Magellan Telescope, the world's largest optical instrument, is being constructed. As in Jennifer Higdon's composition, "blue cathedral", which she wrote in memory of her brother, the structure is sited between earth and sky and serves "as a symbolic doorway into and out of this world."

Visitor Center for Las Campanas Observatory, Atacama Desert, Chile

— August 22, 2010

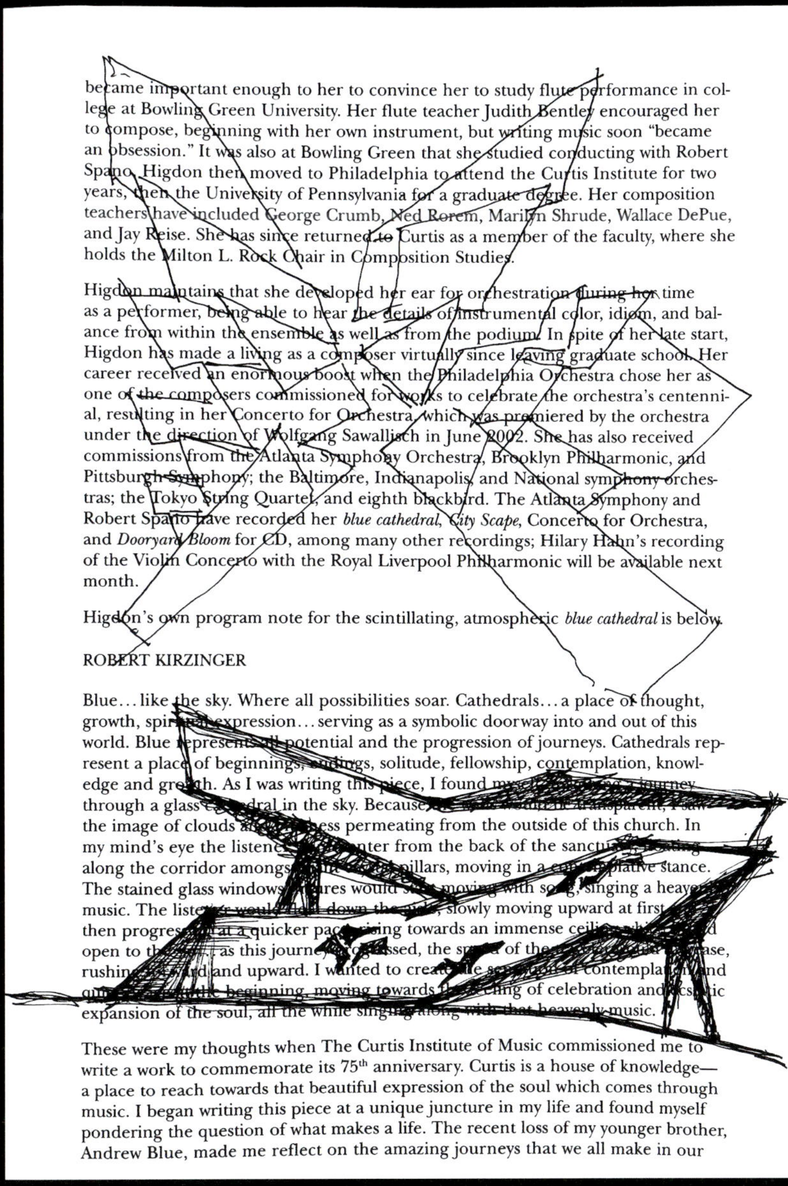

became important enough to her to convince her to study flute performance in college at Bowling Green University. Her flute teacher Judith Bentley encouraged her to compose, beginning with her own instrument, but writing music soon "became an obsession." It was also at Bowling Green that she studied conducting with Robert Spano. Higdon then moved to Philadelphia to attend the Curtis Institute for two years, then the University of Pennsylvania for a graduate degree. Her composition teachers have included George Crumb, Ned Rorem, Marilyn Shrude, Wallace DePue, and Jay Reise. She has since returned to Curtis as a member of the faculty, where she holds the Milton L. Rock Chair in Composition Studies.

Higdon maintains that she developed her ear for orchestration during her time as a performer, being able to hear the details of instrumental color, idiom, and balance from within the ensemble as well as from the podium. In spite of her late start, Higdon has made a living as a composer virtually since leaving graduate school. Her career received an enormous boost when the Philadelphia Orchestra chose her as one of the composers commissioned for works to celebrate the orchestra's centennial, resulting in her Concerto for Orchestra, which was premiered by the orchestra under the direction of Wolfgang Sawallisch in June 2002. She has also received commissions from the Atlanta Symphony Orchestra, Brooklyn Philharmonic, and Pittsburgh Symphony; the Baltimore, Indianapolis, and National symphony orchestras; the Tokyo String Quartet, and eighth blackbird. The Atlanta Symphony and Robert Spano have recorded her *blue cathedral*, *City Scape*, Concerto for Orchestra, and *Dooryard Bloom* for CD, among many other recordings; Hilary Hahn's recording of the Violin Concerto with the Royal Liverpool Philharmonic will be available next month.

Higdon's own program note for the scintillating, atmospheric *blue cathedral* is below.

ROBERT KIRZINGER

Blue… like the sky. Where all possibilities soar. Cathedrals… a place of thought, growth, spir[illegible]expression… serving as a symbolic doorway into and out of this world. Blue [illegible]potential and the progression of journeys. Cathedrals represent a place of beginnings, [illegible]s, solitude, fellowship, contemplation, knowledge and gr[illegible]h. As I was writing th[illegible]piece, I found [illegible] through a glass [illegible]dral in the sky. Because [illegible] the image of clouds [illegible]ess permeating from the outside of this church. In my mind's eye the listene[illegible]nter from the back of the sanctu[illegible] along the corridor amongs[illegible]pillars, moving in a [illegible]plative stance. The stained glass windows[illegible]res would [illegible]with so[illegible]g, singing a heave[illegible] music. The liste[illegible], slowly moving upward at first then progres[illegible]quicker pa[illegible]ing towards an immense ceili[illegible]d open to th[illegible] as this journe[illegible]ssed, the sp[illegible] of the[illegible]ase, rushin[illegible]rd and upward. I wanted to crea[illegible]contempla[illegible]nd [illegible]beginning, moving towards [illegible]ing of celebration and [illegible]tic expansion of the soul, all the while singing [illegible]music.

These were my thoughts when The Curtis Institute of Music commissioned me to write a work to commemorate its 75th anniversary. Curtis is a house of knowledge—a place to reach towards that beautiful expression of the soul which comes through music. I began writing this piece at a unique juncture in my life and found myself pondering the question of what makes a life. The recent loss of my younger brother, Andrew Blue, made me reflect on the amazing journeys that we all make in our

Residential Hall, OCAD University, Toronto, ON

— July 16, 2017

Located on Richmond Street W, a few blocks from Alsop's Sharp Centre for Design, is a proposed new mixed-use Residence Hall with student occupied open space five floors above the street. Street level and above would contain shared university functions, office and commercial spaces. The horizontal platform holds art studios, performing arts and support functions. The form of this building had been percolating for a while before I heard Berlioz's Symphonie Fantastique, but his "idée fixe" in the program notes was a reminder which urged me to draw it.

loved one herself has become a melody to him, an *idée fixe* as it were, that he encounters and hears everywhere.

The *idée fixe*, as much a psychological fixation as a musical one, is introduced in the violins and flute at the start of the first movement's Allegro section. Its appearance "everywhere" in the course of the symphony includes a ball in the midst of a brilliant party; during a quiet summer evening in the country (where it appears against a background texture of agitated strings, leading to a dramatic outburst before the restoration of calm); in the artist's last thoughts before he is executed, in a dream, for the murder of his beloved (at the end of the March to the Scaffold); and during his posthumous participation in a wild witches' sabbath, following his execution, at which the melody representing his beloved appears, grotesquely transformed, to join a "devilish orgy" whose diabolically frenzied climax combines the *Dies irae* from the Mass for the Dead with the witches' round dance.

Today, more than 185 years after its first performance, it is easy to forget that when the *Symphonie fantastique* was new, Beethoven's symphonies had just recently reached France, Beethoven himself having died only in 1827. With its much more specific programmatic intent, Berlioz's work is already a far cry even from Beethoven's own *Pastoral* Symphony of 1808. David Cairns has written that "Berlioz in the 'Fantastic' symphony was speaking a new language: not only a new language of orchestral sound... but also a new language of feeling."

Countless aspects of this score are representative of Berlioz's individual musical style, among them his rhythmically flexible, characteristically long-spun melodies, of which the *idée fixe* is a prime example; the [illegible]xtaposit[illegible] of contrasting harmonies, as in the rapid-fire chords at the end [illegible] March; [illegible]elling [illegible] novel use of particular instruments, whether [illegible]-panied English horn in dialogue with the offs[illegible] in the Country, or the quick tapping of bows [illegible] skeletons of the Witches' Sabbath; and his pre[illegible] dyn[illegible] m[illegible]ngs. And all of this becomes even more striking when one considers that the *Symphonie fantastique* is the composer's earliest big orchestral work, composed when he was not yet thirty, and that the great, mature works—*Roméo et* [illegible], *The Damnation of Faust*, the operas *Les Troyens* and *Béatrice et Benedict* among them—would follow only years and decades later.

MARC MANDEL

Marc Mandel is Director of Program Publications of the Boston Symphony Orchestra.

Stu Rosner

“Song of Hiawatha”, Sioux Falls, SD

— July 28, 2017

Dvorák’s introduction to the New World through Longfellow’s poem formed the inspiration for his 9th Symphony years before he arrived in America. Legends form in one’s imagination quite apart from their realities as this sketch for an apartment building shows. Sioux Falls has a poetic beauty imprinted on its history and seen in bits and pieces of its urban setting. There is something in the sketch as familiar as Dvorák’s music, which nevertheless strives to bring something more to the New World’s (or Sioux Falls’s) landscape through its legends.

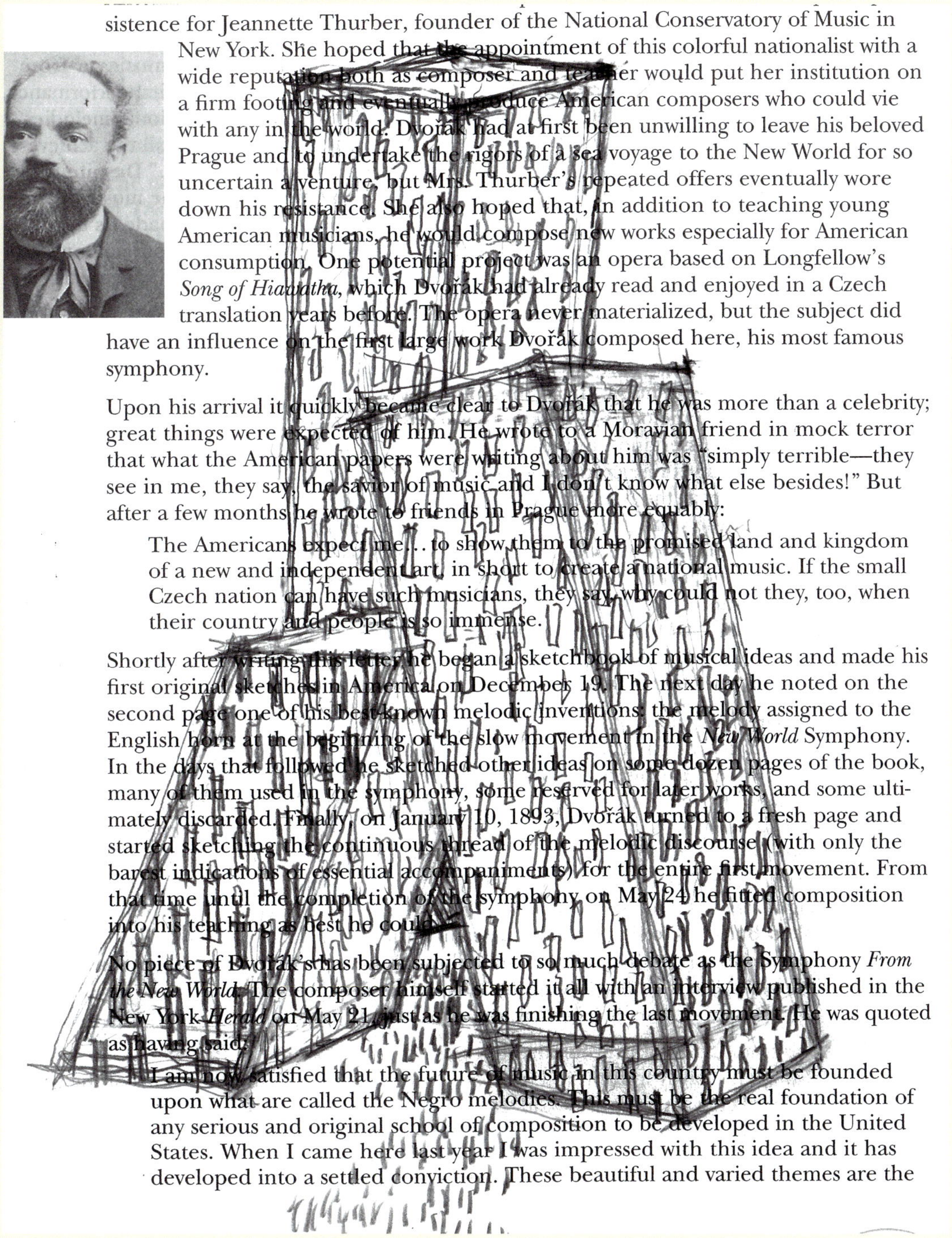

sistence for Jeannette Thurber, founder of the National Conservatory of Music in New York. She hoped that the appointment of this colorful nationalist with a wide reputation both as composer and teacher would put her institution on a firm footing and eventually produce American composers who could vie with any in the world. Dvořák had at first been unwilling to leave his beloved Prague and to undertake the rigors of a sea voyage to the New World for so uncertain a venture, but Mrs. Thurber’s repeated offers eventually wore down his resistance. She also hoped that, in addition to teaching young American musicians, he would compose new works especially for American consumption. One potential project was an opera based on Longfellow’s *Song of Hiawatha*, which Dvořák had already read and enjoyed in a Czech translation years before. The opera never materialized, but the subject did have an influence on the first large work Dvořák composed here, his most famous symphony.

Upon his arrival it quickly became clear to Dvořák that he was more than a celebrity; great things were expected of him. He wrote to a Moravian friend in mock terror that what the American papers were writing about him was “simply terrible—they see in me, they say, the savior of music and I don’t know what else besides!” But after a few months he wrote to friends in Prague more equably:

> The Americans expect me . . . to show them to the promised land and kingdom of a new and independent art, in short to create a national music. If the small Czech nation can have such musicians, they say, why could not they, too, when their country and people is so immense.

Shortly after writing this letter he began a sketchbook of musical ideas and made his first original sketches in America on December 19. The next day he noted on the second page one of his best-known melodic inventions: the melody assigned to the English horn at the beginning of the slow movement in the *New World* Symphony. In the days that followed he sketched other ideas on some dozen pages of the book, many of them used in the symphony, some reserved for later works, and some ultimately discarded. Finally, on January 10, 1893, Dvořák turned to a fresh page and started sketching the continuous thread of the melodic discourse (with only the barest indications of essential accompaniments) for the entire first movement. From that time until the completion of the symphony on May 24 he fitted composition into his teaching as best he could.

No piece of Dvořák’s has been subjected to so much debate as the Symphony *From the New World*. The composer himself started it all with an interview published in the New York *Herald* on May 21, just as he was finishing the last movement. He was quoted as having said:

> I am now satisfied that the future of music in this country must be founded upon what are called the Negro melodies. This must be the real foundation of any serious and original school of composition to be developed in the United States. When I came here last year I was impressed with this idea and it has developed into a settled conviction. These beautiful and varied themes are the

Twin Towers — October 14, 2019

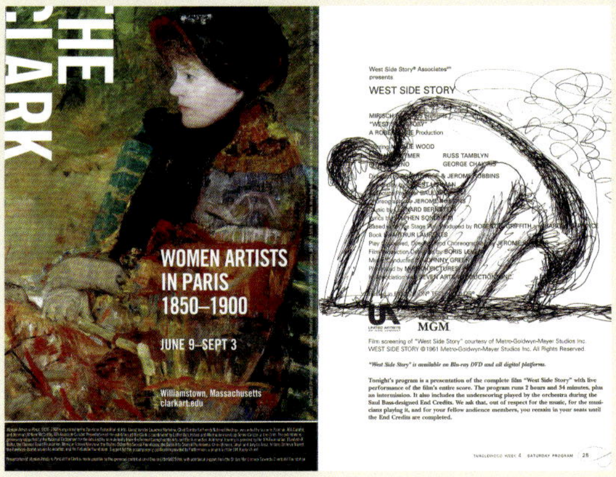

Florencia — September 28, 2018

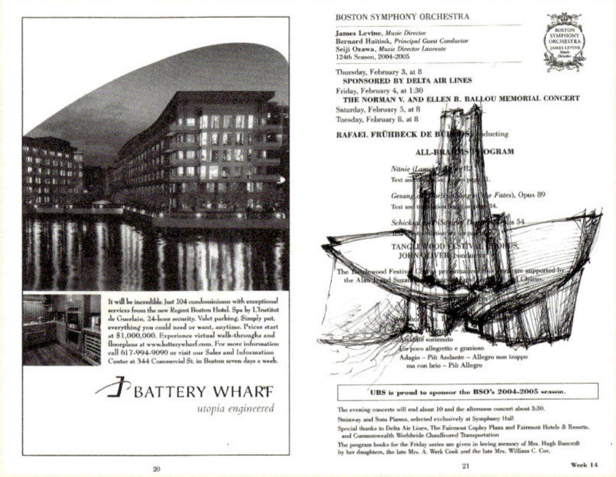

Spanish Monument — February 5, 2005

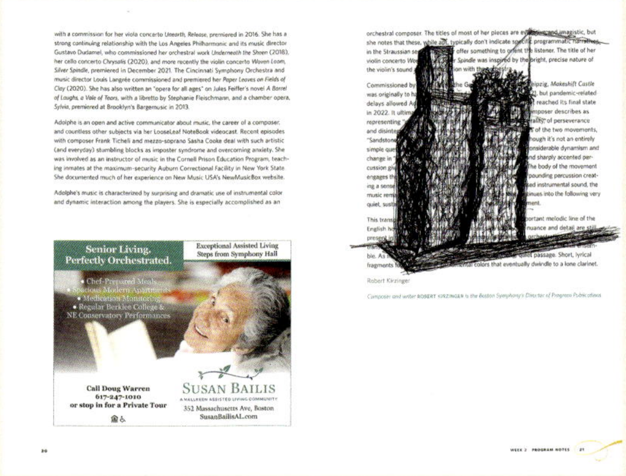

Stone Museum — October 01, 2022

Berlioz's Spark — December 1, 2007

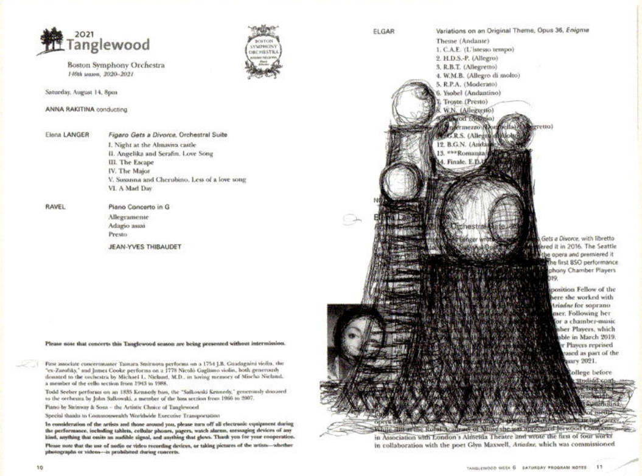

Episodes — August 14, 2021

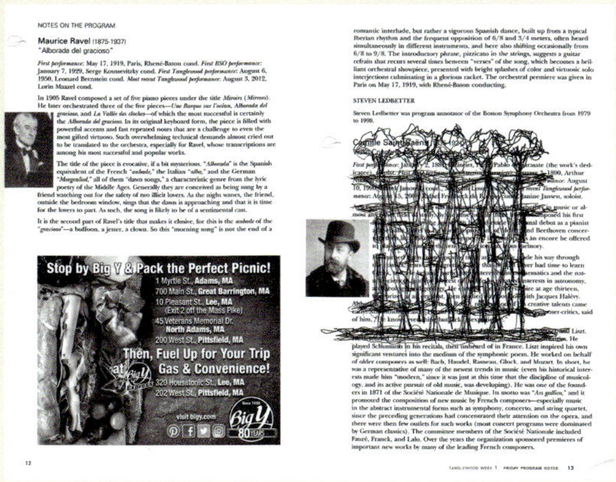

Treehouse 2 — September 08, 2015

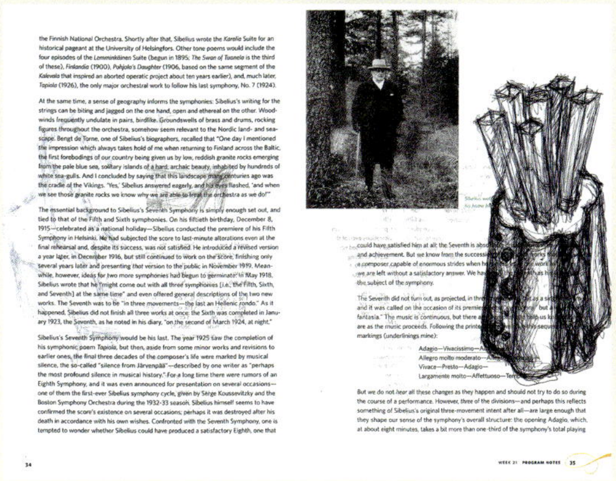

Untitled — April 09, 2022

Play — April 22, 2019

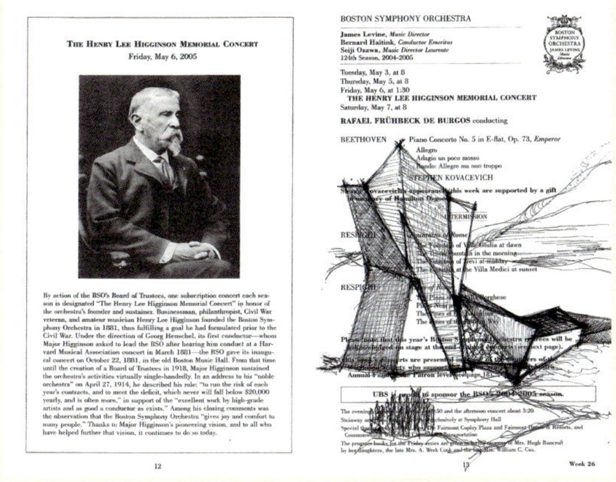

Untitled — May 7, 2005

Fabric Chapel 2 — October 15, 2016

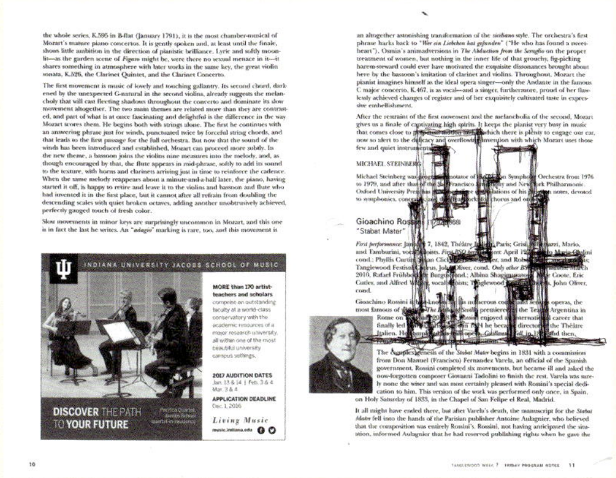

Cubism — August 19, 2016

The Ark

— April 23, 2022

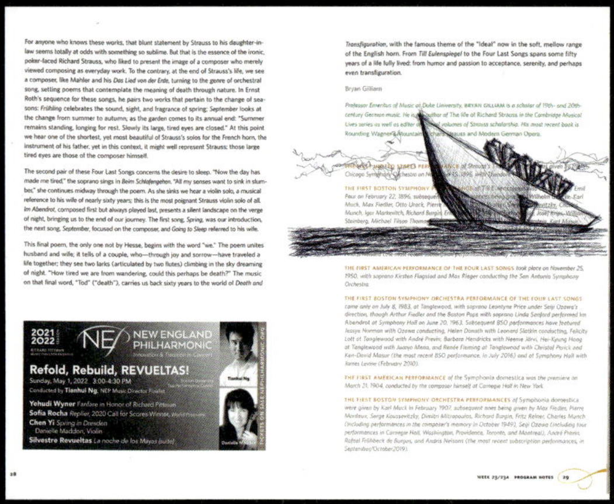
For anyone who knows these works, that blunt statement by Strauss to his daughter-in-law seems totally at odds with something so sublime. But that is the essence of the ironic, poker-faced Richard Strauss, who liked to present the image of a composer who merely viewed composing as everyday work. To the contrary, at the end of Strauss's life, we see a composer, like Mahler and his *Das Lied von der Erde*, turning to the genre of orchestral song, setting poems that contemplate the meaning of death through nature. In Ernst Roth's sequence for these songs, he pairs two works that pertain to the change of seasons: *Frühling* celebrates the sound, sight, and fragrance of spring; *September* looks at the change from summer to autumn, as the garden comes to its annual end: "Summer remains standing, longing for rest. Slowly its large, tired eyes are closed." At this point we hear one of the shortest, yet most beautiful of Strauss's solos for the French horn, the instrument of his father, yet in this context, it might well represent Strauss: those large tired eyes are those of the composer himself.

The second pair of these Four Last Songs concerns the desire to sleep. "Now the day has made me tired," the soprano sings in *Beim Schlafengehen*. "All my senses want to sink in slumber," she continues midway through the poem. As she sinks we hear a violin solo, a musical reference to his wife of nearly sixty years; this is the most poignant Strauss violin solo of all. *Im Abendrot*, composed first but always played last, presents a silent landscape on the verge of night, bringing us to the end of our journey. The first song, *Spring*, was our introduction, the next song, *September*, focused on the composer, and *Going to Sleep* referred to his wife.

This final poem, the only one not by Hesse, begins with the word "we." The poem unites husband and wife; it tells of a couple, who—through joy and sorrow—have traveled a life together; they see two larks (articulated by two flutes) climbing in the sky dreaming of night. "How tired we are from wandering, could this perhaps be death?" The music on that final word, "Tod" ("death"), carries us back sixty years to the world of *Death and*

Transfiguration, with the famous theme of the "Ideal" now in the soft, mellow range of the English horn. From *Till Eulenspiegel* to the Four Last Songs spans some fifty years of a life fully lived: from humor and passion to acceptance, serenity, and perhaps even transfiguration.

Bryan Gilliam

THE FIRST AMERICAN PERFORMANCE OF THE FOUR LAST SONGS *took place on November 25, 1950, with soprano Kirsten Flagstad and Max Rieger conducting the San Antonio Symphony Orchestra.*

THE FIRST BOSTON SYMPHONY ORCHESTRA PERFORMANCE OF THE FOUR LAST SONGS *came only on July 8, 1983, at Tanglewood, with soprano Leontyne Price under Seiji Ozawa's direction, though Arthur Fiedler and the Boston Pops with soprano Linda Sanford performed* Im Abendrot *at Symphony Hall on June 20, 1963. Subsequent BSO performances have featured Jessye Norman with Ozawa conducting, Helen Donath with Leonard Slatkin conducting, Felicity Lott at Tanglewood with André Previn; Barbara Hendricks with Neeme Järvi, Hei-Kyung Hong at Tanglewood with Juanjo Mena, and Renée Fleming at Tanglewood with Christof Perick and Ken-David Masur (the most recent BSO performance, in July 2016) and at Symphony Hall with James Levine (February 2010).*

THE FIRST AMERICAN PERFORMANCE *of the* Symphonia domestica *was the premiere on March 21, 1904, conducted by the composer himself at Carnegie Hall in New York.*

THE FIRST BOSTON SYMPHONY ORCHESTRA PERFORMANCES *of* Symphonia domestica *were given by Karl Muck in February 1907, subsequent ones being given by Max Fiedler, Pierre Monteux, Serge Koussevitzky, Dimitri Mitropoulos, Richard Burgin, Fritz Reiner, Charles Munch (including performances in the composer's memory in October 1949), Seiji Ozawa (including four performances in Carnegie Hall, Washington, Providence, Toronto, and Montreal), André Previn, Rafael Frühbeck de Burgos, and Andris Nelsons (the most recent subscription performances, in September/October2019).*

The Ark is a floating museum designed to display Sandy Sokoloff's paintings and site specific works. The Ark floats from town to town along waterways to riverfront destinations.

Transfiguration, with the famous theme of the "Ideal" now in the soft, mellow range of the English horn. From *Till Eulenspiegel* to the Four Last Songs spans some fifty years of a life fully lived: from humor and passion to acceptance, serenity, and perhaps even transfiguration.

Bryan Gilliam

Professor Emeritus of Music at Duke University, BRYAN GILLIAM *is a scholar of 19th- and 20th-century German music. He is* [illegible] *author of* The life of Richard Strauss *in the Cambridge Musical Lives series as well as editor of* [illegible] *volumes of Strauss scholarship. His most recent book is* Rounding Wagner's Mountain: Richard Strauss and Modern German Opera.

THE FIRST UNITED STATES PERFORMANCE *of Strauss's* Till [illegible] *was given by the Chicago Symphony Orchestra on November 15, 1895, with Theodore* [illegible]

THE FIRST BOSTON SYMPHONY P[illegible]MANCE *of* Till Eulenspiegel *was* [illegible] *Emil Paur on February 22, 1896, subsequent* [illegible] *performances being given by Wilhelm G*[illegible]*cke, Karl Muck, Max Fiedler, Otto Urack, Pierre* [illegible]*, Bruno Walter, Serge* [illegible]*sevitzky, Charles Munch, Igor Markevitch, Richard Burgin, Eri*[illegible]*, Werner Torkan*[illegible]*sky, Josef Krips, William Steinberg, Michael Tilson Thomas,* [illegible] *Joseph* [illegible]*erstein, Kurt Masur, Andrew Davis, Marek Janowski, Daniel* [illegible]*, Roberto Abbado, James Levine, David Robertson,* [illegible] *Graf, Rafael Frübeck de Burgos, Sir Mark Elder, David Zinman, Christoph von Dohnányi, Edward Gardner, Giancarlo Guerrero (the most recent Tanglewood performance, on August 6, 2016), and Andris Nelsons (the most recent subscription performances, in May 2019).*

THE FIRST AMERICAN PERFORMANCE OF THE FOUR LAST SONGS *took place on November 25, 1950, with soprano Kirsten Flagstad and Max Rieger conducting the San Antonio Symphony Orchestra.*

THE FIRST BOSTON SYMPHONY ORCHESTRA PERFORMANCE OF THE FOUR LAST SONGS *came only on July 8, 1983, at Tanglewood, with soprano Leontyne Price under Seiji Ozawa's direction, though Arthur Fiedler and the Boston Pops with soprano Linda Sanford performed* Im Abendrot *at Symphony Hall on June 20, 1963. Subsequent BSO performances have featured Jessye Norman with Ozawa conducting, Helen Donath with Leonard Slatkin conducting, Felicity Lott at Tanglewood with André Previn, Barbara Hendricks with Neeme Järvi, Hei-Kyung Hong at Tanglewood with Juanjo Mena, and Renée Fleming at Tanglewood with Christof Perick and Ken-David Masur (the most recent BSO performance, in July 2016) and at Symphony Hall with James Levine (February 2010).*

THE FIRST AMERICAN PERFORMANCE *of the* Symphonia domestica *was the premiere on March 21, 1904, conducted by the composer himself at Carnegie Hall in New York.*

THE FIRST BOSTON SYMPHONY ORCHESTRA PERFORMANCES *of* Symphonia domestica *were given by Karl Muck in February 1907, subsequent ones being given by Max Fiedler, Pierre Monteux, Serge Koussevitzky, Dimitri Mitropoulos, Richard Burgin, Fritz Reiner, Charles Munch (including performances in the composer's memory in October 1949), Seiji Ozawa (including tour performances in Carnegie Hall, Washington, Providence, Toronto, and Montreal), André Previn, Rafael Frühbeck de Burgos, and Andris Nelsons (the most recent subscription performances, in September/October2019).*

The Ark

Model of the Ark

The gallery is dark, lit by stacks that focus light on the paintings and spill ambient light into the space. The paintings are huge, and represent visual doors that open to the deepest truths of the spirit. The visitor experiences a meditative space combining art and architecture, an environment built to transport one to another reality. —

Study - New Media Library

— October 10, 2015

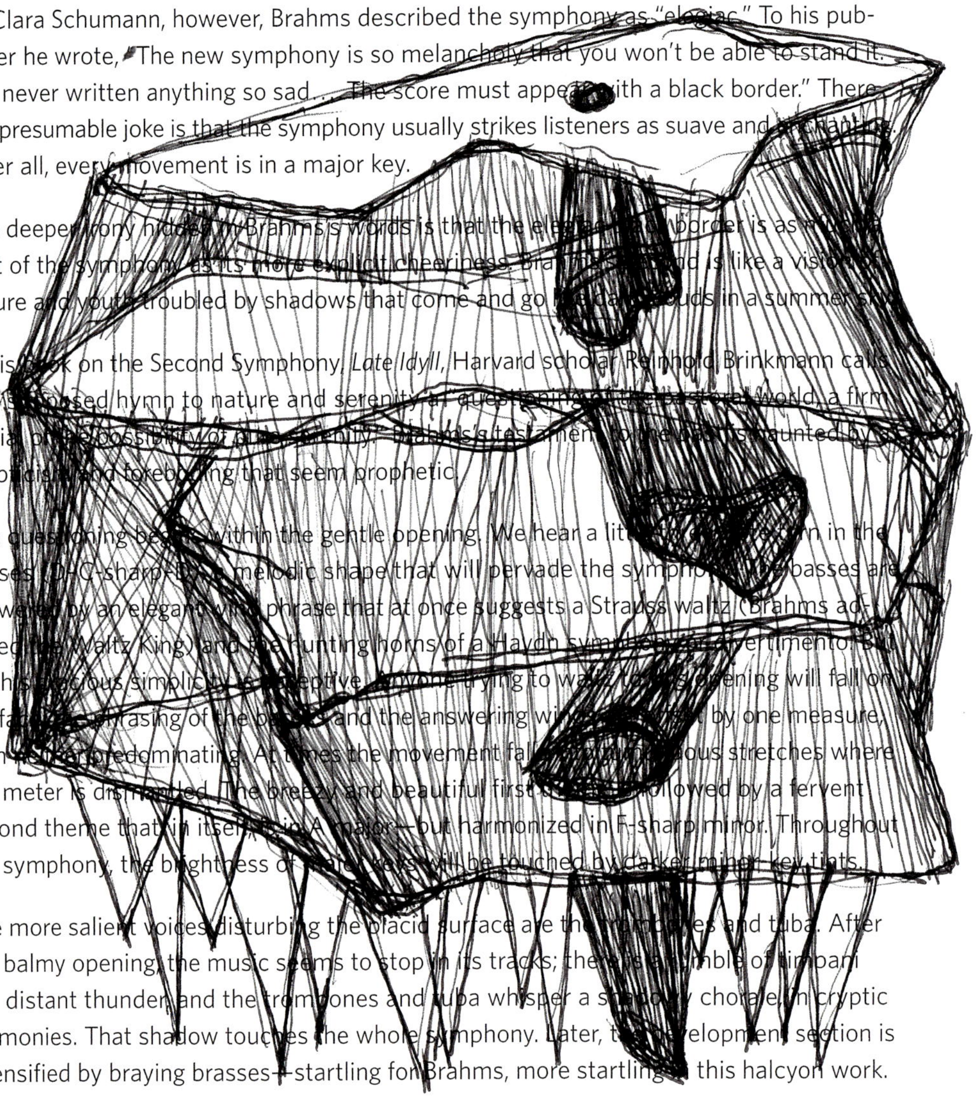

that you will think I wrote it specially for you or even your young lady." He cited the benevolent influence of his composing spot on the Wörthersee: "[there are] so many melodies flying around that you have to be careful not to step on them." Meanwhile, having just finished the First Symphony after some fifteen years of wrestling with it, Brahms completed the Second—and several smaller works—during one delightful four-month working vacation in the summer of 1877.

To Clara Schumann, however, Brahms described the symphony as "elegiac." To his publisher he wrote, "The new symphony is so melancholy that you won't be able to stand it. I've never written anything so sad . . . The score must appear with a black border." There the presumable joke is that the symphony usually strikes listeners as suave and [illegible]. After all, every movement is in a major key.

The deeper irony hidden in Brahms's words is that the elegiac black border is as much a part of the symphony as its more explicit cheeriness. Brahms's Second is like a vision of nature and youth troubled by shadows that come and go like dark clouds in a summer sky.

In his book on the Second Symphony, *Late Idyll*, Harvard scholar Reinhold Brinkmann calls this [illegible] hymn to nature and serenity a questioning of the pastoral world, a firm denial of the possibility of [illegible] serenity." Brahms's testament to the [illegible] is haunted by [illegible] skepticism and foreboding that seem prophetic.

The questioning begins within the gentle opening. We hear a [illegible] turn in the basses [illegible] melodic shape that will pervade the symphony. The basses are answered by an elegant wind phrase that at once suggests a Strauss waltz (Brahms admired the Waltz King) and the hunting horns of a Haydn symphony or divertimento. But all this gracious simplicity is deceptive. Anyone trying to waltz to this opening will fall on his face: [illegible] phrasing of the basses and the answering winds [illegible] by one measure, with [illegible] predominating. At times the movement falls into [illegible] stretches where the meter is dismantled. The breezy and beautiful first [illegible] followed by a fervent second theme that in itself is in A major—but harmonized in F-sharp minor. Throughout the symphony, the brightness of major keys will be touched by darker minor-key tints.

The more salient voices disturbing the placid surface are the trombones and tuba. After the balmy opening, the music seems to stop in its tracks; there is a rumble of timpani like distant thunder, and the trombones and tuba whisper a shadowy chorale in cryptic harmonies. That shadow touches the whole symphony. Later, the development section is intensified by braying brasses—startling for Brahms, more startling in this halcyon work.

From the beginning of the symphony's career there were some who saw the shadows. One of them, conductor and Brahms acquaintance Vincenz Lachner, complained to the composer about "the gloomy lugubrious tones of the trombones" intruding on the tranquility. Brahms replied with one of the most revealing statements he ever made about his music or about himself:

Beethoven Op. 125

— August 29, 2010

A Tower Fantasy

— April 03, 2010

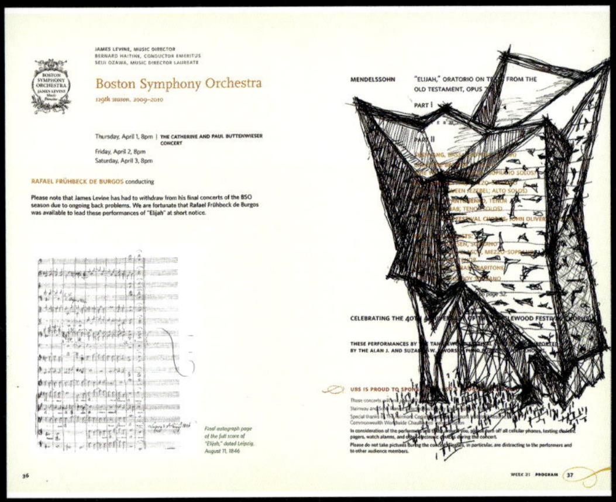

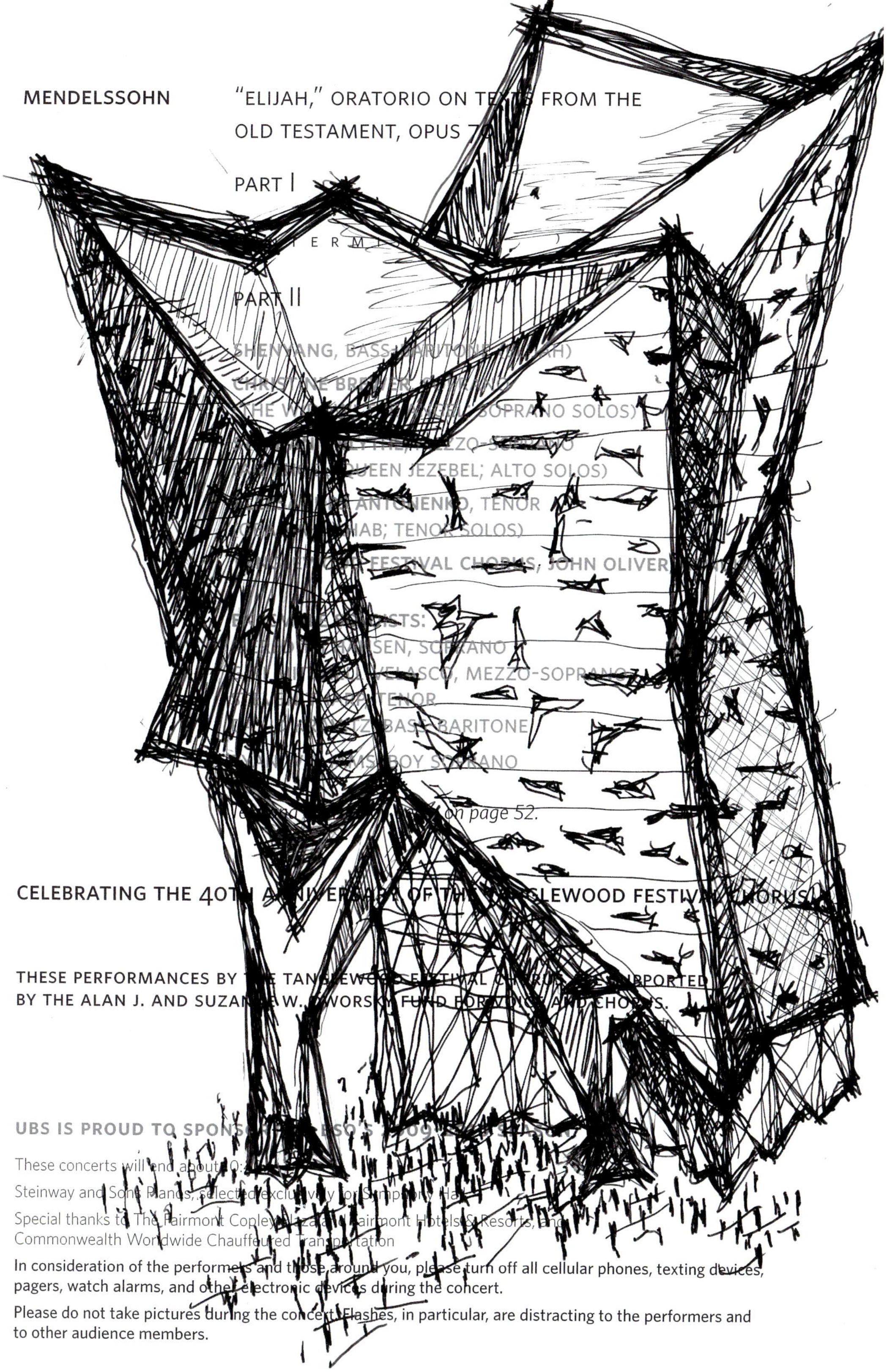

MENDELSSOHN "ELIJAH," ORATORIO ON TE[illegible] FROM THE OLD TESTAMENT, OPUS 7[illegible]

PART I

[illegible]ERM[illegible]

PART II

[illegible]ANG, BASS-[illegible] (ELIJAH)
[illegible]E BREWER, SOP[illegible]
(THE W[illegible] SOPRANO SOLOS)
[illegible]ZZO-SOPRANO
[illegible] QUEEN JEZEBEL; ALTO SOLOS)
[illegible] ANTONENKO, TENOR
[illegible]AB; TENOR SOLOS)
[illegible] FESTIVAL CHORUS, JOHN OLIVER[illegible]

[illegible]STS:
[illegible]SEN, SOPRANO
[illegible]ELASCO, MEZZO-SOPRANO
[illegible] TENOR
[illegible]Z, BASS-BARITONE
[illegible]S, BOY SOPRANO

[illegible] on page 52.

CELEBRATING THE 40TH A[illegible] OF TH[illegible]GLEWOOD FESTIV[illegible] CHORUS

THESE PERFORMANCES BY THE TANGLEWOOD FESTIVAL CHORUS ARE SUPPORTED BY THE ALAN J. AND SUZANNE W. [illegible]WORSKY FUND FOR VOICE AND CHORUS.

UBS IS PROUD TO SPONS[illegible]

These concerts will end about [illegible]
Steinway and Sons Pianos, selected exclusively for Symphony Hall.
Special thanks to The Fairmont Copley Plaza, Fairmont Hotels & Resorts, and Commonwealth Worldwide Chauffeured Transportation
In consideration of the performers and those around you, please turn off all cellular phones, texting devices, pagers, watch alarms, and other electronic devices during the concert.
Please do not take pictures during the concert. Flashes, in particular, are distracting to the performers and to other audience members.

A Midsummer Night's Dreamhouse, Lenox, MA

— August 05, 2017

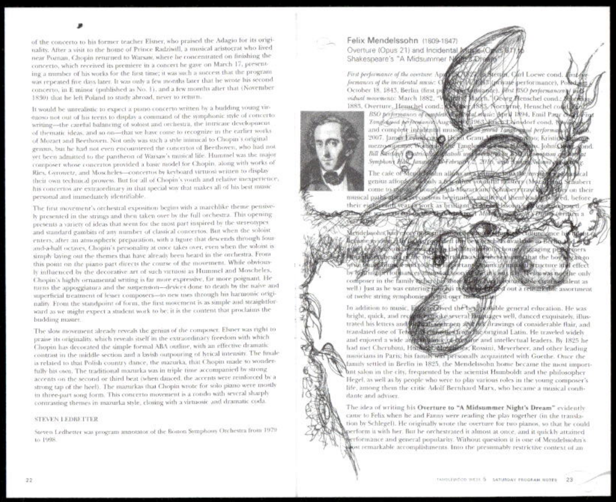

One of the purest musical fantasies inspired a treehouse drawn from Mendelssohn's Incidental Music, Op. 61. An enormous branch suspends carbon fiber sheaves enclosed by glazed carbon fiber netting with woven glass fiber sleeping spheres below.

Felix Mendelssohn (1809-1847)

Overture (Opus 21) and Incidental Music (Opus 61) to Shakespeare's "A Midsummer Night's Dream"

First performance of the overture: April 29, 1827, in Stettin, Carl Loewe cond. *First performances of the incidental music*: October 14, 1843 (private performance), Potsdam; October 18, 1843, Berlin (first public performance). *First BSO performances of individual movements*: March 1882, "Wedding March," Georg Henschel cond.; February 1883, Overture, Henschel cond.; October 1883, Nocturne, Henschel cond. *First BSO performances of complete incidental music*: April 1894, Emil Paur cond. *First Tanglewood performance*: August 10, 1963, Erich Leinsdorf cond. (Overture and complete incidental music). *Most recent Tanglewood performance*: July 6, 2007, James Levine cond.; Heidi Grant Murphy, soprano; Kristine Jepson, mezzo-soprano; Women of the Tanglewood Festival Chorus, John Oliver, cond. *Bill Barclay's theatrical adaptation was premiered in BSO subscription concerts at Symphony Hall, January 28-February 2, 2016, with Andris Nelsons conducting.*

The case of Mendelssohn allows us a glimpse into the mysteries of musical genius afforded by only a few other youthful masters (Mozart and Schubert come to mind). Though both Mozart and Schubert traveled farther on their musical paths after a precocious beginning, neither of them had produced, before their eighteenth year, a work as brilliant as Mendelssohn's Octet (composed when he was sixteen) or the Overture to *A Midsummer Night's Dream* (written a year later).

Mendelssohn had every opportunity to develop his musical culture once his talent became evident. His father provided the best teachers available in Berlin and organized regular Sunday musicales in the Mendelssohn house, engaging performers from the orchestra of the royal court. It was for these events that the boy began to write music himself and to learn important lessons in musical structure and effect by hearing performances almost as soon as the ink was dry. (Felix was not the only composer in the family either; his sister Fanny had a remarkable creative talent as well.) Just as he was entering into his teens, he turned out a remarkable assortment of twelve string symphonies in just over half a year.

In addition to music, Felix received the best possible general education. He was bright, quick, and receptive, spoke several languages well, danced exquisitely, illustrated his letters and journals with pen and ink drawings of considerable flair, and translated one of Terence's comedies from the original Latin. He traveled widely and enjoyed a wide acquaintance of creative and intellectual leaders. By 1825 he had met Cherubini, Hummel, Moscheles, Rossini, Meyerbeer, and other leading musicians in Paris; his family was personally acquainted with Goethe. Once the family settled in Berlin in 1825, the Mendelssohn home became the most important salon in the city, frequented by the scientist Humboldt and the philosopher Hegel, as well as by people who were to play various roles in the young composer's life, among them the critic Adolf Bernhard Marx, who became a musical confidante and adviser.

The idea of writing his **Overture to "A Midsummer Night's Dream"** evidently came to Felix when he and Fanny were reading the play together (in the translation by Schlegel). He originally wrote the overture for two pianos, so that he could perform it with her. But he orchestrated it almost at once, and it quickly attained performance and general popularity. Without question it is one of Mendelssohn's most remarkable accomplishments. Into the presumably restrictive context of an

House Over a Ravine, Richmond, MA

— August 04, 2017

Houses are the piano compositions of architecture. Some, like the works of Chopin, become iconic. And as with Chopin's compositions they can become the main focus and output of an architect's career. As one approaches this house, it's barely noticed as it rises gently from a forest clearing. One can take the path to the roof or choose to enter at grade. Its form in plan stretches over a triangular ravine, with views down, but also out, towards a pond 60' below as the land falls away at the house's far end.

It would be unrealistic to expect a piano concerto written by a budding young virtuoso not out of his teens to display a command of the symphonic style of concerto writing—the careful balancing of soloist and orchestra, the intricate development of [illegible] ideas, and so on—that we have come to recognize in the earlier works of Mozart and Beethoven. Not only was such a style inimical to Chopin's [illegible] but he had not even encountered the concertos of Beethoven. This is not to say that he disliked Beethoven's music; while working on the F minor [illegible] taken part in a private reading of the *Archduke* Trio and wrote to [illegible] Woyciechowski, "I've never heard anything so great; in it Beethoven snaps his fingers at the whole world." But the musical life of [illegible]aw had not yet admitted Beethoven to the pantheon, esp[illegible]rks. Hummel was the [illegible] concertos provided a basi[illegible]g with [illegible] Ries, [illegible], and Moscheles—concertos by keyboard [illegible] written [illegible] prowess.

But for all [illegible]pin's youth and relative inexperience, his concertos are extraordinary in [illegible] way that [illegible] immediately [illegible] key [illegible] shape of the music by setting up the [illegible] first movement, most unusually, keeps to the [illegible] both first and second subjects, a procedure that Donald Francis Tovey regards as "suicidal." Yet it is full of surprising and poetic and majestic moments for all its apparent lack of a strong ground plan. The second movement, "Romance," is nearer to the heart of Chopin, a pure outpouring of elegant and spontaneous melody. The finale, like the middle movement, is in E major. Its most characteristic element appears in the third theme, a krakowiak of great verve and rhythmic subtlety, which brings the concerto to a vigorous close.

STEVEN LEDBETTER

Steven Ledbetter was program annotator of the Boston Symphony Orchestra from 1979 to 1998.

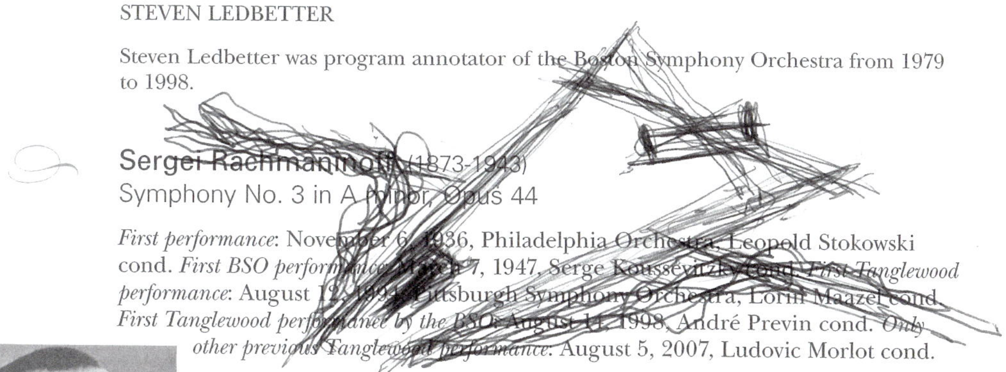

Sergei Rachmaninoff (1873-1943)

Symphony No. 3 in A minor, Opus 44

First performance: November 6, 1936, Philadelphia Orchestra, Leopold Stokowski cond. *First BSO performance*: March 7, 1947, Serge Koussevitzky cond. *First Tanglewood performance*: August 12, 1994, Pittsburgh Symphony Orchestra, Lorin Maazel cond. *First Tanglewood performance by the BSO*: August 14, 1998, André Previn cond. *Only other previous Tanglewood performance*: August 5, 2007, Ludovic Morlot cond.

It is astonishing that, of the three symphonies written by a composer so much loved by concert audiences for his piano concertos, only his Second is reasonably well known. All three of the symphonies are filled with the kind of richly pensive, romantic melody and drenchingly sonorous orchestral colors that audiences love, yet the First and the Third are still stepchildren of the composer's fame.

The three symphonies span most of Rachmaninoff's working life: the First was composed in 1895 and the Third came forty years later, after which his only remaining composition was the *Symphonic Dances*, Opus 45. Upon its première, in November 1936 by the Philadelphia Orchestra led by Leopold Stokowski, the symphony failed to capture the hearts of audiences instantly, as his

Sometimes the urgency of a task is focused by listening to live music, in this case Mozart. In the summer of 2009 there was a competition to design 5 parish libraries for 5 city neighborhoods. One was for Norman-Mayer on a corner site on Gentily Boulevard. Since drive-thru service is at street level, access to the Library's main floor, at Level 2, is from the street corner. Metal screening surrounds the façades and provides sun control. —

Parish Library, New Orleans, Louisiana

— May 02, 2009

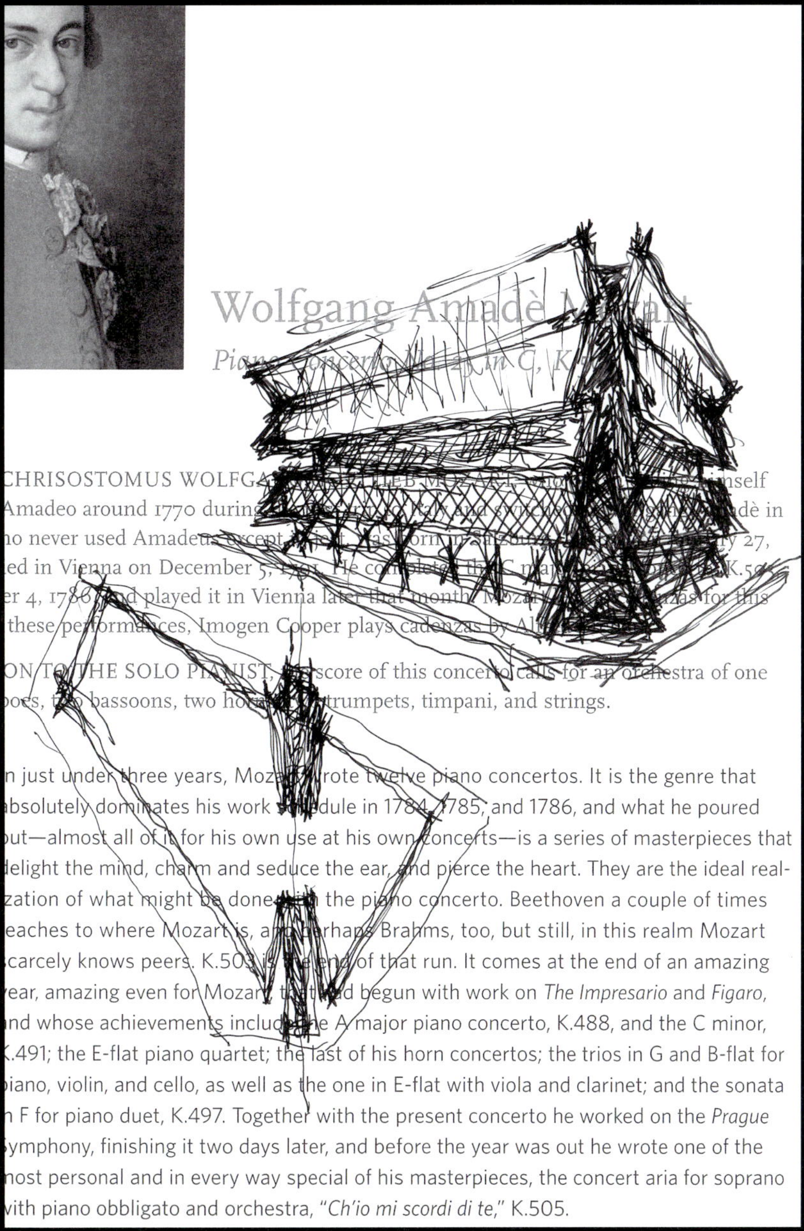

New Media Library, New Orleans, Louisiana

— August 21, 2009

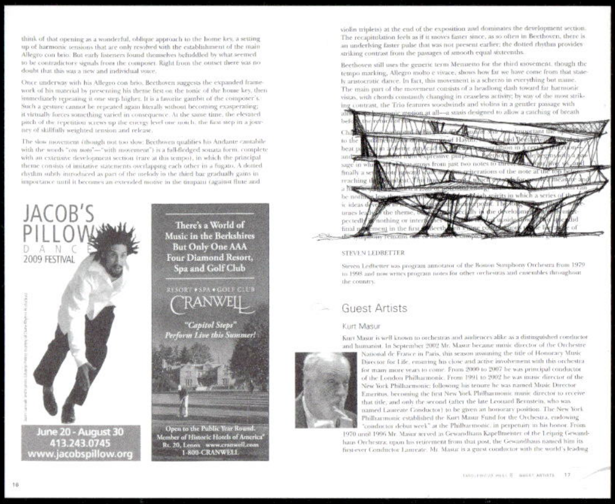

On April 2, 1800, Beethoven began to transform the sound of symphonic music with the first performance of his First Symphony. But as familiar as it seems today, it must have been both surprising and puzzling to the first audiences. So it is with libraries today which are evolving at the pace of technological change to become informational cornucopias. The New Media Library contains everything from books to theaters, transmitting knowledge in an electrochromic glass environment that can be darkened, lightened, or otherwise modified to support the transfer of information.

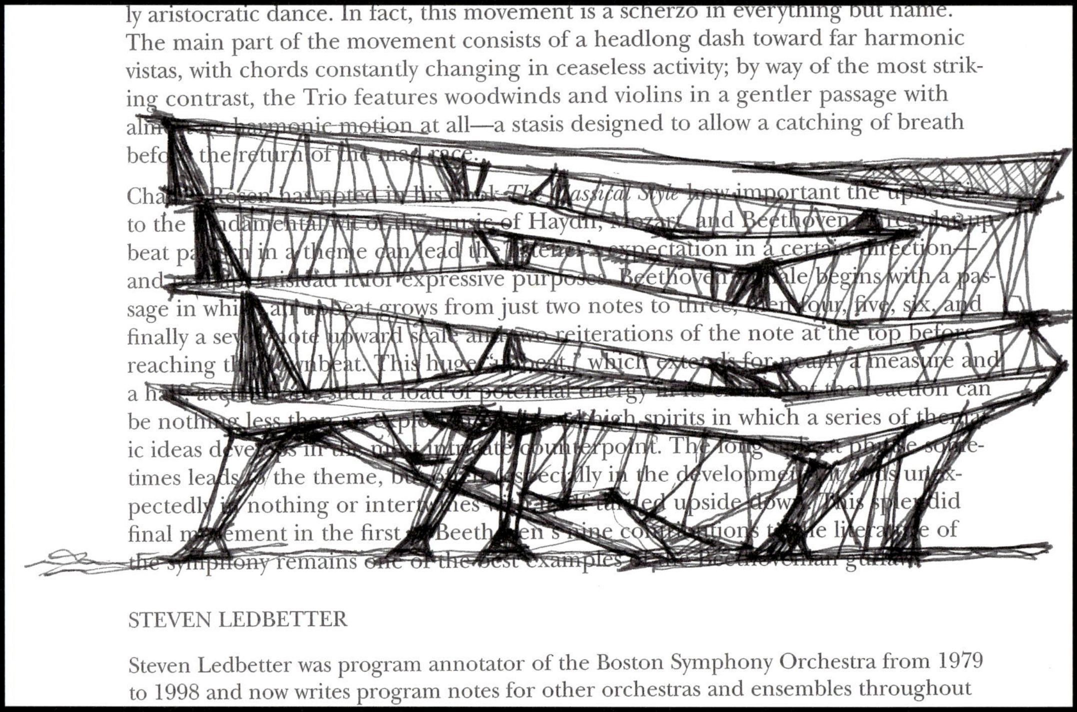

ly aristocratic dance. In fact, this movement is a scherzo in everything but name. The main part of the movement consists of a headlong dash toward far harmonic vistas, with chords constantly changing in ceaseless activity; by way of the most striking contrast, the Trio features woodwinds and violins in a gentler passage with [illegible] harmonic motion at all—a stasis designed to allow a catching of breath before the return of the mad race.

[illegible] *The Classical Style* how important the up[illegible] to the [illegible] of Haydn, Mozart, and Beethoven [illegible] beat pa[illegible] in a theme can lead the listener's expectation in a certain direction—and [illegible] it for expressive purposes. Beethoven's [illegible] begins with a passage in whi[illegible] grows from just two notes to three, [illegible] four, five, six, and finally a se[illegible] upward scale and two reiterations of the note at the top before reaching th[illegible] downbeat. This huge "upbeat," which extends for nearly a measure and a ha[illegible] such a load of potential energy [illegible] the reaction can be nothing less than [illegible] high spirits in which a series of thematic ideas d[illegible] in the [illegible] counterpoint. The long [illegible] phrase sometimes leads to the theme, but [illegible] especially in the development [illegible] unexpectedly in nothing or intert[illegible] upside down. This splendid final movement in the first [illegible] Beethoven's nine contributions to the literature of the symphony remains one of the best examples [illegible]

STEVEN LEDBETTER

Steven Ledbetter was program annotator of the Boston Symphony Orchestra from 1979 to 1998 and now writes program notes for other orchestras and ensembles throughout

Orchidarium and Restaurant, Marie Selby Gardens, Sarasota, FL

— August 31, 2008

As the second work on the program, Mozart's Piano Concerto No. 25 in C became one example of the new, densely rich, intricate, and grand works which characterized the twelve piano concertos of his late twenties. They became as expressive as his symphonies, and hearing this one inspired this sketch. The interwoven structure of concrete, steel and glass is half open and half enclosed as it mimics the tree canopy which serves as an aerial display for exotic orchids and bromeliads. The restaurant accommodates diners on the first and second levels of the building.

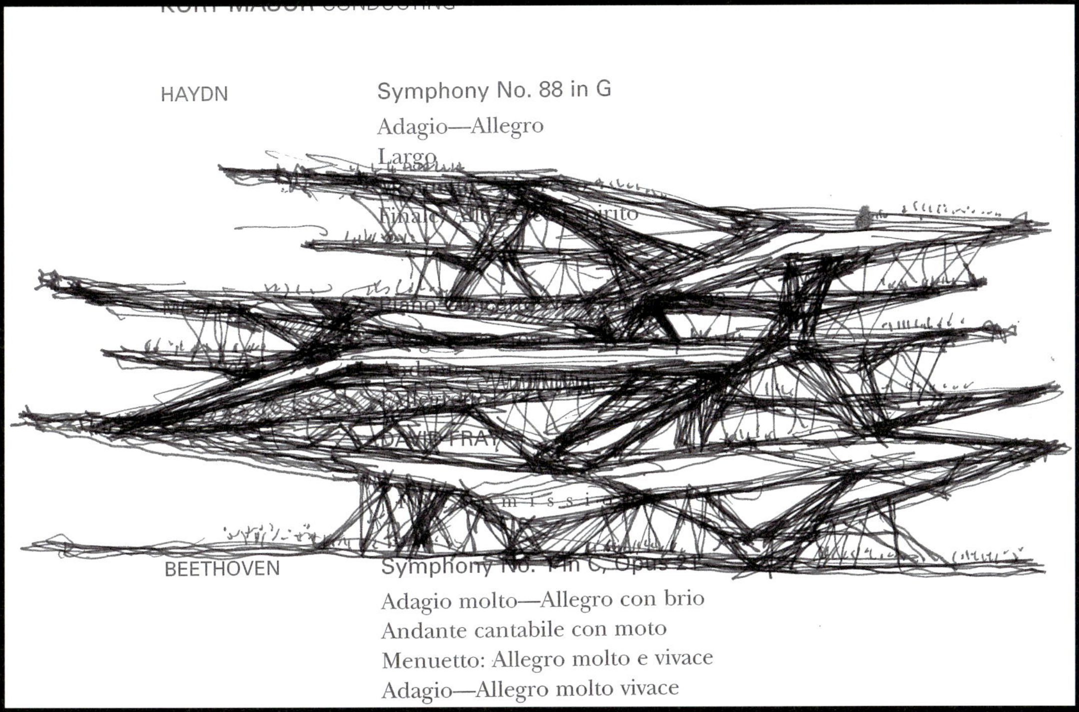

Innovation Hall, Toray Industries, Bangkok, Thailand

— January 13, 2018

Proposed for Bangkok's Lumphini Park is an exhibition center for the fabrics and textiles of Toray's advanced research. Situated high above Bangkok's central garden, the Innovation Museum, as in Stravinsky's Firebird, evokes the alchemy of a magical creature, the Firebird, and the legendary sorcerer Kashchei, who in this case will summon Innovation.

Igor Stravinsky

"The Firebird" (complete)

IGOR FEDOROVICH STRAVINSKY was born at Ora[illegible], Russia, on June [illegible], [illegible] and died in New York on April 6, 1971. He began composition of "The Firebird" in early November 1909, at a country house of the Rimsky-Korsakov family near St. Petersburg. He comp[illegible] score in the city, finishing the actual compo[illegible] the full score a month [illegible]. The final score, somewhat further retouched, bears the date [illegible] 18, 1910. Commissioned by Diaghilev as a ballet in two scenes, the work was first performed on June 25, 1910, by the Ballets Russes at the Paris Opéra, with a cast including Tamara Karsavina (the Firebird), Michel Fokine (Prince Ivan), Vera Fokina (the Tsarevna), and Alexis Bulgakov [illegible]. The scenario was by Fokine in collaboration with Diaghilev [illegible] also created the choreography. Alexandre Golovine designed the settings, [illegible] the costumes. The score is dedicated to Andrei [illegible] who had been Stravinsky's teacher. Stravinsky made [illegible] suites from the ballet on three occasions, the first in 1911 (employing virtually the original [illegible]), the second in 1919 (for a much smaller orchestra), and the third in 1945 (using the same orchestra as the second [illegible] more music).

THE SCORE OF "THE FIREBIRD"—the instrumentation being precisely [illegible]ed by Stravinsky in the original score, including even exact numbers [illegible] instruments—calls for two piccolos (second doubling third flute), two flutes, three [illegible] clarinets (third doubling clarinet in D) and bass clarinet, three bassoons [illegible] second contrabassoon) and contrabassoon, four horns, three trumpets, [illegible] triangle, tambourine, cymbals, bass drum, tam-tam, bells, [illegible] three harps, [illegible] violins, sixteen second violins, fourteen violas, [illegible] double basses, plus an ensemble behind the scenes consisting of [illegible]

The Firebird may be the only case of a major Stravinsky ballet that was not the composer's own idea, at least in its original germ. The Russian legend of the Firebird had been discussed as a possible subject for a ballet by Diaghilev and his staff early in 1909, and Michel Fokine, who was to create the choreography, worked out the scenario combining several Russian fairy tales. The choice of composer was problematic; Diaghilev wanted his old harmony teacher Liadov, but the latter was notoriously slow about finishing

Heartbreak Hotel, Lonely Street, Memphis, Tennessee

— August 17, 2017

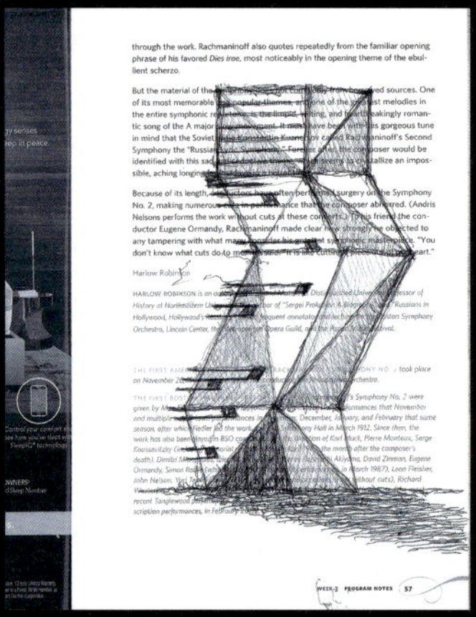

Hearing the achingly beautiful slow movement of Rachmaninoff's Symphony No. 2 recalls the aural mood created by the King in one of his first iconic threnodies. The glass tower thus inspired is clad in a "tonal" range of grays to intensify the hotel's angular form, echoing in silhouette Elvis' performing style.

through the work. Rachmaninoff also quotes repeatedly from the familiar opening phrase of his favored *Dies irae*, most noticeably in the opening theme of the ebullient scherzo.

But the material of the symphony does not come only from borrowed sources. One of its most memorable and popular themes, and one of the greatest melodies in the entire symphonic repertoire, is the limpid, wilting, and heartbreakingly romantic song of the A major slow movement. It must have been with this gorgeous tune in mind that the Soviet critic Konstantin Kuznetsov called Rachmaninoff's Second Symphony the "Russian Lyric Symphony." Forever after, the composer would be identified with this sad and seductive theme, which seems to crystallize an impossible, aching longing for lost love in a better time.

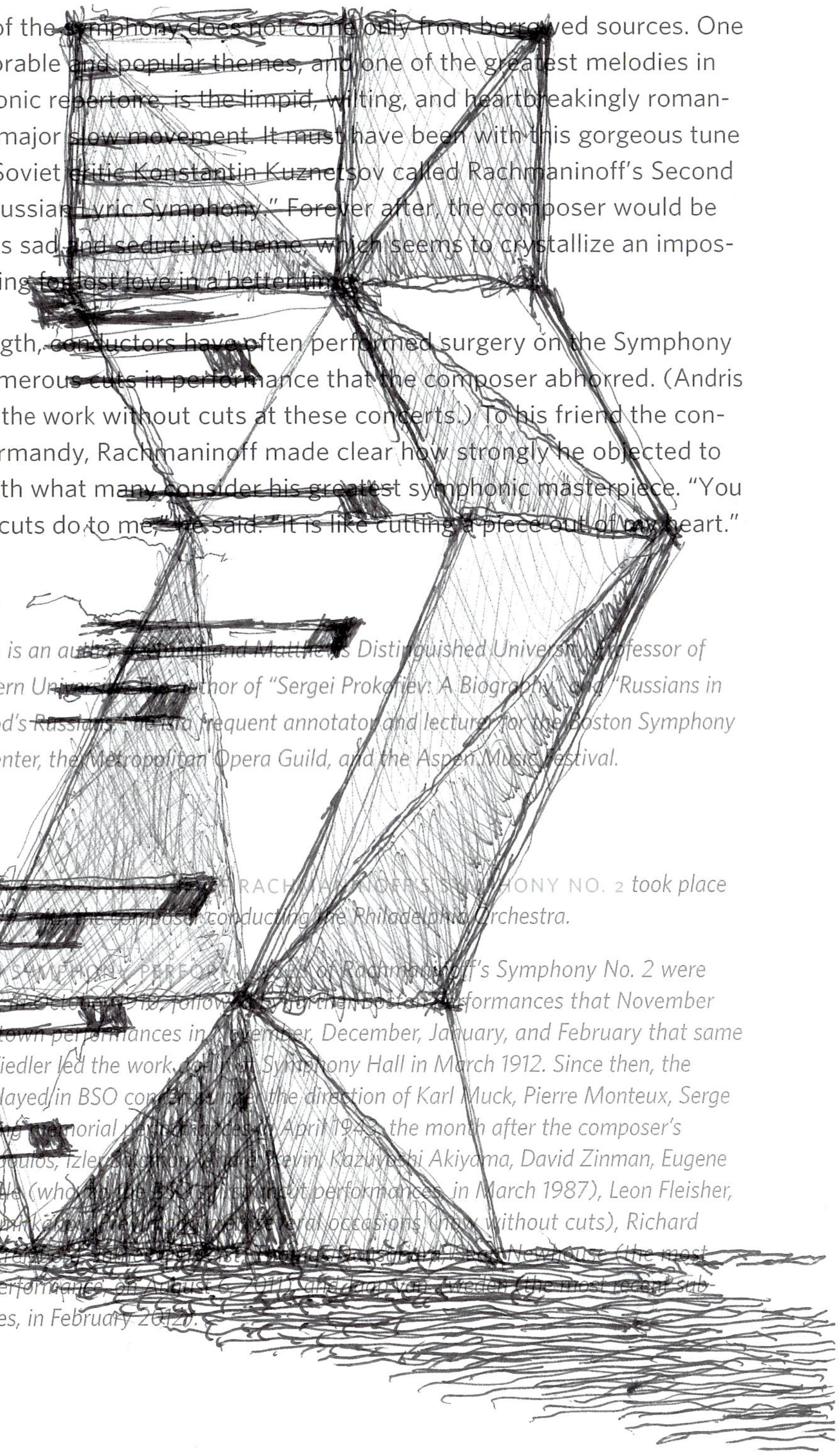

Because of its length, conductors have often performed surgery on the Symphony No. 2, making numerous cuts in performance that the composer abhorred. (Andris Nelsons performs the work without cuts at these concerts.) To his friend the conductor Eugene Ormandy, Rachmaninoff made clear how strongly he objected to any tampering with what many consider his greatest symphonic masterpiece. "You don't know what cuts do to me," he said. "It is like cutting a piece out of my heart."

Harlow Robinson

HARLOW ROBINSON *is an au*[illegible] *Distinguished University Professor of History at Northeastern Uni*[illegible]*thor of "Sergei Prokofiev: A Biography" and "Russians in Hollywood, Hollywood's Russians." He is a frequent annotator and lecturer for the Boston Symphony Orchestra, Lincoln Center, the Metropolitan Opera Guild, and the Aspen Music Festival.*

THE FIRST AMER[illegible] RACH[illegible]'S SYMPHONY NO. 2 *took place on November 26,* [illegible] *conducting the Philadelphia Orchestra.*

THE FIRST BOSTON SYMPHONY PERFORMA[illegible] *of Rachmaninoff's Symphony No. 2 were given by M*[illegible] *formances that November and multiple* [illegible] *performances in November, December, January, and February that same season, after which Fiedler led the work* [illegible] *Symphony Hall in March 1912. Since then, the work has also been played in BSO con*[illegible] *the direction of Karl Muck, Pierre Monteux, Serge Koussevitzky (in*[illegible] *memorial* [illegible] *April 194*[illegible]*, the month after the composer's death), Dimitri Mitropoulos, Izle*[illegible] *Kazuyoshi Akiyama, David Zinman, Eugene Ormandy, Simon Rattle (who* [illegible] *performances, in March 1987), Leon Fleisher, John Nelson, Yuri Te*[illegible] *occasions* [illegible] *without cuts), Richard Westerfield,* [illegible] *Newhouse (the most recent Tanglewood performance, on August* [illegible]*, 2011), and* [illegible] *(the most recent subscription performances, in February 2012).*

Rotch Library, MIT

Kilimanjaro Lodge, near Shira Camp, Tanzania

— January 27, 2018

A concrete structure clad in quarried lava imagines a cliffside retreat on the way to the mountain. Ligeti's Violin Concerto rises in subtly shifting textures and harmonics to a musical peak before returning homeward in uneven rhythmic tones. I tried to capture the sound in the drawing.

György Ligeti

Violin Concerto (1990-1992), with cadenza by Thomas Adès (2011)

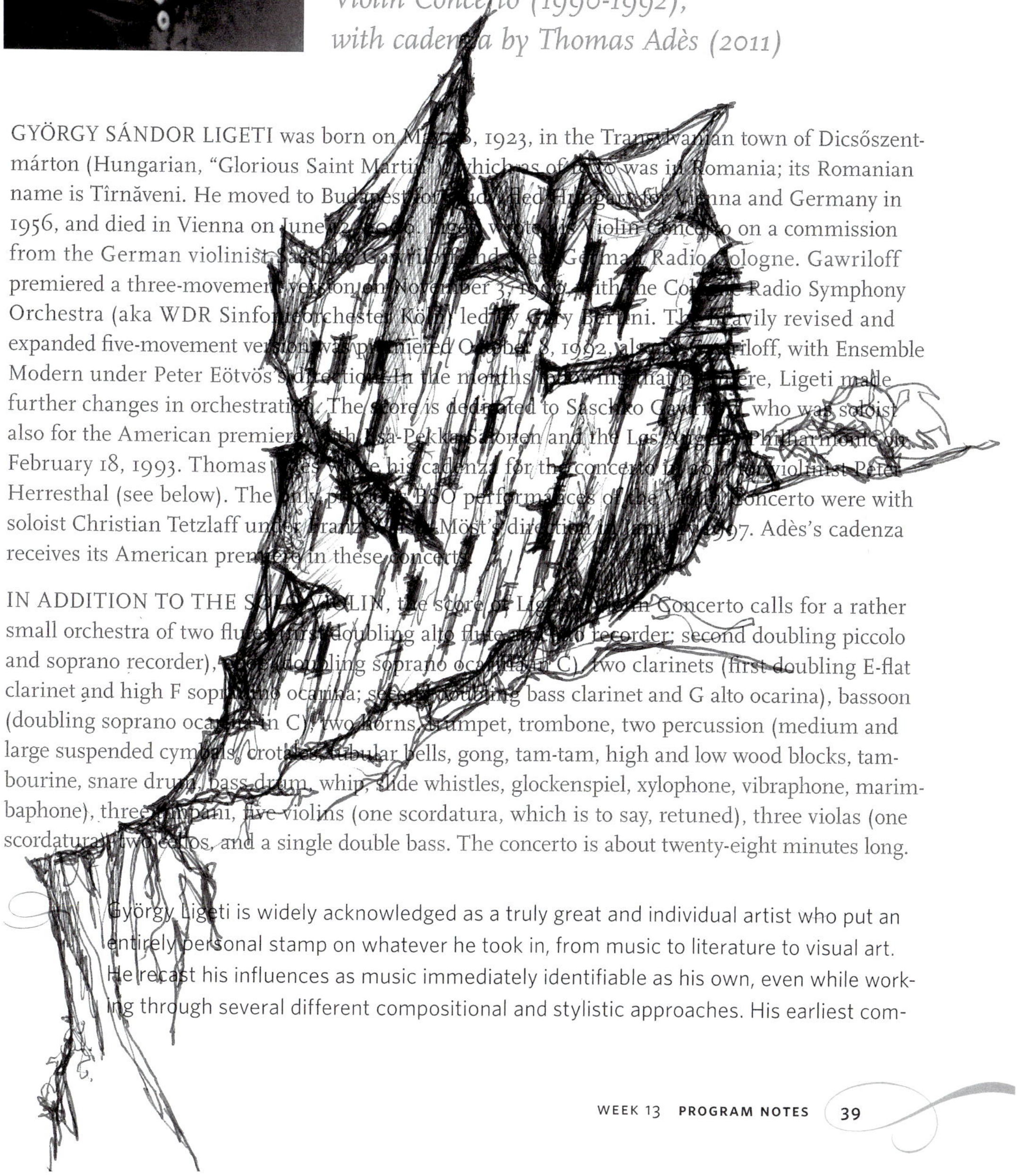

GYÖRGY SÁNDOR LIGETI was born on May 28, 1923, in the Transylvanian town of Dicsőszentmárton (Hungarian, "Glorious Saint Martin"), which as of 1920 was in Romania; its Romanian name is Tîrnăveni. He moved to Budapest for study, fled Hungary for Vienna and Germany in 1956, and died in Vienna on June 12, 2006. Ligeti wrote his Violin Concerto on a commission from the German violinist Saschko Gawriloff and West German Radio Cologne. Gawriloff premiered a three-movement version on November 3, 1990, with the Cologne Radio Symphony Orchestra (aka WDR Sinfonieorchester Köln) led by Gary Bertini. The heavily revised and expanded five-movement version was premiered October 8, 1992, also with Gawriloff, with Ensemble Modern under Peter Eötvös's direction. In the months following that premiere, Ligeti made further changes in orchestration. The score is dedicated to Saschko Gawriloff, who was soloist also for the American premiere with Esa-Pekka Salonen and the Los Angeles Philharmonic on February 18, 1993. Thomas Adès wrote his cadenza for the concerto in 2011 for violinist Peter Herresthal (see below). The only previous BSO performances of the Violin Concerto were with soloist Christian Tetzlaff under Franz Welser-Möst's direction in January 1997. Adès's cadenza receives its American premiere in these concerts.

IN ADDITION TO THE SOLO VIOLIN, the score of Ligeti's Violin Concerto calls for a rather small orchestra of two flutes (first doubling alto flute and alto recorder; second doubling piccolo and soprano recorder), oboe (doubling soprano ocarina in C), two clarinets (first doubling E-flat clarinet and high F soprano ocarina; second doubling bass clarinet and G alto ocarina), bassoon (doubling soprano ocarina in C), two horns, trumpet, trombone, two percussion (medium and large suspended cymbals, crotales, tubular bells, gong, tam-tam, high and low wood blocks, tambourine, snare drum, bass drum, whip, slide whistles, glockenspiel, xylophone, vibraphone, marimbaphone), three timpani, five violins (one scordatura, which is to say, retuned), three violas (one scordatura), two cellos, and a single double bass. The concerto is about twenty-eight minutes long.

György Ligeti is widely acknowledged as a truly great and individual artist who put an entirely personal stamp on whatever he took in, from music to literature to visual art. He recast his influences as music immediately identifiable as his own, even while working through several different compositional and stylistic approaches. His earliest com-

WEEK 13 **PROGRAM NOTES** 39

Space Horizon Cruiser, Mars Orbit

— February 10, 2018

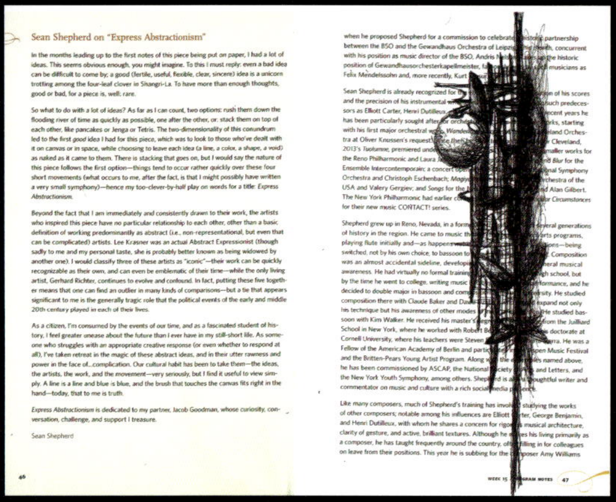

Sean Shepherd on "Express Abstractionism"

In the months leading up to the first notes of this piece being put on paper, I had a lot of ideas. This seems obvious enough, you might imagine. To this I must reply: even a bad idea can be difficult to come by; a good (fertile, useful, flexible, clear, sincere) idea is a unicorn trotting among the four-leaf clover in Shangri-La. To have more than enough thoughts, good or bad, for a piece is, well: rare.

So what to do with a lot of ideas? As far as I can count, two options: rush them down the flooding river of time as quickly as possible, one after the other, or: stack them on top of each other, like pancakes or Jenga or Tetris. The two-dimensionality of this conundrum led to the first *good* idea I had for this piece, which was to look to those who've dealt with it on canvas or in space, while choosing to leave each idea (a line, a color, a shape, a void) as naked as it came to them. There is stacking that goes on, but I would say the nature of this piece follows the first option—things tend to occur rather quickly over these four short movements (what occurs to me, after the fact, is that I might possibly have written a very small symphony)—hence my too-clever-by-half play on words for a title: *Express Abstractionism*.

Beyond the fact that I am immediately and consistently drawn to their work, the artists who inspired this piece have no particular relationship to each other, other than a basic definition of working predominantly as abstract (i.e., non-representational, but even that can be complicated) artists. Lee Krasner was an actual Abstract Expressionist (though sadly to me and my personal taste, she is probably better known as being widowed by another one). I would classify three of these artists as "iconic"—their work can be quickly recognizable as their own, and can even be emblematic of their time—while the only living artist, Gerhard Richter, continues to evolve and confound. In fact, putting these five together means that one can find an outlier in many kinds of comparisons—but a tie that appears significant to me is the generally tragic role that the political events of the early and middle 20th century played in each of their lives.

As a citizen, I'm consumed by the events of our time, and as a fascinated student of history, I feel greater unease about the future than I ever have in my still-short life. As someone who struggles with an appropriate creative response (or even whether to respond at all), I've taken retreat in the magic of these abstract ideas, and in their utter rawness and power in the face of...complication. Our cultural habit has been to take them—the ideas, the artists, the work, and the movement—very seriously, but I find it useful to view simply. A line is a line and blue is blue, and the brush that touches the canvas fits right in the hand—today, that to me is truth.

Express Abstractionism is dedicated to my partner, Jacob Goodman, whose curiosity, conversation, challenge, and support I treasure.

Sean Shepherd

46

when he proposed Shepherd for a commission to celebrate [illegible] partnership between the BSO and the Gewandhaus Orchestra of Leipzig [illegible], concurrent with his position as music director of the BSO, Andris [illegible] the historic position of Gewandhausorchesterkapellmeister, [illegible] musicians as Felix Mendelssohn and, more recently, Kurt [illegible]

Sean Shepherd is already recognized for [illegible] of his scores and the precision of his instrumental [illegible] such predecessors as Elliott Carter, Henri Dutilleux, [illegible] recent years he has been particularly sought after for [illegible] works, starting with his first major orchestral [illegible] *Wonder*[illegible] Cleveland Orchestra at Oliver Knussen's request [illegible] Cleveland, 2013's *Tuolumne*, premiered under [illegible] smaller works for the Reno Philharmonic and Laura [illegible] *Blur* for the Ensemble Intercontemporain; a concert [illegible] Symphony Orchestra and Christoph Eschenbach; *Magiya* [illegible] Orchestra of the USA and Valery Gergiev; and *Songs for the* [illegible] Alan Gilbert. The New York Philharmonic had earlier [illegible] *Circumstances* for their new music CONTACT! series.

Shepherd grew up in Reno, Nevada, in a form[illegible] several generations of history in the region. He came to music th[illegible] arts programs, playing flute initially and—as happens [illegible]—being switched, not by his own choice, to bassoon to [illegible]. Composition was an almost accidental sideline, develop[illegible] general musical awareness. He had virtually no formal training [illegible] high school, but by the time he went to college, writing music [illegible] performance, and he decided to double major in bassoon and com[illegible] University. He studied composition there with Claude Baker and Da[illegible] expand not only his technique but his awareness of other modes [illegible]. He studied bassoon with Kim Walker. He received his master's degr[illegible] from the Juilliard School in New York, where he worked with Robert B[illegible] doctorate at Cornell University, where his teachers were Steven [illegible]. He was a Fellow of the American Academy of Berlin and partic[illegible] Aspen Music Festival and the Britten-Pears Young Artist Program. Along w[illegible] the [illegible] named above, he has been commissioned by ASCAP, the National [illegible] and Letters, and the New York Youth Symphony, among others. Shep[illegible] is a[illegible] thoughtful writer and commentator on music and culture with a rich social media p[illegible]

Like many composers, much of Shepherd's training has invol[illegible] studying the works of other composers; notable among his influences are Elliott [illegible], George Benjamin, and Henri Dutilleux, with whom he shares a concern for rigo[illegible] musical architecture, clarity of gesture, and active, brilliant textures. Although he [illegible] his living primarily as a composer, he has taught frequently around the country, oft[illegible] filling in for colleagues on leave from their positions. This year he is subbing for the [illegible] composer Amy Williams

WEEK 15 [illegible] NOTES 47

Sean Shepherd's recent work "Express Abstractionism" for orchestra (2017) premiered a soundscape projecting music into an aural future. If, in Goethe's terms, "architecture is frozen music" then architecture is fixed, but when music and architecture are intertwined, they are both dynamic in time and space. The Space Horizon creates its own local gravity in various orientations.

when he proposed Shepherd for a commission to celebrate [illegible] historic partnership between the BSO and the Gewandhaus Orchestra of Leipzig. This month, concurrent with his position as music director of the BSO, Andris Nelsons takes up the historic position of Gewandhausorchesterkapellmeister, fa[illegible] such musicians as Felix Mendelssohn and, more recently, Kurt [illegible].

Sean Shepherd is already recognized for th[illegible]ation of his scores and the precision of his instrumental w[illegible] such predecessors as Elliott Carter, Henri Dutilleux, [illegible] recent years he has been particularly sought after for orchest[illegible]orks, starting with his first major orchestral work, *Wanderlu*[illegible]eland Orchestra at Oliver Knussen's request. Since then he [illegible]r Cleveland, 2013's *Tuolumne*, premiered unde[illegible] smaller works for the Reno Philharmonic and Laura Ja[illegible]nd *Blur* for the Ensemble Intercontemporain; a concert open[illegible]ional Symphony Orchestra and Christoph Eschenbach; *Magiy*[illegible]rchestra of the USA and Valery Gergiev; and *Songs* for the [illegible]nd Alan Gilbert. The New York Philharmonic had earlier co[illegible]*ular Circumstances* for their new music CONTACT! series.

Shepherd grew up in Reno, Nevada, in a form[illegible]veral generations of history in the region. He came to music th[illegible]ool arts programs, playing flute initially and—as happens [illegible]ions—being switched, not by his own choice, to bassoon to [illegible]. Composition was an almost accidental sideline, developi[illegible]neral musical awareness. He had virtually no formal training [illegible]gh school, but by the time he went to college, writing music [illegible]erformance, and he decided to double major in bassoon and comp[illegible]versity. He studied composition there with Claude Baker and Dav[illegible] expand not only his technique but his awareness of other modes [illegible]. He studied bassoon with Kim Walker. He received his master's [illegible] from the Juilliard School in New York, where he worked with Robert B[illegible]is doctorate at Cornell University, where his teachers were Steven [illegible]rra. He was a Fellow of the American Academy of Berlin and partic[illegible]spen Music Festival and the Britten-Pears Young Artist Program. Along w[illegible] the e[illegible]les named above, he has been commissioned by ASCAP, the National [illegible]ociety [illegible]s and Letters, and the New York Youth Symphony, among others. Shepherd is a[illegible] thoughtful writer and commentator on music and culture with a rich social media p[illegible]nce.

Like many composers, much of Shepherd's training has involv[illegible] studying the works of other composers; notable among his influences are Elliott [illegible]ter, George Benjamin, and Henri Dutilleux, with whom he shares a concern for rigor[illegible]s musical architecture, clarity of gesture, and active, brilliant textures. Although he [illegible]kes his living primarily as a composer, he has taught frequently around the country, oft[illegible] filling in for colleagues on leave from their positions. This year he is subbing for the [illegible]poser Amy Williams

WEEK 15 [illegible]GRAM NOTES 47

“Titan” Office Tower, Mitte, Berlin

— September 23, 2017

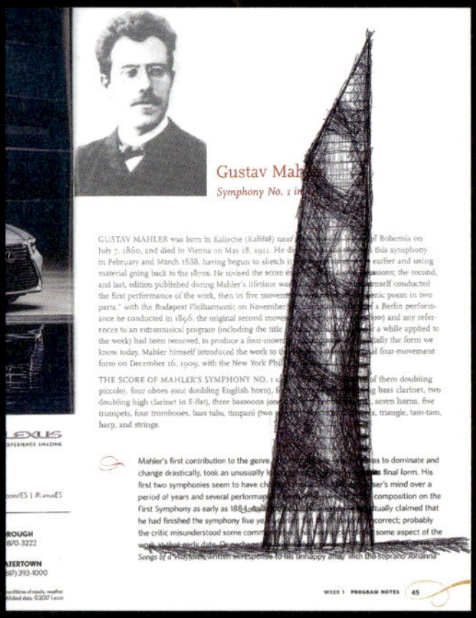

Mahler referred to his first symphony, composed over a period of years in his twenties, as a symphonic poem. Critics praised its “lively imagination” but criticized its oblique musical references, the composer offering no greater guidance to the listener. Deciding that he needed more programmatic description, Mahler titled it in later performances “Titan, a tone poem in symphonic form,” and ultimately, “Symphony in D for large orchestra.” The Tower, owing to the expanse and monumentality of Mahler’s composition, is its architectural equivalent in an urban setting.

Gustav Mah

Symphony No. 1 i

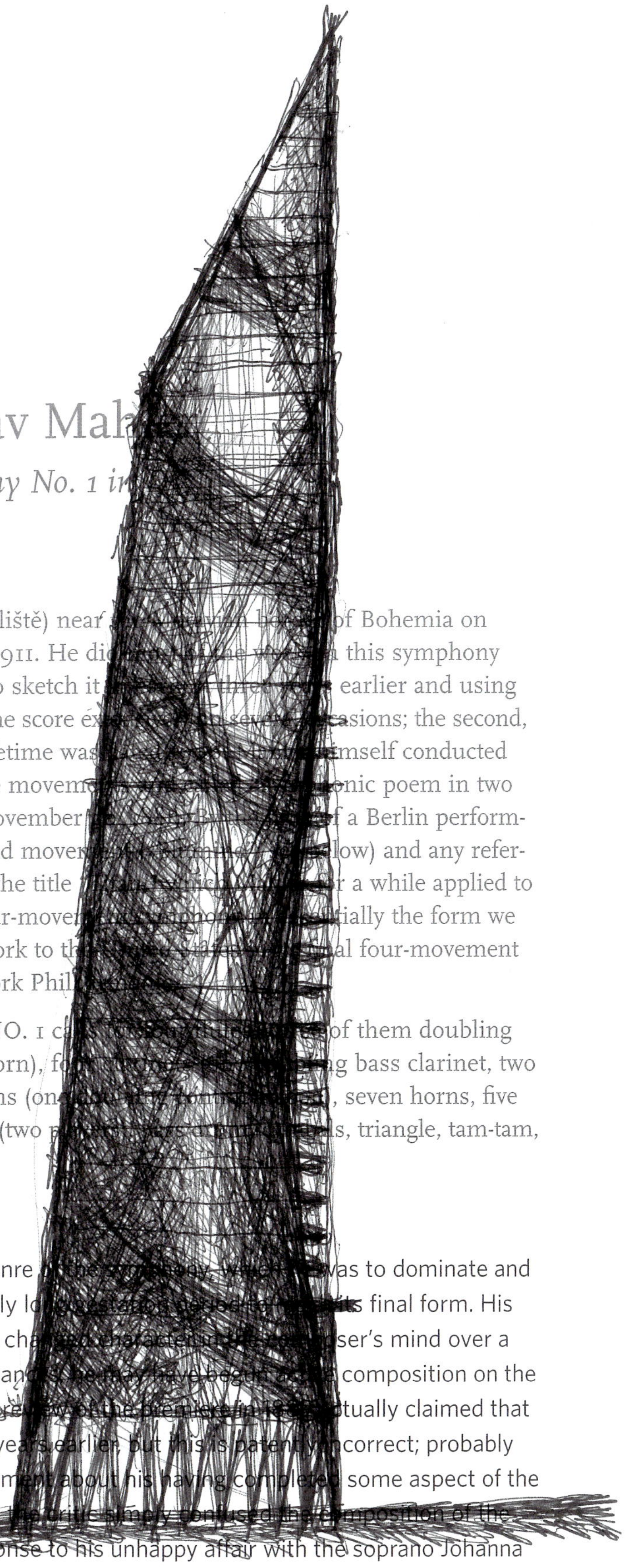

AHLER was born in Kalische (Kaliště) near … of Bohemia on
, and died in Vienna on May 18, 1911. He di… this symphony
and March 1888, having begun to sketch it … earlier and using
ng back to the 1870s. He revised the score ex… casions; the second,
tion published during Mahler's lifetime was … imself conducted
formance of the work, then in five moveme… onic poem in two
the Budapest Philharmonic on November … f a Berlin perform-
ducted in 1896, the original second movem… low) and any refer-
extramusical program (including the title … r a while applied to
ad been removed, to produce a four-move… ially the form we
Mahler himself introduced the work to th… al four-movement
cember 16, 1909, with the New York Phil…

E OF MAHLER'S SYMPHONY NO. 1 c… of them doubling
ır oboes (one doubling English horn), f… g bass clarinet, two
gh clarinet in E-flat), three bassoons (on…), seven horns, five
ur trombones, bass tuba, timpani (two … s, triangle, tam-tam,
rings.

Mahler's first contribution to the genre of the symphony, which … was to dominate and change drastically, took an unusually l… its final form. His first two symphonies seem to have ch… ser's mind over a period of years and several performan… composition on the First Symphony as early as 1884. A review of the premiere in 18… tually claimed that he had finished the symphony five years earlier, but this is patently incorrect; probably the critic misunderstood some comment about his having completed some aspect of the work at that early date. Or perhaps the critic simply confused the composition of the *Songs of a Wayfarer*, written in response to his unhappy affair with the soprano Johanna

Residential Tower

— November 10, 2018

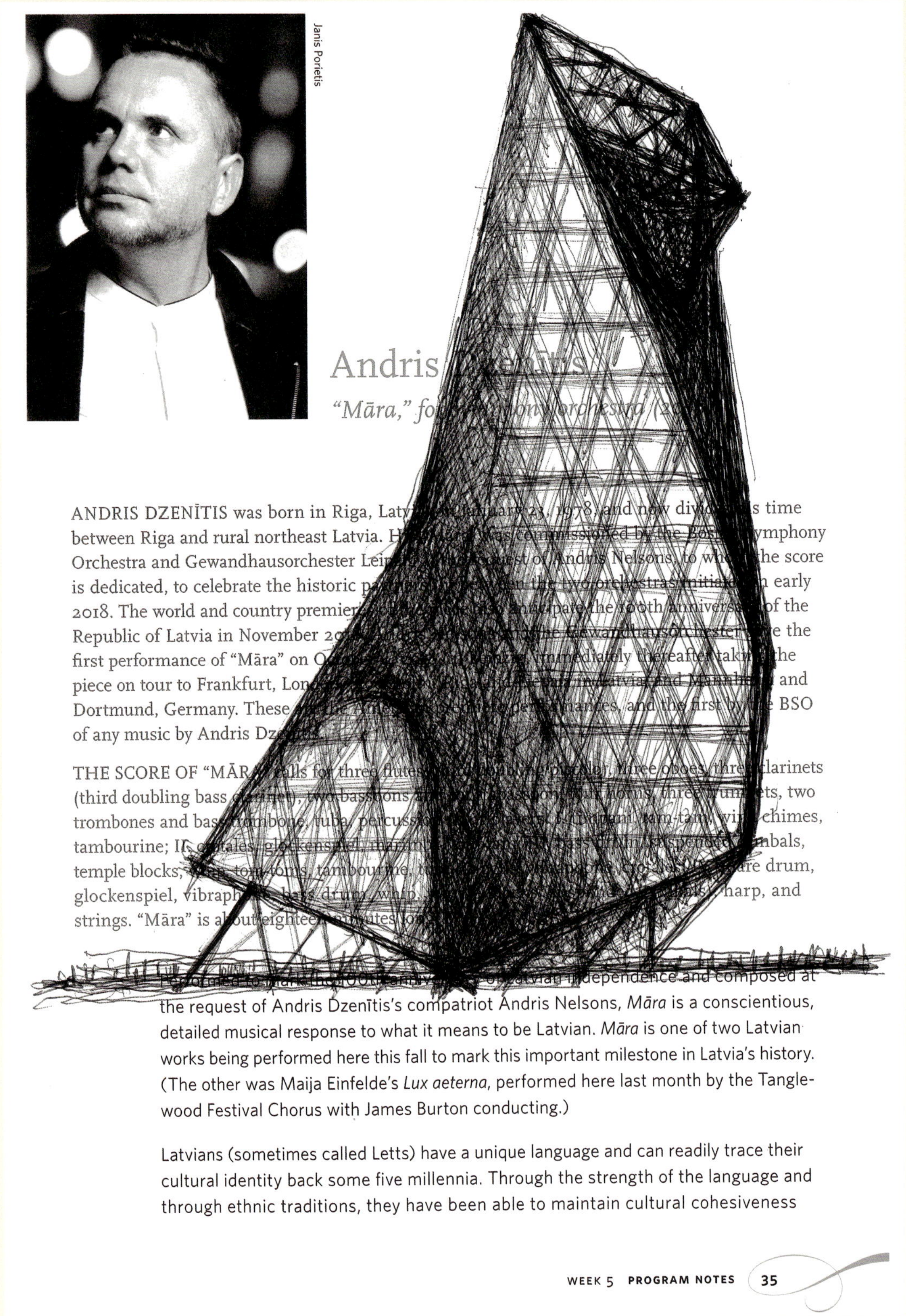

Glass Museum

— March 31, 2012

Witold Lutosławski rehearsing the Boston Symphony Orchestra for a program of his music in October 1990

"row" are somewhat clear at the start of the movement), but the textures are very different, a series of increasingly active episodes with first one, then each subsequent string section doubling its pulse—from quarter-note to eighth-note to sixteenth. The movement flows right into the next, Apogee, which as the title suggests is really the climax of the preceding episode. Less than a minute long, this movement is a series of chords, *fff*, for the whole string body, surging, then abating in energy to a held chord. The Epilogue, which ensues without pause, is similar to the Prologue but in reverse, diminishing from full string orchestra to solo cello at the end, where we clearly hear the main motif (here as A-A-sharp-E) giving way to entropy.

Robert Kirzinger

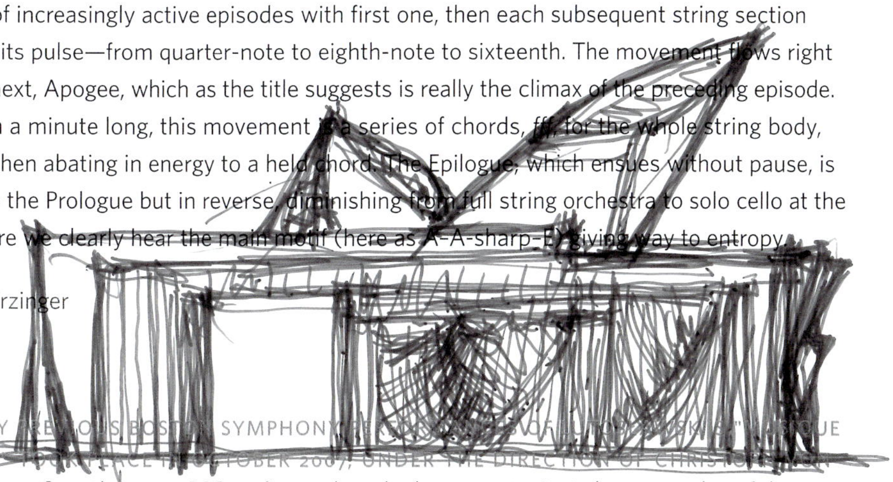

THE ONLY PREVIOUS BOSTON SYMPHONY PERFORMANCES OF LUTOSŁAWSKI'S "MUSIQUE FUNÈBRE" TOOK PLACE IN OCTOBER 2007, UNDER THE DIRECTION OF CHRISTOPH VON DOHNÁNYI. *Over the years, BSO audiences have had an opportunity to hear a number of the composer's works, including, among other things, the Symphony No. 3 (led here by Esa-Pekka Salonen in January 1988); "Chain 2" for violin and orchestra (given its United States premiere in 1987 by BSO violinist Ronan Lefkowitz with the Tanglewood Music Center Orchestra, Lefkowitz later repeating the work with the BSO as part of an all-Lutosławski program led here by the composer in October 1990); the Symphony No. 4 (led here most recently by Seiji Ozawa in February 1995 in memory of the composer, who had died the previous year); the Cello Concerto (played here by Mstislav Rostropovich with Seiji Ozawa conducting in February 1987, and by Lynn Harrell under James Levine's direction in November 2004), and the Concerto for Orchestra (led here most recently by Christoph von Dohnányi in April 2005).*

Party Pavilion, Kensington Gardens, London

— July 22, 2018

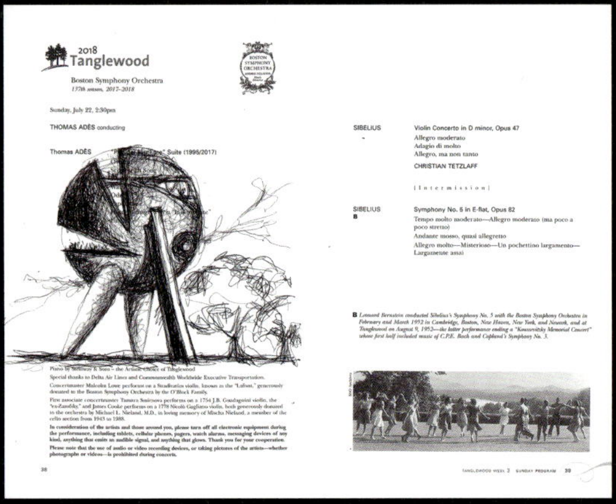

The architectural subject matter was drawn entirely from listening to Thomas Adès' Suite "Powder Her Face," which characterizes in a musical composition the opulent and dissolute lifestyle of the real-life Duchess of Argyll. Not one to celebrate or emulate, he borrows or "steals" freely from a number of musical sources and synthesizes them into his own unique composition. Attempting to reflect what I heard musically transformed Adès' composition into seriously frivolous architecture.

2018 Tanglewood

Boston Symphony Orchestra
137th season, 2017–2018

BOSTON SYMPHONY ORCHESTRA
ANDRIS NELSONS Music Director

Sunday, July 22, 2:30pm

THOMAS ADÈS conducting

Thomas ADÈS — "Powder Her Face" Suite (1995/2017)

Overture
Scene with Song
Wedding March
Waltz
Ode
Paper Chase
Hotel Manager's Aria "It is too late"
Finale

Piano by Steinway & Sons – the Artistic Choice of Tanglewood

Special thanks to Delta Air Lines and Commonwealth Worldwide Executive Transportation.

Concertmaster Malcolm Lowe performs on a Stradivarius violin, known as the "Lafont," generously donated to the Boston Symphony Orchestra by the O'Block Family.

First associate concertmaster Tamara Smirnova performs on a 1754 J.B. Guadagnini violin, the "ex-Zazofsky," and James Cooke performs on a 1778 Nicolò Gagliano violin, both generously donated to the orchestra by Michael L. Nieland, M.D., in loving memory of Mischa Nieland, a member of the cello section from 1943 to 1988.

In consideration of the artists and those around you, please turn off all electronic equipment during the performance, including tablets, cellular phones, pagers, watch alarms, messaging devices of any kind, anything that emits an audible signal, and anything that glows. Thank you for your cooperation.

Please note that the use of audio or video recording devices, or taking pictures of the artists—whether photographs or videos—is prohibited during concerts.

38

Saguaro Tower, La Paz, Mexico

— August 17, 2018

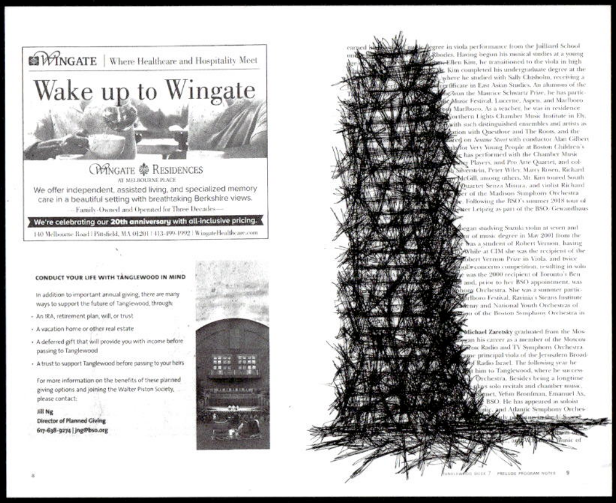

From a sketch made during a 2018 Tanglewood performance of Shostakovich's 4th Symphony

There is nothing modest or cautious about the Shostakovich 4th Symphony. Its premiere was postponed 25 years for political reasons.

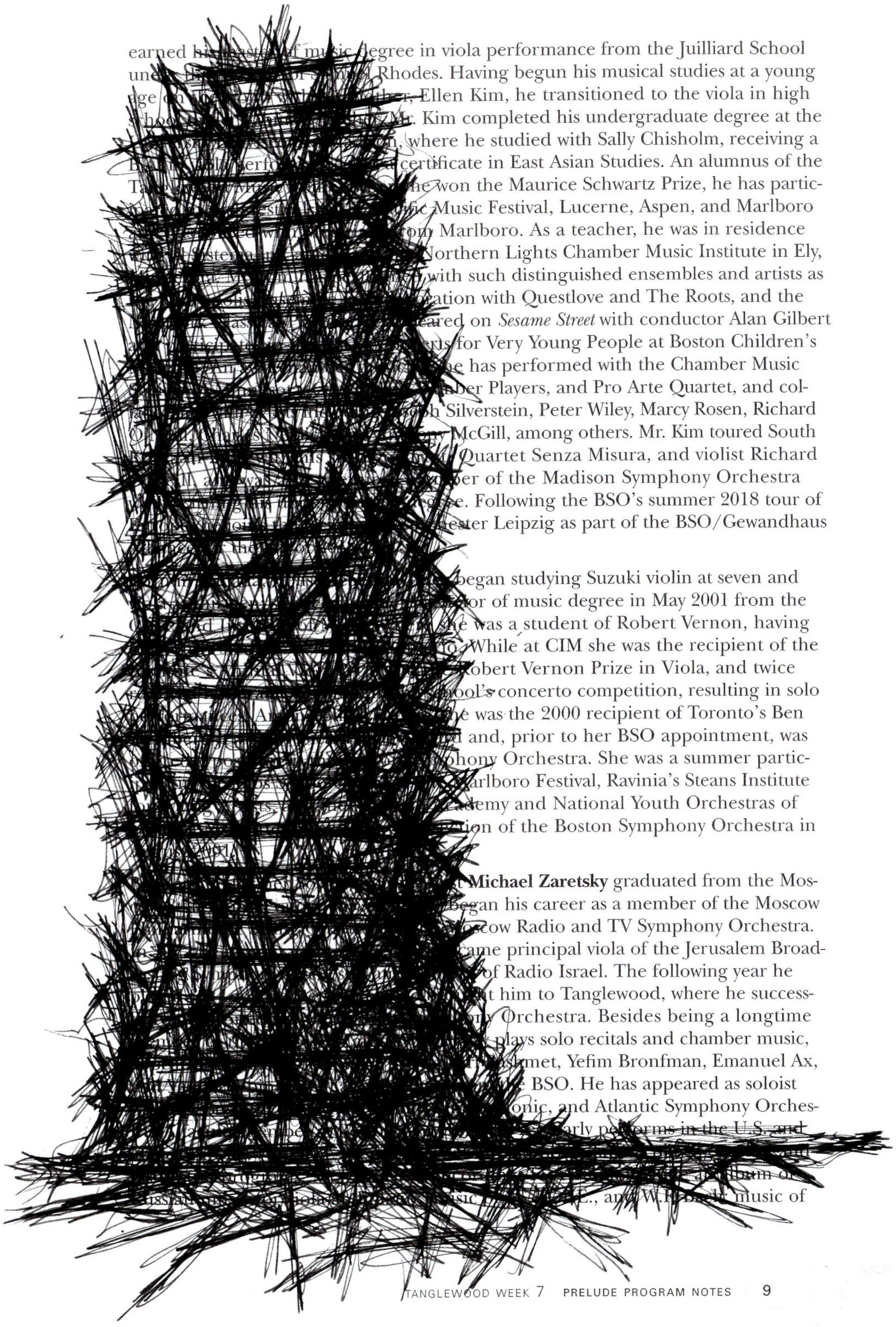
degree in viola performance from the Juilliard School
Rhodes. Having begun his musical studies at a young
Ellen Kim, he transitioned to the viola in high
Kim completed his undergraduate degree at the
where he studied with Sally Chisholm, receiving a
certificate in East Asian Studies. An alumnus of the
won the Maurice Schwartz Prize, he has partic-
Music Festival, Lucerne, Aspen, and Marlboro
Marlboro. As a teacher, he was in residence
Northern Lights Chamber Music Institute in Ely,
with such distinguished ensembles and artists as
ation with Questlove and The Roots, and the
on Sesame Street with conductor Alan Gilbert
for Very Young People at Boston Children's
has performed with the Chamber Music
Players, and Pro Arte Quartet, and col-
Silverstein, Peter Wiley, Marcy Rosen, Richard
McGill, among others. Mr. Kim toured South
Quartet Senza Misura, and violist Richard
of the Madison Symphony Orchestra
Following the BSO's summer 2018 tour of
Leipzig as part of the BSO/Gewandhaus
began studying Suzuki violin at seven and
of music degree in May 2001 from the
was a student of Robert Vernon, having
While at CIM she was the recipient of the
Robert Vernon Prize in Viola, and twice
concerto competition, resulting in solo
was the 2000 recipient of Toronto's Ben
and, prior to her BSO appointment, was
Orchestra. She was a summer partic-
Marlboro Festival, Ravinia's Steans Institute
emy and National Youth Orchestras of
of the Boston Symphony Orchestra in
Michael Zaretsky graduated from the Mos-
began his career as a member of the Moscow
Radio and TV Symphony Orchestra.
principal viola of the Jerusalem Broad-
of Radio Israel. The following year he
him to Tanglewood, where he success-
Orchestra. Besides being a longtime
solo recitals and chamber music,
met, Yefim Bronfman, Emanuel Ax,
BSO. He has appeared as soloist
and Atlantic Symphony Orches-
music of
TANGLEWOOD WEEK 7 PRELUDE PROGRAM NOTES 9

So nothing less ambitious in architectural terms could begin to reflect the Symphony's formidable sound. Thus, the spiny office/hotel tower takes cues from La Paz's desert climate and indigenous cactus to provide deep shade for the windows and balconies of the Saguaro Tower's façade. —

New Symphony Hall, Turin, Italy

— August 09, 1997

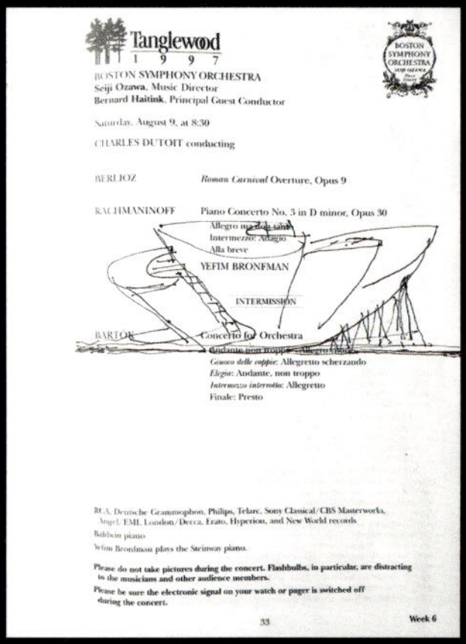
Tanglewood 1997

BOSTON SYMPHONY ORCHESTRA
Seiji Ozawa, Music Director
Bernard Haitink, Principal Guest Conductor

Saturday, August 9, at 8:30

CHARLES DUTOIT conducting

BERLIOZ — *Roman Carnival* Overture, Opus 9

RACHMANINOFF — Piano Concerto No. 3 in D minor, Opus 30
Allegro ma non tanto
Intermezzo: Adagio
Alla breve
YEFIM BRONFMAN

INTERMISSION

BARTÓK — Concerto for Orchestra
Andante non troppo — Allegro vivace
Giuoco delle coppie: Allegretto scherzando
Elegia: Andante, non troppo
Intermezzo interrotto: Allegretto
Finale: Presto

RCA, Deutsche Grammophon, Philips, Telarc, Sony Classical/CBS Masterworks, Angel/EMI, London/Decca, Erato, Hyperion, and New World records

Baldwin piano

Yefim Bronfman plays the Steinway piano.

Please do not take pictures during the concert. Flashbulbs, in particular, are distracting to the musicians and other audience members.

Please be sure the electronic signal on your watch or pager is switched off during the concert.

33 Week 6

As exuberant as Berlioz's Roman Carnival Overture, Turin's New Symphony Hall would become the new home of the RAI National Symphony Orchestra. Reflected in the Po adjacent to Turin's Parco de la Confluenza, the new hall builds on the cultural successes of Italy's second largest city and provides a regional counterpoint to Milan's world famous La Scala.

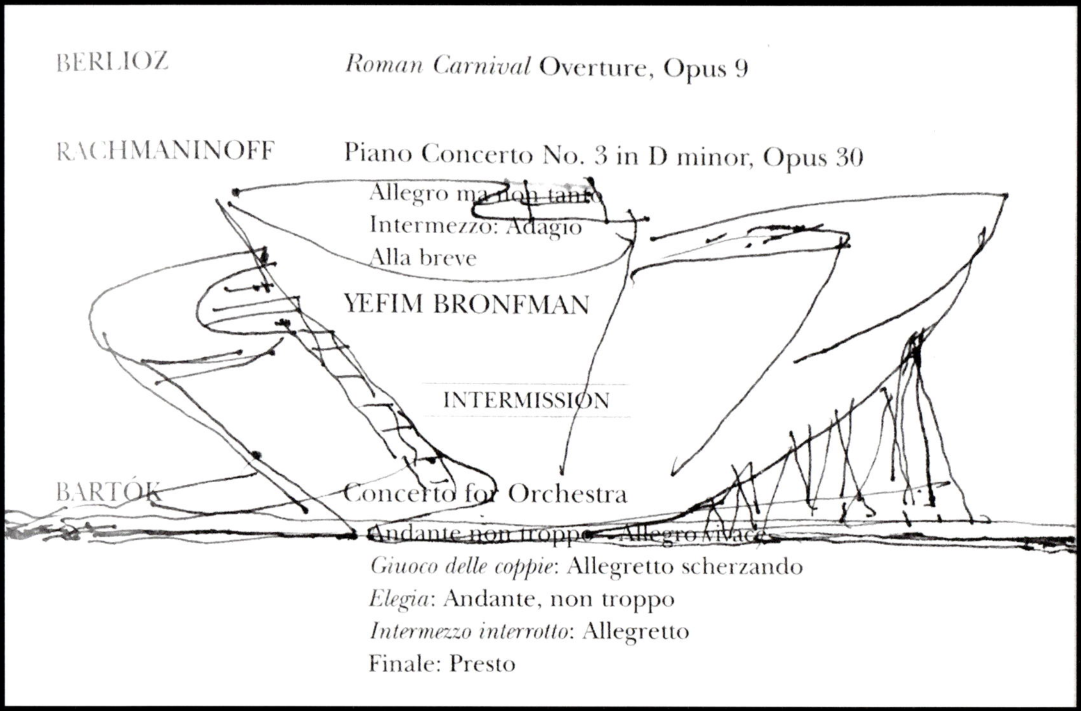
BERLIOZ — *Roman Carnival* Overture, Opus 9

RACHMANINOFF — Piano Concerto No. 3 in D minor, Opus 30
Allegro ma non tanto
Intermezzo: Adagio
Alla breve
YEFIM BRONFMAN

INTERMISSION

BARTÓK — Concerto for Orchestra
Andante non troppo — Allegro vivace
Giuoco delle coppie: Allegretto scherzando
Elegia: Andante, non troppo
Intermezzo interrotto: Allegretto
Finale: Presto

Music Pavilion, Tippet Rise Art Center, Fishtail, MT

— January 19, 2019

Owing more to the golden eagles of Montana than to its geological formations, this broadly spreading music pavilion perches lightly in contrast to the other monumental concrete acoustic structures of the preserve. Designed in accordance with the acoustic principles of Presence Sound, a multi-pier base structure supports outstretched tapering canopies of carbon fiber composite shaped to project and reflect ensemble music to audiences gathered in the open landscape.

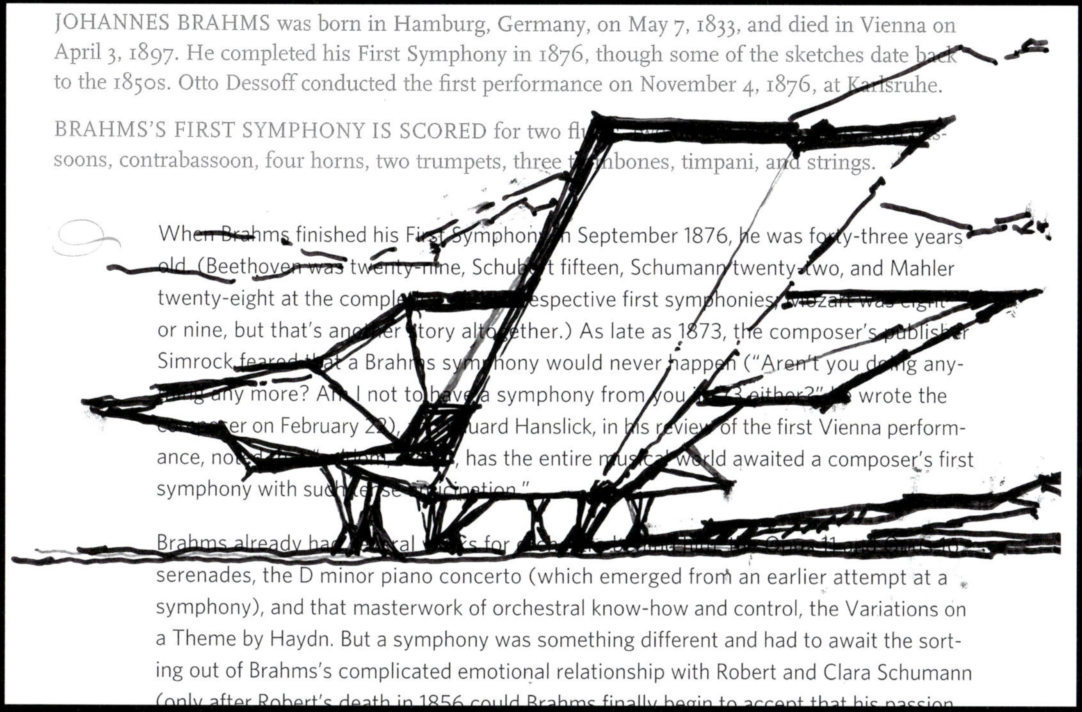

Vertical Food Festival, Shinjuku, Tokyo

— March 24, 2018

Some time ago, while listening to Shostakovich's intensely textured Symphony #4, I was reminded of the famous Izakaya Alley near Shinjuku Station in which 50 or more restaurants are packed closely together. Sited just off Omoide Yokocho with the intention of creating an even denser food experience (if that's possible) is a new vertical restaurant cluster. Accessed from elevators at grade and starting at an entrepôt at the top, visitors encounter a winding path downward through five stories of Izakaya back to street level.

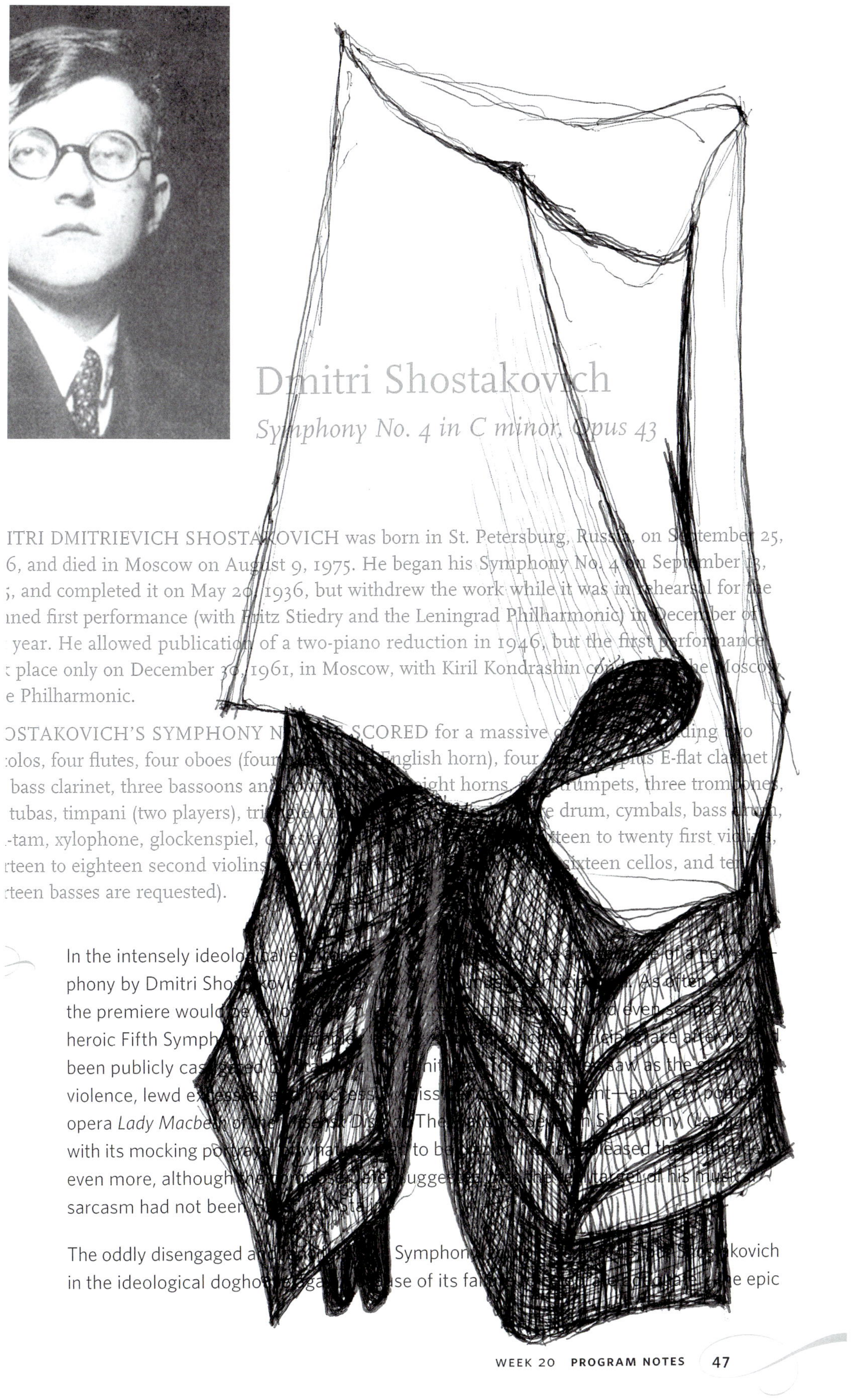
Dmitri Shostakovich
Symphony No. 4 in C minor, Opus 43
WEEK 20 PROGRAM NOTES 47

Office Building, St Petersburg, Russia

— January 12, 2019

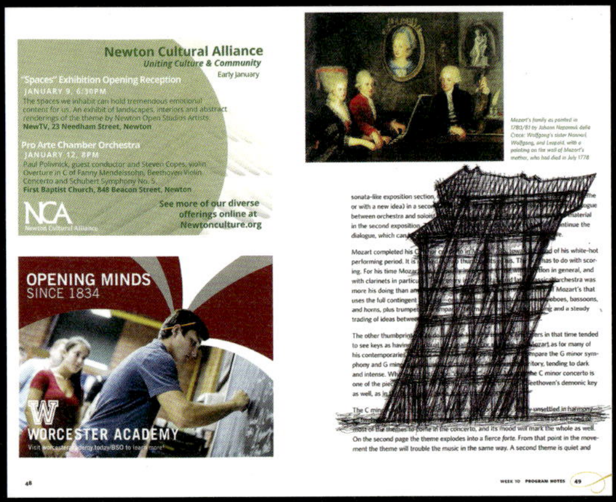

Channeling the constructivist monument to the Third International is probably the impulse for this sketch of a 14-story office building in St. Petersburg.

Sometimes the music generates the drawing, sometimes it supports it.

Mozart's family as painted in 1780/81 by Johann Nepomuk della Croce: Wolfgang's sister Nannerl, Wolfgang, and Leopold, with a painting on the wall of Mozart's mother, who had died in July 1778

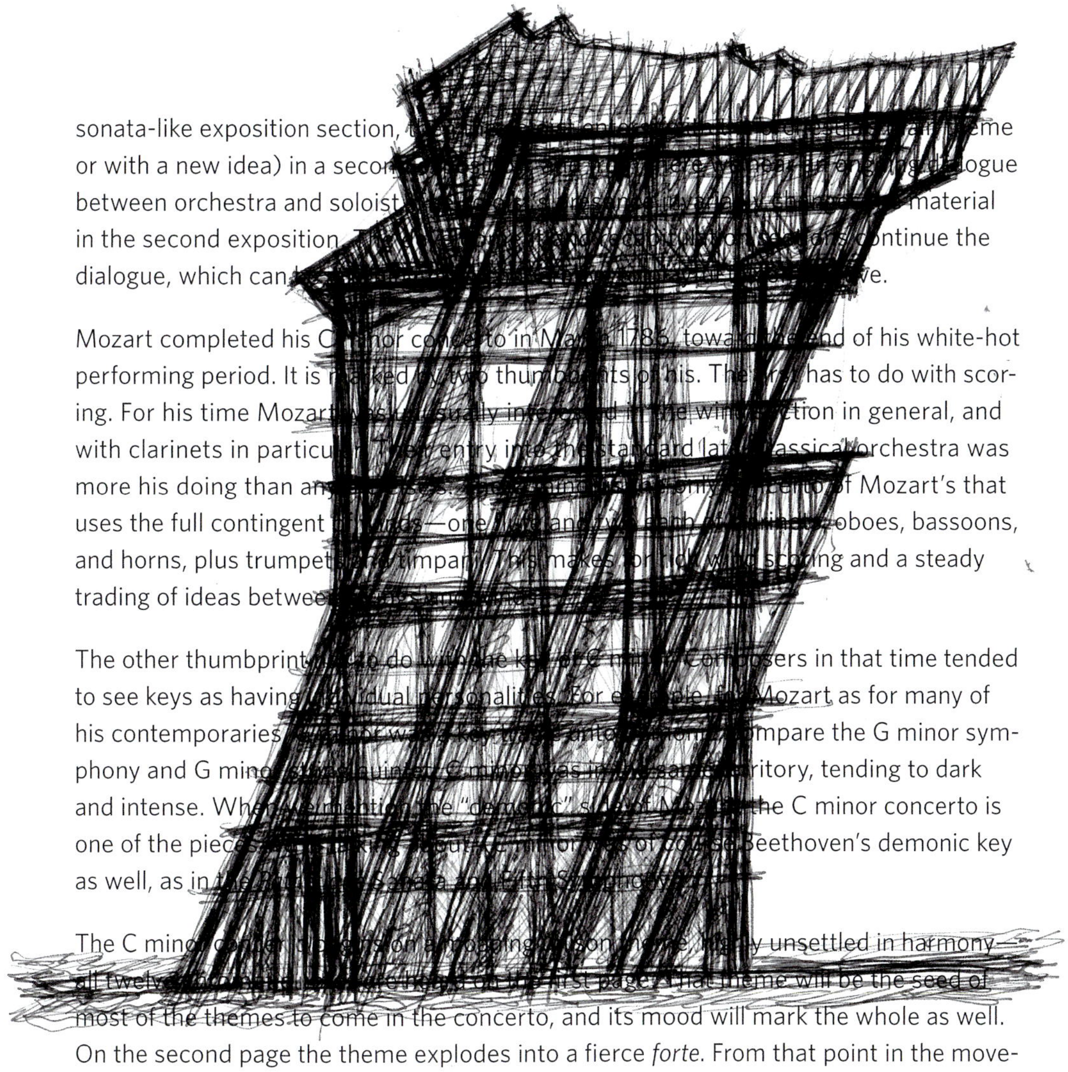

sonata-like exposition section, [illegible] eme or with a new idea) in a seco[illegible] ogue between orchestra and soloist [illegible] material in the second exposition [illegible] ontinue the dialogue, which can [illegible] ve.

Mozart completed his C [illegible] nor co[illegible]to in Ma[illegible] 1786, towa[illegible] end of his white-hot performing period. It is [illegible] ked [illegible] two thumb[illegible] ts of his. The [illegible] has to do with scoring. For his time Mozart [illegible] in general, and with clarinets in particu[illegible] entry into the stan[illegible] ard lat[illegible] assical orchestra was more his doing than an[illegible] f Mozart's that uses the full contingent [illegible] —one [illegible] oboes, bassoons, and horns, plus trumpet[illegible] timpani. This makes for [illegible] ng and a steady trading of ideas betwee[illegible]

The other thumbprint [illegible] Composers in that time tended to see keys as having [illegible] dual personalities. For e[illegible] Mozart as for many of his contemporaries [illegible] mpare the G minor symphony and G mino[illegible] ritory, tending to dark and intense. Wh[illegible] the C minor concerto is one of the piec[illegible] Beethoven's demonic key as well, as in [illegible]

The C mino[illegible] unsettled in harmony—all twelv[illegible] e heard on the first page. That theme will be the seed of most of the themes to come in the concerto, and its mood will mark the whole as well. On the second page the theme explodes into a fierce *forte*. From that point in the movement the theme will trouble the music in the same way. A second theme is quiet and

Earth Island Institute - Philippines, Manila Bay, Las Piñas

— March 09, 2019

An international advocate for environmental education and activism, the new Center promotes dolphin-safe fishing practices worldwide. With operations and administration on the lower floors, the upper domed space is programmed as a virtual aquarium and introduction to Freedom Island Bird Sanctuary, promoting the work of the organization through ecotourism.

Pyotr [illegible]yich T[illegible]haik[illegible]

Sym[illegible]ony No. 4 i[illegible] F mi[illegible]or, O[illegible]

PYOTR ILYICH TCHAIKOVS[illegible] born a[illegible] Kamsko[illegible]otkinsk[illegible] Vyatka [illegible] May [illegible] 1840, and died in St. Petersburg o[illegible] 6, 18[illegible]. He began the S[illegible]phony [illegible] in May 187[illegible] and completed the score on Ja[illegible] 187[illegible]. Nicolai Rubinstein conducted the [illegible] performance [illegible] March 4 that year, in M[illegible]

THE SCORE OF TC[illegible] SYMPHONY NO. 4 ca[illegible] for two [illegible] and piccolo, two oboes, two clarinet[illegible] bass[illegible] four ho[illegible]s, two trumpet[illegible] three t[illegible]bones, tuba, timpani, triangle, cymbals, [illegible] drum, and strings.

For [illegible], the [illegible]phony No. 4 was a bre[illegible] through [illegible] work, [illegible] bounding creative lea[illegible] his first [illegible] symphonies [illegible] scale, [illegible] ntrol of [illegible] inte[illegible] it [illegible] above any symphonies [illegible] previous[illegible] produced by other Russian composers, [illegible] of [illegible] the symphonic form in favor of operas and programmatic works. He[illegible] masterpieces [illegible], Tchaikovsky combines his strong se[illegible] theatrical (already demonstrated in *Romeo a[illegible]et*, *Fra[illegible] Rimini* an[illegible]) with a heightened mastery of orchestrat[illegible] and thematic development.

The [illegible] the Fourth Sym[illegible] has been [illegible] fatef[illegible] composer's eventful and emotionally volatile life. It was in 187[illegible] he ma[illegible] and ultimately tragic decision to marry Antonina Ivanovna Milyukova, a woma[illegible] kn[illegible] did so (on July 18) in a panic-stricken attempt to conceal— or even o[illegible] his homosexual inclinations.

Not surprisi[illegible] Tchaikovsky's lack of sexual in[illegible] women and [illegible] unbal- anced personal[illegible] marriage ende[illegible] ere two months, at the en[illegible]kovsky attempt[illegible] into the frigid Moscow River in the [illegible] tracting [illegible] a. [illegible] have seen Ken Russell's film-bio of Tchaikovsky, *The Music Lovers*, will no doubt remember the

Gastown Hotel, Vancouver, BC

— March 23, 2019

A sketch of a tall waterfront hotel began from hearing Roberto Sierra's Concerto for Saxophones and Orchestra with the Boston Symphony Orchestra. Characterized by the unique drama and extraordinary variety of sounds coming from a largely familiar but rarely heard instrument in concert, the sketch reflects the classical concerto form infused with the freedom of jazz.

Florence Price

"Symphonic Reflections" from Symphony No. 3
(selected by Thomas Wilkins)

FLORENCE BEATRICE PRICE was born in Little Rock, Arkansas, on April 8, 1887, and died in Chicago, Illinois, on June 3, 1953.

THE INSTRUMENTATION OF FLORENCE PRICE'S SYMPHONY NO. 3 includes piccolo, three flutes, two oboes, English horn, two clarinets, bass clarinet, two bassoons, four horns, three trumpets, three trombones, tuba, timpani, percussion (tambourine, snare drum, cymbal, bass drum, triangle, crash cymbals, wood block, sandpaper, castanets, slapstick, gong, orchestral bells, xylophone), celesta, [illegible], and strings. "Symphonic Reflections" from Symphony No. 3 is about eighteen [illegible].

Boston can boast a strong connection to the African-American composer Florence Price: after graduating as valedictorian of her high school at fourteen, she attended Boston's New England Conservatory, where she studied organ and piano and took composition lessons with Wallace Goodrich and Frederick Converse. She also studied privately with George Whitefield Chadwick. (Converse and Chadwick were particularly prominent Boston composers; the BSO performed their work on many occasions.) Decades later, she wrote several letters to BSO conductor Serge Koussevitzky in hopes of his programming her music, but never received a reply. In the recent resurgence of interest in Price's life and music, these letters are frequently cited to epitomize the change in her fortunes following a promising beginning to her career. Until recently, her orchestral works have rarely been performed, and this is the first BSO performance of any of her music, although BSO musicians programmed her String Quartet in chamber music co[illegible]ing 2017. Part of the renewed interest in Price's work was triggered by the discovery of a trove of the composer's music and papers in a semi-derelict house outside of Chicago in 2009.

Growing up in Arkansas, Florence Smith received her first musical training from her mother. After earning her diploma in organ performance and a teaching degree for piano, she returned to Little Rock to teach. The musicologist Rae Linda Brown, in her article "Lifting the Veil: The Symphonies of Florence B. Price" (printed in the score of the Third Symphony), relates that after her father's death in 1910, [illegible] moved to Indianapolis, where she was able to pass for white because of her light skin. (Her mother was mulatto.) From [illegible] to Atlanta to teach at Clark University, where she proved herself a gifted administrator as well, but in 1912 she returned to Little Rock and married Thomas Price, a lawyer, with whom she had two daughters, as well as a son who died in infancy. She continued to teach pi[illegible] [illegible]pose small pieces during this time, but [illegible]ause of her race was barred from many professional activities. She made several trips to Chicago to advance her musical training further, and in 1927 the family moved there, where she immediately continued to teach. She also played organ in movie theaters.

The Shaw Center

— March 26, 2005

BOSTON SYMPHONY ORCHESTRA

James Levine, *Music Director*
Bernard Haitink, *Conductor Emeritus*
Seiji Ozawa, *Music Director Laureate*
124th Season, 2004-2005

Thursday, March 24, at 8
Friday, March 25, at 1:30
Saturday, March 26, at 8

JAMES LEVINE conducting

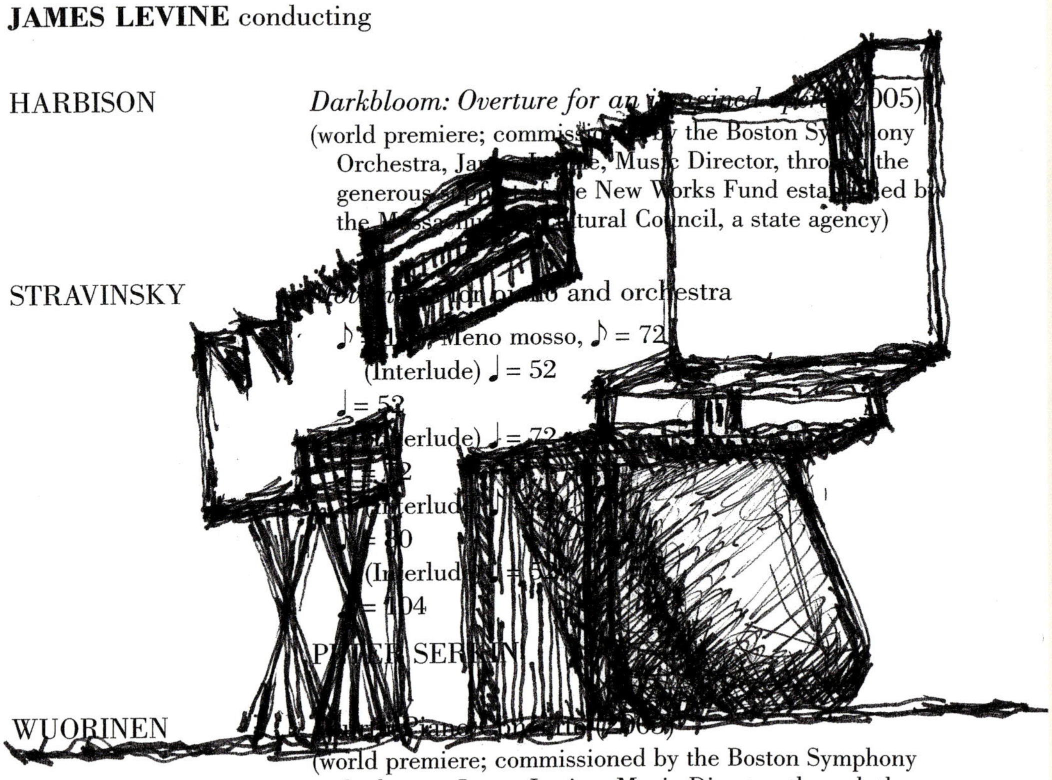

HARBISON *Darkbloom: Overture for an i... (2005)*
(world premiere; commiss... the Boston Sy...ony Orchestra, Ja... Music Director, thro... the generous ... e New Works Fund esta... ed b... the M... tural Council, a state agency)

STRAVINSKY ... and orchestra
♪ ... Meno mosso, ♪ = 72
(Interlude) ♩ = 52
♩ = 52
(...erlude) ♩ = 72
... 2
...erlud...
... = 80
(In...erlud... = 5...
... = 104
P... SER...

WUORINEN ... Piano ... (2005)
(world premiere; commissioned by the Boston Symphony Orchestra, James Levine, Music Director, through the generous support of Catherine and Paul Buttenwieser)

Part I –
Part II –
Part III

Mr. SERKIN

The world premiere performances of the new works on this program are supported in part by an award from the National Endowment for the Arts, which believes that a great nation deserves great art.

INTERMISSION

Igor Stravinsky
Movements for piano and orchestra

Igor Stravinsky was born at Oranienbaum, Russia, on June 18, 1882, and died in New York City on April 6, 1971. He began composing Movements *in 1958, completing it on July 30, 1959. He dedicated it to Margrit Weber, who was soloist at the first performance on January 10, 1960, with the composer conducting, as part of a Stravinsky Festival at New York's Town Hall. The only previous Boston Symphony performances featured pianist Michel Béroff in April 1976 under the direction of Seiji Ozawa and Joseph Silverstein, and Peter Serkin in December 1995 with Ozawa conducting. In addition to the solo piano, the score calls for two flutes (second doubling piccolo), oboe, English horn, clarinet, bass clarinet, bassoon, two trumpets, three trombones, harp, celesta, and strings, of which Stravinsky specifies six each of first and second violins, four violas, five cellos, and two double basses. The piece lasts about 8 minutes.*

Until the early 1950s, Stravinsky was generally regarded as the most important "hold-out" against Schoenberg's twelve-tone system, which had begun to attract ever wider attention in Europe and America following World War II. At that time, Stravinsky was putting the cap on his neoclassical orientation with the largest of all his neoclassical works, his opera *The Rake's Progress*, completed in 1951. This was a definite ending point: Whether because he felt he could say no more in the musical language derived from the two centuries past, or because of critical reaction to the opera implying that he was completely written out, Stravinsky never again wrote in an historicizing style. Instead, partly through the influence of his amanuensis Robert Craft, who was an enthusiastic admirer of the works of Schoenberg, Berg, and Webern, he began a close study of their work and of the possibilities of serial technique.

His next several works, while not built on a complete twelve-tone row, emphasized the kind of contrapuntal treatment normally given to the tone row in the work of Schoenberg—especially retrograde and retrograde-inversion (i.e., playing a figure backwards, or backwards and upside down), which are relatively rare in tonal counterpoint. This efflorescence of contrapuntal writing, though by no means entirely new in Stravinsky's

The Shaw Center

Model of the Shaw Center

The Shaw Center became the catalyst for downtown redevelopment by concentrating the fine and performing arts on Baton Rouge's central block, with direct views of the Mississippi River. —

Study - Toledo Courthouse Annex

— November 19, 2016

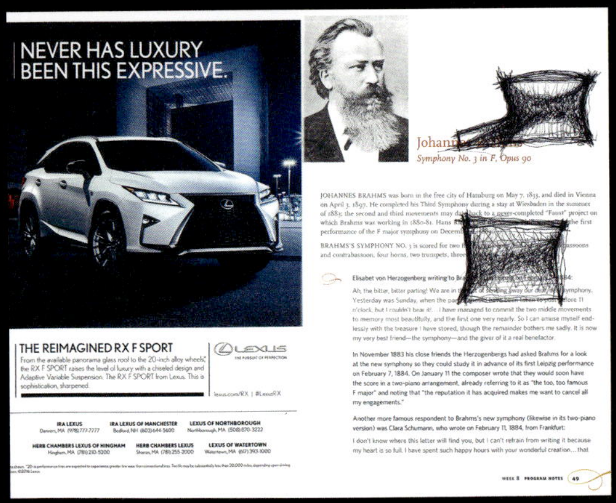

Johannes Brahms

Symphony No. 4 in E minor, Opus 98

JOHANNES BRAHMS was born in the free city of Hamburg on May 7, 1833, and died in Vienna on April 3, 1897. The first mention of his Fourth Symphony is in a letter of August 19, 1884, to his publisher, Fritz Simrock. The work must have been completed about a year later, and in October 1885 he gave a two-piano reading of it with Ignaz Brüll in Vienna for a small group of friends including the critic Eduard Hanslick, the surgeon Theodor Billroth, the conductor Hans Richter, and the historian and Haydn biographer C.F. Pohl. Brahms conducted the first [illegible] performance on October 25, 1885, at Meiningen.

THE SCORE OF BRAHMS'S SYMPHONY NO. 4 calls for two flutes [illegible] clarinets, two bassoons and contrabassoon, four horns, two trumpets, [illegible] triangle, and strings. Piccolo and triangle appear in the third movement [illegible] the third and fourth movements only, and the trombones in [illegible]

When [illegible] friends [illegible] was forthcoming [illegible] he was apt to be most flip and ironic concerning the works [illegible] cared about, such as the Fourth Symphony. In August 1885, from [illegible] [illegible] Brahms sent his adviser Elisabet von Herzogenberg the [illegible] movements of a symphony: "Would you... tell me what you think of it?... Cherries never get ripe for eating in these parts, so don't be afraid to say if you don't like the taste. I'm not [illegible] eager to write a bad No. 4." Back in Vienna, when a friend asked if he'd done a string quartet or the like over the summer, Brahms replied, "Nothing so grand as that! Once again I've just thrown together a bunch of polkas and waltzes."

Like any composer, Brahms worried about the reception of a new work. He was more anxious than usual about the Fourth Symphony. His previous two symphonies had scored immediate successes, and that upped the ante for this one. Meanwhile, Brahms perhaps suspected he did not have a Fifth in him. And in its tone and import, the Fourth was the darkest and most densely crafted symphonic work he had put before the

WEEK 8 **PROGRAM NOTES** 61

Toledo Courthouse Annex

Model of Toledo Courthouse Annex

Toledo, nicknamed "The Glass City", is known for its long history of glass manufacturing. As such, the Federal Courthouse Annex is conceived in glass, as a lantern that lights the path of justice. —

AFTERWORD

— by Warren Schwartz

I never really kept a sketchbook. And I never really threw anything away. So when I discovered that I'd kept most of the Symphony programs from the time Sheila and I met, I realized that I had been keeping sketchbooks, literally, for decades.

The sketches grew in size, as did the programs after a decade or two, and instead of drawing on the white areas only, I gave myself the freedom to make marks wherever it felt best. Mostly, they were on the pages with lots of print and a portrait of a composer. These pages were the most fertile places to visualize the music I was hearing. I was never so happy to make sketches of architecture without over thinking, over designing, or over editing. All that the music demanded was that I listen. Many times I made sketches that I hated, but all I needed to do was to turn the page. Maybe the next page would yield a better sketch. And when the concert was over, I applauded the Orchestra and took the program home.

The programs became neatly stacked piles, and the piles became my unwitting sketchbook. And there was enough time between concerts that I could go about the other business of architecture: the thinking, the designing and the editing. I began to consider doing something with the sketches, collecting them in some more organized way, maybe posting some of the better ones on the web.

Although some of the music generated visual soundscapes for me, I was most excited to turn what I was hearing into buildings without program or agenda. After the fact, I looked at each sketch and decided what kind of a building it could be, where it could be sited, and how it might be built. And each had its own nature and narrative. I was a little surprised by some of the building forms that emerged from the music. Most took unusual formal freedoms, unencumbered as they were by program or budget. Some of these sketches have become buildings, but not in their original form.

And so the idea of a book took shape, slowly, by accumulation, sketch by sketch. And if the design process has a parallel in music composition, then at their best, the sketches echo the shape of the music.

All sketches were made during Boston Symphony concerts at Symphony Hall, Boston, or at The Tanglewood Music Shed, Lenox, MA —

Left to right from top Boston Symphony Orchestra stage and proscenium, 2019. Symphony Hall stage with the Tanglewood Festival Chorus, 2016. Symphony Hall, 2,625 seating capacity. Andris Nelsons, Music Director. Boston Symphony Hall, 2023. John Williams, Film Night at Tanglewood, 2023. Tanglewood Music Shed, view from the lawn. John Williams, Film Night at Tanglewood, 2023. John Williams at 91, conducting the Boston Symphony Orchestra at Tanglewood, 2023.

AUTHOR

WARREN SCHWARTZ

Warren is a Florida native and a Founding Principal of Schwartz/Silver. When he arrived at Cornell University, he discovered to his surprise that the only thing of interest in the course catalogue was architecture. The amount of snowfall in Ithaca was a second surprise. Now an adapted New Englander, Warren is the project designer of several of the firm's most honored projects, including the Shaw Center for the Arts and MIT's Rotch Architecture Library. He is a frequent juror for AIA awards and scholarships and is actively involved in a range of professional and civic organizations. He is a National Design Peer of the General Service Administration and a Fellow of the American Institute of Architects.

SHEILA FIEKOWSKY — ADVISOR

A member of the Boston Symphony Orchestra since 1975, Sheila Fiekowsky was born in Detroit and began studying the violin at the age of nine when she was offered a violin through a public school program. Her musical studies quickly progressed when her teacher, a bass player, insisted she begin lessons with Emily Mutter Austin, a violinist with the Detroit Symphony Orchestra. Her summers were spent at the Meadowmount School of Music, where she studied violin with Ivan Galamian and chamber music with Joseph Gingold. She appeared as a soloist with the Detroit Symphony at 16 and that same year won the National Federation of Music Clubs Biennial Award. Currently, in addition to performing with the Boston Symphony, Sheila is frequently heard in chamber music concerts in Boston and the Berkshires.

CONTRIBUTORS

MARK VOLPE

Mark Volpe served as CEO of the Boston Symphony Orchestra from 1997-2021. In his role, he was responsible for the Boston Symphony Orchestra, Boston Pops and Tanglewood as well as the real estate holdings of the BSO, the most extensive of any orchestra in the world. Previously, he held leadership positions with the orchestras of Detroit, Minnesota, and Baltimore. He is a frequent lecturer at major universities in the U.S. and Europe. Volpe has written articles that have appeared in various periodicals and recently co-authored a book, "Fundraising for the Arts", which was published by Bocconi University Press (Milan, Italy). His degrees include a JD from the University of Minnesota, a BM from the Eastman School and five honorary doctorates. In 2017, he was elected to the American Academy of Arts and Sciences and was named a Chevalier of the Order of Arts and Letters by France's Minister of Culture in 2019.

NICHOLAS URIE

As an active composer and arranger, Nicholas Urie has been commissioned to write music for concerts, recordings, and television broadcasts in collaboration with Cory Wong, Kurt Elling, John Scofield, Lucienne Renaudin Vary, Donny McCaslin, Queen Latifah, Lavinia Meijer, Steve Vai, Trijntie Oosterhuis, Warner Classics, the Metropole Orchestra, WDR Symphony Orchestra, the Boston Pops, Luzerner Sinfomieorchester, the Boston Symphony Orchestra community concert series, and the Aarhus Jazz Orchestra, among others. Urie's recordings of original music, Excerpts from an Online Dating Service (2009), My Garden (2012), Quintet (2019), and Two Songs (2022), earned wide critical acclaim. He received both bachelors and masters degrees from the New England Conservatory of Music and is an Associate Professor at the Jazz Composition department at Berklee where he has been teaching since 2012. Nicholas's book *Harmony for Arrangers* will be published by Oxford University Press.

BOOK CREDITS

Graphic design by Florencia Damilano
Art direction by Oscar Riera Ojeda
Copy editing by Kit Maude and Julia Schwartz

Unlike sketches, buildings are always works of collaboration. Photographs and renderings of buildings within the book are the result of the collaborative effort of Schwartz/Silver Architects, notably including my partners Angela Hyatt, Peter Kleiner, Mark Schatz, Robert Silver and Jon Traficonte.

In addition, these firms collaborated on the following projects:
The A.H. McCoy Federal Building - CDFL Architects + Engineers / The National Music Museum - Koch Hazard Architects / The River Center, Library - WHLC Architecture / The Shaw Center - Eskew Dumez Ripple + / The Toledo Federal Courthouse Annex - Schooley Caldwell

Photography credits:
Alan Karchmer: pages 2-3, 6-7, 12-13, 76-77, 80-81 and 174-175.
Matt Wargo: pages 32-33.
Tim Mueller: pages 58-59.
Chuck Choi: pages 130-131.
Timothy Hursley: pages 158-159.

Rendering credits:
Schwartz/Silver Architects: pages 20-21 and 164-165.
Young and de la Sota: pages 110-111 and 112.

OSCAR RIERA OJEDA
PUBLISHERS

ISBN 978-1-946226-81-5
Published by Oscar Riera Ojeda Publishers Limited
Printed in China

Oscar Riera Ojeda Publishers Limited
Unit 1331, Beverley Commercial Centre,
87-105 Chatham Road South, Tsim Sha Tsui, Kowloon, Hong Kong

Production Offices
Suit 19, Shenyun Road,
Nanshan District, Shenzhen 518055, China

International Customer Service & Editorial Questions: +1-484-502-5400

www.oropublishers.com | www.oscarrieraojeda.com
oscar@oscarrieraojeda.com